Palgrave Studies in Literature, Culture and Human Rights

Series Editor
Alexandra S. Moore
Binghamton University
New York, USA

This series demonstrates how cultural critique can inform understandings of human rights as normative instruments that may at once express forms of human flourishing and be complicit with violence and inequality. The series investigates the role of genre and the aesthetic in shaping cultures of both rights and harm. Essential to this work is an understanding of human rights as at once normative and dynamic, encompassing egregious violations as well as forms of immiseration that have not always registered in human rights terms.

Muhammad Waqar Azeem
Editor

Human Rights in the Age of Drones

Critical Perspectives on Post-9/11 Literature, Film and Art

palgrave
macmillan

Editor
Muhammad Waqar Azeem
Binghamton University
Binghamton, NY, USA

ISSN 2524-8820 ISSN 2524-8839 (electronic)
Palgrave Studies in Literature, Culture and Human Rights
ISBN 978-3-032-08190-2 ISBN 978-3-032-08191-9 (eBook)
https://doi.org/10.1007/978-3-032-08191-9

This Palgrave Macmillan imprint is published by the registered company Springer Nature Switzerland AG.
The registered company address is: Gewerbestrasse 11, 6330 Cham, Switzerland

This book is dedicated to all who lost their life, freedom, and happiness to unjust violence.

Preface

In 2013 while travelling in a public bus on the Mall Road, Lahore, Pakistan, I glanced at an Urdu newspaper with a headline: "A US Drone Strikes in Hangu." I experienced empathic fear that just like this and many other strikes in North Waziristan, South Waziristan, Khyber Agency and Bajaur Agency, another drone could hit this very bus while targeting a suspect insurgent in the vicinity. This feeling stuck with me forever. I spent more than ten years thinking, discussing, and writing to understand what makes the lives of the people in Pakistan, as well as many Middle Eastern and African countries, so cheap that they could be wiped out as collateral damage with the push of a button thousands of miles away from the impact. This book is an outcome of that research, and it attempts to mollify the fear that my fellow citizens, and citizens of many countries, harbor for an unannounced strike that could eliminate them any moment.

Many teachers, colleagues, and friends joined hands with me in this pursuit. Let me begin by thanking David Bartine whose seminars at Binghamton University encouraged me to consider my ideas worth sharing. The session at MLA 2018 (Drone Warfare and Post-9/11 Cultural Practices) provided the impetus, material, and exceptional contributors for this book. Thanks to Dr Waseem Anwar for travelling all the way from Pakistan to preside this session at MLA Convention. I must mention South Asian Literary Association's 2016 annual conference where I first presented my work on Drone Art and was fortunate enough to receive Barbra Harlow's precious comments. I am thankful to Monika Mehta who motivated me to start this book project despite my best efforts to postpone it. Special thanks to my seminar professor Peter E. Gordon (Harvard) at SCT 2018 (Cornell) for letting me present on Drone Art in front of my brilliant seminar fellows. Input from other SCT faculty, especially Samuel Moyn (Yale) and Eduardo Cadava (Princeton), was precious and instrumental in advancing this project.

This book could not have been possible without Alexandra Moore's active mentorship for more than four years. She reviewed the proposal numerous times and every time her feedback was rigorous. My heartfelt thanks to Alex Adams (also a contributor) who very generously reviewed the book proposal, made very productive comments, and added strength and vitality to it. I am also grateful to Sadiq Khan, Timothy A. Lavis, and Mushtaq Bilal for reviewing the introduction on a very short notice and giving their valuable insights. This book could not have the quality and content without the watchful attention of Palgrave's anonymous external reviewer; I really appreciate their deep involvement in the project, concise and expert feedback, and their encouragement in teasing out the concepts with clarity and confidence. My utmost thanks to Molly Beck, executive editor, Felicity Plester, editorial director, and Esther Rani and Sasikala Thopu, production editors, and the rest of the Palgrave/Springer Nature team who facilitated and supported this project with patience and care.

My sincere appreciation for all the contributors for trusting me with their innovative work and staying committed to the project despite the endless time it took.

Finally, my deepest thanks to one person who is behind everything I can be proud of, my wife, Zunaira. I am thankful to her for bearing with my preoccupation with this project for five long years. I owe this book to Zohaib, Maryam, and Haider, the lights of my life; we could not achieve much without the positivity and hope they bring in our life every single moment. And we cannot thank enough for our parents' prayers; their blessings are the prizest treasure.

Binghamton, NY, USA
June 1, 2024

Muhammad Waqar Azeem

Contents

Notes on Contributors

Alex Adams is an independent researcher based in the UK. He has published widely on securitization, torture, drone warfare, and popular culture, including three monographs: *Political Torture in Popular Culture: The Role of Representations in the Post-9/11 Torture Debate* (Routledge, 2016), *How to Justify Torture: Inside the Ticking Bomb Scenario* (Repeater, 2019) and *Death TV: Drone Warfare in Contemporary Popular Culture* (2021).

Jenna Ann Altomonte is an Assistant Professor of Art History at Mississippi State University. She received her Master of Arts in Art History (2009) and Ph.D. in Interdisciplinary Arts (2017) from Ohio University. Her primary area of research centers on global contemporary art and digital performance studies with a specialization in political and social intervention practices. Her current research endeavors examine responses to contested, occupied, and conflicted spaces in the post-9/11 era. Her recent and forthcoming publications include, "Conflict Fetishization and the Politics of Graffiti," in *Dust, Scratch and Paint: Street Art in the Global South*, (eds. Cynthia Gabbay and Tom Penfold, 2023); "Identity Politics and Digital Space: Adel Abidin's *Abidin Travels: Welcome to Baghdad*," in *Cultural Production and Social Movements After the Arab Spring: Nationalism, Politics and Transnational Identity* (ed. Eid Mohamed, IB Tauris, 2021), and "Playing *Killbox*: Didactic Gaming and Drone Warfare" in *Video Games and the Global South* (ed. Phillip Penix-Tadsen, Carnegie Mellon University ETC Press, 2020).

Muhammad Waqar Azeem is an adjunct lecturer at Binghamton University where he teaches twentieth-century American and Asian American literature, film, and art. His research interests include 9/11 literature, postcolonial and ethnic studies, human rights, and critical theory.

Lopamudra Basu is Professor of English at University of Wisconsin-Stout. She grew up in Kolkata, India, and attended the University of Delhi, India, where she received B.A. and M.A. degrees. She received her Ph.D. in English from the City University of New York. She is the author of *Ayad Akhtar, the American Nation and its Others After 9/11: Homeland Insecurity* (Lexington Books, December, 2018). She is the co-editor of *Passage to Manhattan: Critical Essays on Meena Alexander* (Cambridge Scholars Publishing, UK, 2009). Her articles, interviews, and reviews have been published in *South Asian Review, Nebula, Social Text, Journal of Commonwealth and Postcolonial Studies, Remarkings* and in the anthologies *Rites of Passage in Postcolonial Women's Writing* (Rodopi, 2010), *Drawing From Life: Memory and Subjectivity in Comic Art* (University of Mississippi Press, 2013), *Masks of Threat: South Asian Racialization and Belonging after 9/11* (Lexington, 2016), *A History of Indian Poetry in English* (Cambridge University Press, 2016). Her current scholarly interests include trauma studies, post 9/11 American literature, and postcolonial poetry.

Inderpal Grewal is Professor Emeritus of Women's, Gender, and Sexuality Studies at Yale University. She is also Professor in the Ethnicity, Race and Migration Studies Program, the South Asian Studies Council, and affiliate faculty in the American Studies Program. She is the author of *Home and Harem: Nation, Gender, Empire and the Cultures of Travel* (Duke University Press, 1996), *Transnational America: Feminisms, Diasporas, Neoliberalisms* (Duke University Press, 2005), and *Saving the Security State: Exceptional Citizens in Twenty-First century America* (Duke University Press, 2017). With Caren Kaplan, she has written and edited *Gender in a Transnational World: Introduction to Women's Studies* (Mc-Graw Hill 2001, 2005) and *Scattered Hegemonies: Postmodernity and Transnational: Feminist Practices* (University of Minnesota Press, 1994). With Victoria Bernal, she has edited *Theorizing NGO's: States, Feminism and Neoliberalism* (Duke University Press, 2014). She is one of the editors of the Duke University Press book series entitled *Next Wave: New Directions in Women's Studies* (Bio adapted from: https://wgss.yale.edu/people/inderpal-grewal).

Marcus Heiligenthal is a PhD Candidate in English at the State University of New York at Binghamton. His dissertation project, titled "Unsettling Economies: Exceptionalism, Neoliberalism, and the Grammar of the Frontier in American Literature," focuses on the relationships between the myth of the American frontier, the rise of a particularly American-style of neoliberalism, and literatures that render this overlap legible while imagining possibilities for resistance. Outside of his dissertation project, Marcus's research interests include transnational American studies, critical finance studies, economic history, critical drone studies, and contemporary American and global literature.

S. F. Maxwell writes about visual culture and political aesthetics, with a focus on the post-9/11 digital age and networks of the technological and the human. She has published in the *Journal of War and Culture Studies* and *ASAP/J*. She earned her Ph.D. from the University of Sheffield.

Daniel O'Gorman is Lecturer in Contemporary Literature at the University of Leeds. His research focuses on literatures of the global contemporary, with a particular interest in literary responses to terrorism and counterterrorism. He is the author of *Fictions of the War on Terror: Difference and the Transnational 9/11 Novel* (Palgrave, 2015) and co-editor of *The Routledge Companion to Twenty-First Century Literary Fiction* (Routledge, 2019). His work has appeared in *Textual Practice*, *Critique: Studies in Contemporary Fiction*, *The European Journal of English Studies*, *The Journal of Commonwealth Literature*, and *The Journal of Postcolonial Writing*.

Susanne Schwertfeger is an art historian whose work spans art history from the Early Modern Period to contemporary of the twentieth century. She earned her Ph.D. from Kiel University with a dissertation on seventeenth-century Dutch trompe-l'oeil painting. Her postdoctoral project focuses on the illustration of the Gothic Novel. Schwertfeger is co-editor of *CLOSURE: e-Journal für Comicforschung* (since 2014), and has co-edited special issues such as *Gothic Studies on Gothic and Comics* (2023). Her publications on the Gothic furthermore include '"No spoilers, please": The Crux of Illustrating the Explained Gothic Without Explaining the Mystery' (Studies in Horror and the Gothic, 2017). Other topics of her research are animal ethics in art, the aesthetics of illusion, photography, public art, comic studies, and text-image relations.

Rachel Ann Walsh is an Assistant Teaching Professor in the English Department and the Interim Director for the International Studies Program at Bowling Green State University. Her scholarship on contemporary global literature, South African apartheid literature, racial capitalism, precarity, and post-9/11 technologies of surveillance, policing, and militarized border control has appeared in *Contemporary Literature*, *Twentieth-Century Literature*, *Environment and Planning D*, and *Radical Philosophy Review*. Her current book project is on autofiction and global archives of precarity in contemporary literature.

Anne Scott Wilson is an artist, academic, and curator who sustained a live performance career before studying at university. Transitioning from performance to visual art, her practice explores what it is to be in a body through a lens of dance, studio practice (visual arts) and years of live performance. She explores the dichotomous relationship between movement and meaning experienced within a transition from performance to the performative in curation and solo practice using video, sound, photography, AI and installation in public and gallery contexts. She has received several public commissions, grants, and residencies in Australia and overseas and is currently exploring artificial intelligence in artistic practice supported by the Australia Council for the Arts and ARS Electronica Australia. Her works are held in public and private collections and she is represented by Conny Dietzschold Gallery in Sydney, Hong Kong, and Cologne.

List of Figures

CHAPTER 1

Introduction: Drones, Rights and Culture

Muhammad Waqar Azeem

The use of weaponized drones appeared as a significant human rights issue in the wake of 9/11 attacks in the US and with the start of America's Global War on Terror in 2001. The spike in drones was unprecedented in the history of warfare when the US deployed them as counter-insurgency tools in Pakistan, Yemen, Somalia, the Philippines, Libya and Iraq. Armed drones became controversial in terms of their legality, ethics and appropriateness for target killing on or off the battlefield. One of the outcomes of a vague legal framework was that, in Mahmood Ahmad's words, the US "set a dangerous example, one that empowers states to disregard International Law as well as fundamental human rights" (Ahmad 2014, 253). The violence committed outside a well-defined legal framework became a precedent for other nations and de-sanctified the concept of sovereignty. Historical evidence already shows that since 9/11 there has been a steep rise in the use of armed drones. In the latest Russia-Ukraine conflict (Feb 2022–), Israel-Hamas conflict (October 2023–) and India-Pakistan skirmishes (2025), all the countries involved have deployed armed and surveillance drones profusely, with impunity, and total

M. W. Azeem (✉)
Binghamton University, Binghamton, NY, USA
e-mail: mazeem1@binghamton.edu

M. W. Azeem (ed.), *Human Rights in the Age of Drones*, Palgrave Studies in Literature, Culture and Human Rights,
https://doi.org/10.1007/978-3-032-08191-9_1

indifference to the rights of the citizens. Just in June 2025, Russia launched hundreds of drones in Ukraine, at times over 400 drones in a single night ("Russia Launches Record Drone and Missile Strike on Ukraine," *The New York Times*, June 9, 2025), Ukraine retaliating with its own drones, though with less number and frequency (*The New York Times*, June 2, 2025). Pakistan has intensified "a deadly drone campaign" apparently against Islamic jihadists and separatists inside its own borders to curb political dissent (*The New York Times*, June 19, 2025). This is the age of autonomous war with boundless territory and unlimited timeframe.

The debates about drones have emerged in law, ethics, security studies, international relations and cultural expressions, this last category being the major focus of this book, with attention to literature, film and art. The volume proposes a contrapuntal critical reading of the cultural representations of drones to examine their violent interventions in societies, cultures, and nations. Borrowed from Edward Said (1935–2003), contrapuntal reading method makes it possible that "texts and worldly institutions are seen working together" (Said 1994, 318). A contrapuntal reading may analyze cultural texts in the context of the law and policies which enable violence by the powerful nations (Global North) against the weaker nations (Global South). We interpret the cultural texts about drones in the context of the United States' control over the legal, political and media discourse with the aim to convince international organizations and rights activists to "enforce clear limits on the government's authority" to commit an irreversible act of killing with a drone (Jaffer & Sponsoring Body American Civil Liberties Union 2016, 55).

The basic tenet of the contrapuntal method is that an interpretation is an act of resistance. Obviously, an interpretation could take any side; even the defenders of drone-strikes interpret ground realities to make a case for drone strikes. That is why it is so important to situate an interpretative practice within a critical tradition. Although each chapter in this volume offers a unique perspective, our interpretive practices are inspired from Said's contrapuntal method that identifies imperial violence through a cultural text. The chapters in this book offer interpretations of cultural texts to critique the imperial power of the US. By analyzing narratives, performances and visuals, the authors argue that drones violate the rights of civilians, noncombatants, and innocent people in the Global South. The contrapuntal reading of cultural texts in connection with the legal memos, journalistic reports, and congressional proceedings exposes the hypocrisy of the Empire in its shallow claims to defend democracy and rights around the world. Our central position, that this introduction addresses and expands on, is that America's drone operations evacuate their targets of their humanity, thus depriving them of the status of a subject worthy of human rights privileges and protections.

From a human rights perspective, drone strikes have been widely recognized to be controversial and in violation of the civil liberties, privacy and sovereignty of the people. Against the United States' claims of extreme caution in the selections of targets, scholars have argued that many drone strikes against the so-called insurgents targeted noncombatants and without any substantial threat. The loss of civilians' life suggests, as Craig Martin contends, that "the drone strike operations may indeed be characterized by systemic violations" of International Humanitarian Law and International Human Rights Law (Martin 2015). As De Groof, a researcher at Brussels-based Research and Information Group on Peace and Security, argues, drone strikes do not depend on any specific information about "the participation of the targeted individuals in hostilities" and do "not require the presence of an established and imminent threat" (De Groof 2016, 137).

Part of the legal controversy about drones comes from the unconventional nature of the conflict between the US and the countries under drone strikes. As Charles G Kels argues, the US' "worldwide fights against al-Qaeda can only be a noninternational armed conflict, or else something short of armed conflict altogether" (Kels 2012). Understood like this, the US was not involved in an armed conflict with terrorists outside Afghanistan and Iraq. Therefore, the drone strikes outside the active battlefield clearly disregarded the sovereignty of the people. DeShaw in *Analyzing the Drone Debates* (2014) also concurs that "disagreements persist" whether the drone strikes were legal in countries not engaged in declared war with the United States. Through almost two decades of drone strikes, the central argument put forward by the United States, as evidenced by the Obama administration's instructions to CIA, was that they could use drones if "the local government is not equipped to address the threat" ("The Secret Rules of the Drone War," *The New York Times,* July 9, 2016). The United States' belligerence toward other states is, in DeShaw's words, a "harkening back to an orientalist binary of civilized and uncivilized, the latter being an 'empty land where Western powers could plunder without legal constraint'" (2014, 73, 74).

To counter this orientalist attitude, the volume magnifies the targets of drones through the analysis of the representation of drones in literature, performances and visual texts. Cultural representations of drone violence make visible, in Gregoire Chamayou's words, "discursive efforts" of the US "for ensuring the social and political acceptability of" drones (Chamayou 2015, 17). The American administration manipulated media, expert opinions and official directives to present drones as an efficient tool that could target terrorists in the regions inaccessible to the soldiers on the grounds. The official White House Archives state President Geroge W. Bush's justification for drones: to "take out the enemy while sparing the innocent." In various news conferences on *WSJ* (May 23, 2013), *CBS* (May 24, 2013) and *CNN* (April 1, 2016), President Barack Obama repeatedly admired the accuracy and limited collateral damage of the drones. However, the strategy of the United States to shape social and political discourse to justify drone-operations only shows how the US follows the colonial paradigm of "necro-ethics", a guiding principle of engendering death rather than life (Chamayou 2015, 17). I connect necro-ethics to Achille Mbembe's elaboration of necropolitics (Mbembe 2019), which, according to him, is the power of the sovereign to create conditions which expose certain bodies to death. In other words, under necropolitical control, a sovereign governs the people not by protecting them but by implementing the tools to kill them, so that the population lives not with the reassurance of its rights but the constant realization of their absence. In Mbembe's own expression, necropolitics, or necropower, encompasses "various ways in which, in our contemporary world, weapons are deployed in the interest of maximally destroying persons and creating death-worlds, that is, new and unique forms of social existence in which vast populations are subjected to living conditions that confer upon them the status of the living *dead*" (Mbembe 2019, 92).

A necropolitical governance devalues the life of racialized bodies, providing a rationale for their death without requiring the killer to furnish a legal or moral reason, except the racial identity of the target. Chamayou's "necro-ethics" is thus a philosophical basis of rules, laws, and policies which informs necropolitics of a sovereign (Chamayou 2015). Chamayou's observation reveals how drones are a technology of necro-ethics as they combine jury and executioner for quick termination of the racialized bodies. The weaponized drones contribute to the conditions which turn an entire population into "a living *dead*" (Mbembe 2019), a subject considered dead even before the actual strike takes place. And that is the point of necro-ethics which essentially is a process of, in Jamie Allinson's words, identifying "populations as *less than life*, or as dangerous life whose extinguishing must be managed in order for valuable life to flourish" (Allinson 2015, italics are in the original quotation). Drones are technology of necro-ethics which actualize a symbiosis between aerial violence and the history of racialization and colonization.

The complicity between aerial view and colonial paradigm has received renewed attention in the human rights debates. Moore and Pinto in *Writing Beyond the State* (2020) analyze Theophilus Marboah's representation of "Brookes" slave ship and Massimo Sestini's photograph of a ship carrying asylum seekers to draw comparison between slaves and immigrants as situated in statelessness. Their argument that "the medium of aerial photography" draws on "the colonial formal point of view" and thus shows the crisis in human rights provides a useful theoretical background to our discussion of drone technology as a tool of colonial violence (5). The United States' use of drones has purposely extended the racialization on the ground, in Feldman's words, into a vertical factor. The contours of the vector include a compromise on targeted killing without due process, redefinition of the concept of sovereignty, renegotiation of right to life and racialization of the enemy populations (Feldman 2011). As a result, drone warfare redefines populations' relationship with space into a "psychopathological relationship to airspace" (Amin and Downey 2020, 65). This is how the citizens and subjects experience surveillance and violence from the airspace as necropolitical control. This "region-wide phenomenon" makes people live in a state of constant emergency, and a "condition of paranoia" permeates the populations (Amin and Downey 2020, 68, 69).

The part of the complexity involved in drone warfare and its targets comes from their connection with sovereignty. The executive powers vested in the President of the United States to sign each order for a drone strike seems to point fingers at the exceptional powers of the president and state of exception as legal rationalization of the strikes. Giorgio Agamben's elaboration of the state of exception as the effect of an executive order for a drone strike runs short of explaining the kill list of targets reviewed and approved by the president of the United States. State of exception has a nationalist frame; the president projects themselves as a sovereign who decides on the exception without congressional support, but at the same time their sovereign right is supported by the congress through its validation of the president's right to act as a sovereign under the emergency situations. Drone operations in the context of the war on terror almost always either traverse or take place on national borders. As the cultural geographer Derek Gregory observes, drone warfare is a "borderland war" inspired from imagining borders as dangerous. “Neither will it be – nor is it – clear where the battlespace begins and ends” (Gregory 2011). Such characteristics of drone operations complicate the notion of state of exception; the executive orders do not appear to be fully applicable to the wars with undefined enemy and range. That is why, as Ian Shaw shows us, drone strikes depend on a disposition matrix that identifies the pattern of life of the potential terrorists, thus subjecting whole populations to drone violence. Enabled by a network of technology, drone pilots, military command, image analysis, bureaucrats and the government, drone warfare is less of a temporary arrangement under an emergency rule and more of a permanent norm that “becomes the new face of an old Empire (Shaw 2013).”

Other than the above political, juridical and geographical approaches to drone violence, an architectural approach may also show the intervention of the Empire in the Global South. This method digitally reconstructs the sites impacted by drone strikes and measures the extent of damage to the buildings and places. This approach is predicated on what Fuller and Weizman call “investigative aesthetics” that employs visual and spatial analysis to produce evidence against drone attacks (Fuller & Weizman 2021). An architectural method comes very close to the working of a fact-finding commission by providing evidence where there is very little or none. Such procedures combine aesthetics and forensic architecture to study mass violence, atrocities, genocides, and drone strikes and produce evidence for the forgotten or covertly committed imperial violence. This model, despite its advancement and exceptional output, depends on scientific discourse and does little to engage the humanities perspective.

On the other hand, a humanities-based contrapuntal reading highlights the contours of the subject of a drone strike by permitting an interplay between cultural forms and social forms, a literary plot and a political plot, and fictional characters and historical characters. This volume produces a contrapuntal relationship between subjects of drone violence and their cultural representations in film, drama, theater, fiction, performance and dance. Edward Said borrows the notion of “counterpoint” from Western music with an intent to be simultaneously aware “of the metropolitan history that is narrated” and “other histories against which…the dominating discourse acts” (Said 1994, 51). To advance his contrapuntal method, Said approves CLR James’ suggestion that “Beethoven belongs as much to West Indians as he does to Germans, since his music is now part of the human heritage” (Said 1994, XV). Said exploits his contrapuntal method to reflect the tensions between the colonizer and the colonized in cultural domain. In conversation with Said, Daniel Barenboim argues that music is an isolated phenomenon but it "mirrors" as well as "anticipates" the social development too (Barenboim et al. 2004, 41). Said, referring to Theodore Adorno, admires music that does not reflect hierarchy and that maintains "atonality where all twelve tones are equal" (Barenboim et al. 2004, 41). Barenboim agrees with Said, indicating that the tonal system is not a "law of nature" and "(d)issonance stretched to its extremes becomes a kind of consonance as in Schoenberg" (Barenboim et al. 2004, 43, 44).

Let me now situate our discussion about drone violence and its victims in the contrapuntal framework summarized above. In the context of post-9/11 drone strikes, the vague category of suspect terrorists and their so-called sympathizers belong to the "other" whose "histories" (Said 1994) are hardly narrated except as anomalies, abnormalities, and deviations in the so-called grand march of Western civilization. To resist the dominant American discourse that justifies killing on suspicion of uncommitted crime, we use contrapuntal reading to regard an anomalous musical note (metaphorically speaking) as worthy of existence in the overall "tonal system" of human civilization. The Empire invokes the notion of a co-called suspect (terrorist) to keep disadvantaged, economically underdeveloped, and mostly Muslim populations outside the mainstream history, and treat them as a cancerous organ of the human race. As academics, we insist that this category of humans—a suspect—is an imperial construct, and we contrapuntally analyse drone violence of the Empire *and* the condition of its subjects within the same framework ("tonal system") in the hope that a suspect emerges as a valid category of serious reflection in the contemporary discourse of human rights.

To assess human rights debates on drones from a contrapuntal perspective, this volume considers literary and cultural representations as sites where gross violations become visible. We (the contributors and the editor) analyze the representations of the victims of the armed drones within the context of racialization and othering of their targets. The targets of the strikes are not socially, politically and culturally significant enough to be eligible for what Judith Butler calls a grievable life (2010). Muslim populations, especially those residing in the war-torn regions, are mostly presented in the Western media as sympathizers and collaborators of the terrorists, and therefore unworthy of the privileges and rights the citizens of the developed world (Europe and the United States) enjoy. Such devaluation of human life in the Global South will continue to make rights work irrelevant, unnecessary and superfluous. The lives whose safety cannot be apprehended, and whose death does not provoke any consequential global reactions, are likely to be terminated without invoking human rights. Our task, as this volume proposes, is to animate, humanize and make visible the potential targets of the Hellfire, MQ-9 Reaper, and other drones used in and since the start of war on terror. Moreover, the literary and visual analyses offered in the chapters enhance our understanding of the ways human rights are violated. In the context of this book, the primary human rights question is, in Moore and Dawes' words in the *Technologies of Human Rights* (2022): "what counts as representable?" (6). Our focus on the subjects objectified as mere suspects in America's war on terror allows a bottom-up perspective, the view from the ground that defies drone violence just by disseminating the viewpoint of the victim.

A contextual explanation of how certain subjects lose their right to represent themselves would be President George W. Bush's use of "a dual rhetoric of retaliatory pay back and generous humanitarianism" in connection with the war on terror (McClennen and Slaughter 2009, 3). His double-speak could portray the very violation of rights as protection of rights by silencing the viewpoint of the Afghans who, as the president would say, received US bombs and food at the same time. This way of depicting the war as a humanitarian mission rather than an imperial invasion is a classic example of how a false representation deprives people in the Global South of their right to life. Bush's statement obviously represents his position. The Afghans' failure to represent themselves automatically disqualifies them from deserving both life and rights. This volume contrapuntally analyzes the representations of drone victims and targets to discuss the rights of a subject maligned—mostly without any concrete evidence—as a suspect terrorist or a suspect collaborator or a suspect sympathizer. As cultural representations—literature, art, film—are imagined forms, they conceive the possibility of recognizing a subject who gets disqualified as a rights-bearing subject and gets killed before the process of claiming rights even begins. These representations therefore are sites of reflection to navigate human rights of the subject devoid of subjectivity, that is, bereft of human agency that makes them a rights-bearing individual.

In *Theoretical Perspectives on Human Rights and Literature* (2012), Goldberg and Moore suggest that humanists should find and apply relevant critical and theoretical reading practices to "parse the implications of subjectivity as a political problem for human rights" (8). Sophia and Moore further argue in *The Routledge Companion to Human Rights and*

Literature (2016) that "the use of literature as a vehicle for human rights advocacy is at once a way to illuminate the humanity of the speaking subject as it is a mode of reflecting a true "story" that has been erased by official "history"" (12). This thread of scholarship centering on the subject of human rights provides us impetus to narrow down our scholarly reflections on the subjectivity of the victims of drone strikes in the context of 9/11 and war on terror. I argue that the United States considers the potential targets of drones—killed or not—as lacking human subjectivity. Walter Benjamin in his "Critique of Violence" postulates that nation-states exist by maintaining their monopoly over violence (Benjamin 1986). What makes an individual a citizen is their submission to the state violence and protection against violence from other states. If an individual is exposed to a foreign country's violence in a way where their own state becomes helpless, this citizen is no more a protected citizen and therefore no more a rights-bearing subject. In the post-9/11 world where citizens of many countries are not protected from America's drones, the subject of human rights is complex, and our volume addresses that complexity with focus on the victims of drone strikes.

The legal, biopolitical, postcolonial and investigative approaches explain how the concept of warfare undergoes significant changes due to remote combat, and how aerial violence has supported US imperialism in Africa, the Middle East and Asia. However, this volume brings attention to the unique subject position of the victim of a drone strike which not only combines the power to surveil and inflict violence but also bypasses the human rights paradigm. A drone strike is mostly predicated on suspicion, rather than a proven crime. The subject of a drone strike is almost forever a suspect unless proven guilty retrospectively. This object of suspicion is complex because the existing categories of human rights subject—stateless individuals, untrialed detainees, refugees, victims of state violence—do not neatly align with a suspect (terrorist or sympathizer) who becomes a victim of drone violence not for an actual crime but for an imagined potentiality of a crime. All the chapters in the book expand on, complicate and make visible the category of a suspect and the implications of such a subject for drone warfare in the post-9/11 human rights discourse.

Foundational documents of Human Rights, like Universal Declaration of Human Rights, and much of legal discourse do not address the complexity surrounding a subject of a drone strike who is targeted on the grounds of suspicion. In her critique on the Universal Declaration of Human Rights, Hannah Arendt demands a human individual's "right to have rights, or the right of every individual to belong to humanity" (Arendt 1973, 298). A subject is not a given; geographical locations, ideological contexts, theoretical elaborations, systems of governance and archives continue to shape and reshape which bodies deserve to be a subject, and more importantly, a rights-bearing subject. The apprehension and recognition of subjects is motivated by "a differential politics of subject formation" (32) as Judith Butler reminds us in *Frames of War* (2009). Frames and their iteration assign value to bodies. Referring to Michel Foucault's *The Order of Knowledge*, Butler further posits that it is disciplining through framing that predetermines how we rate certain bodies and consider them worthy of our attention, recognition, sympathy, and solidarity. Taking Bush-era war on terror as an example, they argue that framing allows the viewing of the suspected terrorists and their families as bodies, which can be disposed of without provoking any moral or legal backlash. An unequal distribution of precarity produces a differential sense of lives, "subjects who are living, but not yet regarded as "lives"" (32).

Framing however is not just one directional imposition; rather, in Butler's opinion, framing is also an act of "breaking out" of a representation from its point of origin. The photographs of Abu Ghraib or those of Guantanamo, for example, once released, initiate the process of framing and reframing as they circulate through various forms of media. Framing is not just recognition of life as livable or grievable but also an act of countering the dominant representations through art, culture, photography, film or literature. The US frames the Vietnamese or Iraqis or Afghanis or Pakistanis as a potential threat and positions these racial configurations as unmournable lives. The chapters in this volume reframe the subjects of drone violence, assign them apprehension, recognition and precarity, and rupture the dominant discourse to generate a rights-bearing subject.

The Bush administration actively framed and interpreted 9/11 and the war on terror to justify killing of people on mere suspicion of terrorism. Jacques Derrida, in his interview with Giovanna Borradori, reminded us repeatedly that the "impression" that 9/11 was a "major event" was manufactured. On the one hand, "our sadness and condemnation" over 9/11 "should be without limits, unconditional, unimpeachable," but on the other hand, "there is interpretative and conditional evaluation that makes us believe that this is a "major event."" Derrida further points out that "Bush speaks of 'war,' but he is in fact incapable of identifying the enemy against whom he declares that he has declared war." Such war is especially useless because "technoscience...blurs the distinction between war and terrorism." Derrida's notion that "the event" as "a major event" was configured through an act of interpretation leads us in this volume to take interpretation seriously. There is no absolute interpretation that will defy the power of the Empire; but a myriad of interpretations demonstrate, as in this book, a critical consciousness that will help readers see through unjust violence the US can exercise due to its technoscientific advancement.

This volume is based on a thematic tripod: rights, drones and culture. In this triangular schema, we are suggesting that interpretation of the representation of drones delineates a reading practice that combines legal, technological and cultural discourse. By applying such reading practice, we follow Beryl Pong's suggestion in *The Art of Drone Warfare* (2022), a special issue of *Journal of War and Culture Studies* that "cultural products need to be seen and scrutinized again in order to intervene in the prevailing logic underpinning autonomous military systems which are becoming entrenched." Our volume aligns with that volume's objective to scrutinize "aesthetics" of drone art to "make(s) politics perceptible." But our volume also extends this worthy objective of intervening into the logic and politics of autonomous weapons by showing that aesthetics is a means to recreate a subject of drone violence discursively annihilated well before it is exposed to a physical/psychological harm through an actual strike.

The contributors through their experimental readings of visual art, films, drama, literature and performing art invite readers to think about various forms of violence unleashed by drones. The use of drone technology in African, Middle Eastern and South Asian territories revives the history of Western colonialism along with the use of force against racialized bodies. The categories of violence discussed in the chapters include technopolitical control, torture, racialized killing, trauma, dehumanization of the target, gendering and othering of the enemy, militarized surveillance, constriction of freedom and subversion of culture. The contributors connect these forms of drone violence with narratives and plays, films and seasons, memoirs and archives, performing art, short-videos and visual art, and drone art. Those who justify drone violence present it as a humane weapon that causes minimum collateral damage. To challenge such a naive representation of drones, this book offers counter-interpretations. As Robert Sullivan reminds us, stressing a mutually reinforcing relation between literature and human rights, "Words are a powerful weapon."

To illustrate the objective of the book further, I will follow Malone and Braeunert's position that drone art is a "countermeasure" (2019). Discussing the art exhibition titled *To See Without Being Seen* that they themselves curated, they argue the drone-art provokes "new ways of thinking about how to recognize, critique, and subvert while also alerting us to the fact that we are in the midst of a change in perception that will ultimately affect not only the way we see, but also the way we live and relate to each other" (Malone and Braeunert 2019). They further posit that the "dominant Western perspective" persists in a "scopic regime" facilitated by a drone's camera (2019). The United States, in collaboration with NATO countries, exercises its technological superiority over the Global South to subject it to its control. The drone camera, both symbolically and literally, represents the imperial gaze of the West, watching the people underneath through a lens of suspicion and imagining them as terrorists. Drones are invisible to naked eyes, but art and literature can switch the "machine vision" of a drone from the realm of invisibility to visibility, impressing on human senses an aesthetics that is simultaneously political (Malone and Braeunert 2019). Human vision thus counters machine vision through visual art.

The chapters in the book critically evaluate the Western superiority and control over the Global South, by framing cultural forms (fiction, film, drama, theater, art, performance, and dance) in a contrapuntal relation with the politics, history, and society. The critical perspectives in the book spotlight the question of human rights by dilating the contradictions, contestations and obscurities, which surround the remotely controlled technologies of violence.

The book is divided into three sections as outlined below:

Part I, Drones, Violence and Imaginary of the Future, focuses on drone technology and its role in empowering the Empire. The chapters in this section discuss how advanced war technology rationalizes imperial control. The section questions the tendency in the popular cultural representations to normalize the colonial logic of us vs. them, imperial technological superiority, and imaginary of the future that Empire produces to justify its use of violence.

Inderpal Grewal in Chap. 2 (reprint) analyzes George Brant's play *Grounded* and Hari Kunzru's short story "Drone" to enable "a literary and cultural critique" of weaponized drones, the agents of the "technoscientific rationality" of the US Empire. Through her close reading of both the texts, she argues that the use of drones by the United States manifests not only its desire for imperial power but also its anxieties about surveillance and dominance. She further argues that drone visuality is "captured by power and violence, and there is no counter visuality that can escape this power" (346). She also shows that a drone-pilot is an emerging subjectivity that is both accomplice and victim of "U. S. Empire's lethal military and policing power" (348).

Chapter 3 by Lopamudra Basu focuses on the victims of the Empire by critically reading the visuals of Showtime's *Homeland* Season 4. Using Butler, Agamben, Chamayou, Gregory and Pease, Basu argues that the season presents the logic of differential vulnerability. In this logic the non-White Muslims are considered collateral damage whose killing does not evoke any moral questions. Basu argues that *Homeland* instills in the audience "the ideology of the Homeland Security State" that sets aside civil rights and privacy, justifying America's absolute control over space. At the same time, the season does not apologize for or rationalize the excesses of security agencies, stamping America as a global Empire. This chapter explains how the United States' claim on human rights is racialized as it values lives based on their national and racial identity.

Chapter 4 by Marcus Heiligenthal draws connections between Empire and periphery via the concept of the imaginary of the future. The US privileges its right to security by capitalizing on the vulnerability of the subjects targeted through war on terror. Extending the logic of preemption, Heiligenthal argues that drone warfare also follows the financial imperative to minimize the cost of war. The US intervenes into the imaginary of the future by naming, finding and eliminating the potential threat, through a complete disregard to the right to life of the suspects. He notices an "imperial arbitrage" in the US' deployment of drones as a strategy to take zero risk for its own citizens and shifting the risk in its entirety to the suspects and people who surround them. Here we see an economic logic that dictates that capital could move from one market to another, depending on where it faces the minimum risk and maximum profit. Drone war, in this context, moves to others, minimizing harm to American soldiers and the economy. The reaction to drone strikes in the form of further terrorist activities produces further precarity, rationalizing the use of drone-technology on a permanent basis, and thus providing a logic to imperialism. This chapter proposes that the imperial project is essentially rooted in an imaginary that the Empire nourishes through culture and media.

Part II, Drone Aesthetics: Resistance and Counter-Archive, focuses on the resistive potential of aesthetics in compiling an archive that challenges the algorithmic profiling of the populations from the Global South.

Chapter 5 by Jenna Ann Altomonte analyzes the artwork of Afridi, Bridle and Chishty to argue that their art magnifies the interventions of American drones in the social and culturals lives of the people in Pakistan. This chapter positions each art piece as a didactic tool that informs the viewers of the effects of drones on noncombatants. Altomonte argues that Afridi's installation *#NotABugSplat*, a huge portrait of a child, killed by one of the drone strikes in Pakistan, makes visible the victims of drone strikes. This portrait was spread over farmland facing upwards in the hope that a drone's camera should see one of its victims. Similarly, Bridle's *Dronestagram*, an app linked with Instagram makes visible on screen drone strikes in Pakistan and Afghanistan. This app engages public discourse, inviting civilians in debate about the rights violations. To show how drones shrink cultural festivals and celebrations, Chisthy's painting depicts kites in the skies symbolizing nostalgia about the tradition of kite flying in Pakistan. The writer interprets the painting about kite flying as freedom of the people and the skies as a spectacle of that freedom. However, the ubiquitous but secretive presence of drones in the skies has curtailed people's freedom for traditional festivity.

Chapter 6 by Rachel Ann Walsh analyzes Atef Abu Saif's *Drones Eat with Me: A Gaza Diary* (2016) and *Don't Look Left: A Diary of Genocide* (2023) to argue that Israel uses drones to create an archive of the life of Palestinians based on their "pattern of life". The entries in the diaries produce a counter archive, chronicling the human rights crises caused by the use of drones by the Israeli military. Walsh frames Gaza as a necropolitical site violently excluded from international human rights discourse or only marginally included in it.

In Chap. 7, S.F. Maxwell analyzes James Bridle's art series "Drone Shadows" through the lens of verticality, invisibility, and subjecthood. She contextualizes the artwork in the colonial history of the Imperial Museum. She also equates art viewership with an act of resistance against the drone operations which themselves function by viewing the target with their electronic eye. Referring to the exhibit of a Predator drone, "one thick white line painted onto the floor of the grand atrium," Maxwell argues that the viewer of this artwork embodies a counterpoint to a drone pilot as the former establishes a bond with the space where the art piece is on display while the latter ruptures the very connection of the bodies from their space. Maxwell's work is ethnographic as she captures her own experience of viewing the exhibit.

Chapter 8 by Daniel O'Gorman's uses spatial violence and justice theories to analyze George Brant's play *Grounded*. O'Gorman argues that drone warfare conflates terrorism with Islam, as the warfare broadens its scope globally, assuming conflation between Muslims and terrorists. Intrigued by the question of agency, he also contemplates the unique position the drone pilots have occupied: they appear to be the victims of "perpetrator trauma" even though the decision to kill is being increasingly outsourced to machines.

O'Gorman's most vital contribution is his critical reading of the literary element in the play—the stage—as refreshing our gaze on the pilot, so that we conceive her/him not as a gendered binary (attacker-attacked) but a multiplicity (embodied network of violence). The machine and the human become "co-constituting," as O'Gorman puts it. Here is an anticipation, in the form of the literary piece that synthesizes technology and human, presaging a just global coexistence between the oppressors and the oppressed. As the classical tragedy has shaped the world view of the West, *Grounded* destabilizes our perception of the justice executable through machines.

Part III, Disrupting Binaries: Self, Gender, Drone, advances the feminist, postcolonial and minority perspectives on drone warfare. The chapters here focus on the binaries of self and gender with reference to drone pilots and targets.

Anne Scott Wilson in Chap. 9 captures "a sense of embodied cognition" by videorecording with a camera-fitted drone the moves of a dancer. She observes that a drone-camera is a recorder of truth in a menacing manner. The drone views from angles inaccessible to the human eye. She foregrounds her "virtual self" that has been as tangible to her as her physical body engaged in dance moves. The purpose of the project is to see how an interaction with a drone changes a human's feelings. She infers from this experimental project that the relation between emotions, dance and drones gets pronounced in the post-9/11 cultural practices, and that relation challenges the notion that machine and human are absolutely distinct from each other.

In Chap. 10, Susanne Schwertfeger employs a Gothic framework to underscore the relevance between human rights and art. Through a close reading of the photographs by Trevor Paglen, Schwertfeger's chapter delves into the unsettling juxtaposition of beautiful landscapes and dreadful weapons. This not only evokes an atmosphere of the Sublime but also exemplifies the Uncanny and transgressive elements concerning time, space, and the body, which are key concepts in the Gothic. She also demonstrates how this transgression finds parallel in potential infringements upon human rights within the respective contexts. By incorporating contemporary drone theory (e.g., Chamayou 2015) and analyzing artworks by James Bridle, Mahwish Chishty, Forensic Architecture, and other relevant artists, this chapter explores in visual art a detachment of surveillance and the act of killing from the human body of the perpetrator.

Alex Adam in Chap. 11 offers a compelling analysis of Gavin Hood's 2015 film *Eye in the Sky* and shows the Empire's exploitation of the ethics of torture for its self-serving agendas. He shows conflict between the military and civil authorities over the ethics of drone strikes in populated areas. The risk posed by the terrorists required the United States to deploy drones, thus necessitating "emergency ethics." Adam argues that a weaponized drone offers "the ticking bomb scenario" because their presence over a region keeps the populations under constant fear of being hit by a drone any time. He posits that we should not reflect about drones in terms of when they can be used and when they cannot be; rather we should think in terms of "the relations of power that they enable." The total power vested in the state shows us only two options: who to kill and who to spare. The film under analysis reduces this debate to precisely these two options, foreclosing any possibility of critical inquiry into the more foundational debates like: Should the state concentrate and exercise unlimited power?

This chapter contributes to the broader premise of the book—the need to rethink drone violence not as a one-time act of destroying or sparing life, but as a persistent fear of a ticking bomb to be exploded any moment. The chapter invokes a new paradigm of human rights violations by drone strikes, which subvert the binary between survival and death, and instead expose the simultaneity of torture (ticking bomb) and elimination.

This volume focuses on the cultural representations of drones because, in addition to dealing with the words, representations are politically aligned. As McClennen and Slaughter observe: "If there has been one ongoing thread in humanities research in the past three decades, it is that culture cannot be understood without reference to the politics of representation. Symbolic forms, societal contexts, and representational meanings are intimately tied to relations of power" (2009). To materialize the task of showing the connections between symbolic and social forms, the chapters in this volume engage the cultural texts with their social and political contexts, demonstrating how the cultural forms conceal or reveal the violation of rights of the subjects in the Global South struggling for a simple recognition of being human at par with the dignified notion of humanity in the West.

References

Ahmad, Mahmood. 2014. The Legality of Unmanned Aerial Vehicles Outside the Combat Zone: A Case Study of the Federally Administered Tribal Areas of Pakistan. *Defense & Security Analysis* 30 (3): 245–253. https://doi.org/10.1080/14751798.2014.921448.

Allinson, Jamie. 2015. The Necropolitics of Drones. *International Political Sociology* 9 (2): 113–127. https://doi.org/10.1111/ips.12086.

Amin, Heba Y, and Anthony Downey. 2020. Contesting Post-Digital Futures: Drone Warfare and the Geo-Politics of Aerial Surveillance in the Middle East. *Digital War* 1 (1–3): 65–73. https://doi.org/10.1057/s42984-020-00021-y.

Arendt, Hannah. 1973. *The Origins of Totalitarianism*. New edition/with added prefaces. New York: Harcourt Brace Jovanovich, Publishers.

Barenboim, Daniel, Edward W Said, and Ara Guzelimian. 2004. *Parallels and Paradoxes: Explorations in Music and Society*, 1st Vintage books ed. New York: Vintage Books.

Benjamin, Walter. 1986. Critique of Violence. In *Reflections*. Translated by Edmund Jephcott, 283. New York: Schochen Books.

Butler, Judith. 2010. *Frames of War*. London: Verso.

Chamayou, Grégoire. 2015. *A Theory of the Drone*. La Vergne: The New Press. Accessed January 30, 2025. ProQuest Ebook Central.

De Groof, Mélanie. 2016. Death from the Sky: International Legal and Practical Issues on the Use of Armed Drones. In *Drones and Unmanned Aerial Systems: Legal and Social Implications for Security and Surveillance*, ed. Aleš Završnik, 205–241. Cham: Springer.

DeShaw Rae, James. 2014. *Analyzing the Drone Debates: Targeted Killing, Remote Warfare, and Military Technology*. 1st ed. New York: Palgrave Macmillan US. https://doi.org/10.1057/9781137381576.

Feldman, Keith P. 2011. Empire's Verticality: The Af/Pak Frontier, Visual Culture, and Racialization from Above. *Comparative American Studies* 9 (4): 325–341.

Fuller, Matthew, and Eyal Weizman. 2021. *Investigative Aesthetics: Conflicts and Commons in the Politics of Truth*. London: Verso.

Goldberg, Elizabeth Swanson, and Alexandra Schultheism Moore. 2012. In *Theoretical Perspectives on Human Rights and Literature*, ed. Elizabeth Swanson Goldberg. Routledge.

Gregory, Derek. 2011. The Everywhere War. *The Geographical Journal* 177 (3): 238–250. https://doi.org/10.1111/j.1475-4959.2011.00426.x.

Jaffer, Jameel, and Sponsoring Body American Civil Liberties Union. 2016. In *The Drone Memos: Targeted Killing, Secrecy, and the Law*, ed. Jameel Jaffer. New York: The New Press.

Kels, Charles G. 2012. Drone Warfare: One Fight or Many? *The National Law Journal & Legal Times* 34 (43): 35.

Malone, Meredith, and Svea Braeunert. 2019. To See Without Being Seen. *Media-N: The Journal of the New Media Caucus* 13 (1): 39–56. ISSN: 1942-017X.

Martin, Craig. 2015. A Means-Methods Paradox and the Legality of Drone Strikes in Armed Conflict. *The International Journal of Human Rights* 19 (2): 142–175. https://doi.org/10.1080/13642987.2014.998864.

Mbembe, Achille. 2019. *Necropolitics.* Translated by Steve Corcoran. Durham: Duke University Press.

McClennen, Sophia A., and Alexandra Schultheis Moore, eds. 2016. *The Routledge Companion to Literature and Human Rights.* Abingdon, Oxon: Routledge.

McClennen, Sophia A., and Joseph R. Slaughter. 2009. Introducing Human Rights and Literary Forms; or, the Vehicles and Vocabularies of Human Rights. *Comparative Literature Studies* 46 (1): 1–19.

Moore, Alexandra S., and James Dawes, eds. 2022. *Technologies of Human Rights Representation.* Albany: State University of New York Press.

Pong, B. 2022. The Art of Drone Warfare. *Journal of War & Culture Studies* 15 (4): 377–387. https://doi-org.proxy.binghamton.edu/10.1080/17526272.2022.2121257.

Said, Edward. 1994. *Culture and Imperialism.* New York: Vintage Books.

Shaw, I. G. R. 2013. Predator Empire: The Geopolitics of US Drone Warfare. *Geopolitics* 18 (3): 536–559. https://doi.org/10.1080/14650045.2012.74924.

PART I

Drones, Empire and Power

CHAPTER 2

Drone Imaginaries: The Technopolitics of Visuality in Postcolony and Empire

Inderpal Grewal

For every scholar or writer who sees drones as manifestations of militarized state power,[1] there are those who see these technologies as useful for social justice projects, rescue operations, or environmental protection. While there are those who claim that even in war, drones can reduce violence and death through their greater precision and accuracy, others view technological advancement as a good in and of itself, or see drones as simply a commodity.[2] While much of the debate around drones in the United States concerns their use by the military, the power of privatized capital and corporations in this new century suggests that entities other

[1] Benjamin, *Drone Warfare.*
[2] Naylor, "Look, Up in the Sky!"

I. Grewal (✉)
Professor Emeritus, Women's, Gender, and Sexuality Studies, Yale University, New Haven, CT, USA
e-mail: inderpal.grewal@yale.edu

M. W. Azeem (ed.), *Human Rights in the Age of Drones*, Palgrave Studies in Literature, Culture and Human Rights,
https://doi.org/10.1007/978-3-032-08191-9_2

than the state are developing and profiting from these technologies. Consequently, the consumption and production of these drones raises serious concerns. In the militarization of everyday life, the military and the consumer product are entangled not simply in the history of their origins or production but also in the technopolitics of visuality, that is, the ways that digital technologies become harnessed to struggles over power and inequality to address the violence of empire and postcolony. In the contemporary phase of intensified economic and financial globalization and inequality, cultural critique has turned to drone technology to examine the operations of both empire and capital. Postcolonial, neocolonial, and national differences, allied to the material places, geographies, and deployments of war and global capital, have produced divergent drone aesthetics and imaginaries. In particular, a debate has emerged between those who advocate a more humanist response to militarized drones and those who locate resistance in narratives of the emergent subjects of this technology.[3]

The latter subjects may be posthuman or postnational, with the implication that liberal subjects and their institutions (legal, political, cultural) cannot respond adequately to the new sensoria and powers of neoliberal capital as it is allied with the practices and processes of empire and sovereignty that together subtend the drone. As much as some argue for visual witnessing of human rights abuses and assertions of national sovereignty to resist the military use of drones by the United States, there are others for whom these forms of liberal rights seem outmoded and ineffective against the dispersed and massive onslaught of violence by technosecuritized, neoliberal states, individuals, and corporations. In this debate, the drone has emerged as the latest avatar for a literary and cultural critique of technoscientific rationality, the security state as both empire and postcolony, and its imbrication with neoliberal economic processes.

As the chapters in this collection suggest, there is much to be learned from understanding how military drones produce both empire and its targets in national, regional, and global contexts. Transnational news organizations provide readers and viewers in the United States and in many other regions with narratives of drones dropping bombs in Pakistan, Yemen, and Afghanistan as part of the argument that this is a "smart" way to wage war, even though we learn that many civilians are being killed in the process. The drone as a "domestic" threat has emerged in the United States as well; one was found hovering over the White House and police have used

[3] Evangelista and Shue, *The American Way of Bombing*.

these to monitor protests and crowds.[4] Yet the power of empire, so lethal for many outside the United States—and for minorities inside it—is also anxious and insecure precisely because the state is not the only sovereign entity that can use drones, since they are in the hands of individuals, corporations, NGOs, and states. Although many writers and scholars imagine the affective power of drones as a global, ubiquitous, and borderless technology, drones also produce insecurity for the empire since they contain the power of technologies and algorithms to create dispersed forms of sovereignty that challenge state and empire.[5] In such a context, the extreme privatization of aeromobility offered by the drone that is being sold globally as a part of consumer culture is both a promise and a threat to imperial power.[6] Imbricated within neoliberal economic processes and rationalities of private and corporate power that are both national and transnational, the power of such aeromobility threatens the sovereignty of the imperial state by breaking down the distinction between empire and postcolony, even as it adds to the securitization of everyday life that extends state power.

To examine the power and anxiety of empire and postcolonial states, I turn to two cultural texts: a short story set in a dystopic India of the future and a play about the contemporary politics of drone warfare within the United States. In bringing these together, I reveal the disparate and transnational effects of empire and capital. I do so to address the cultural imaginaries produced by two different national contexts as they grapple with the drone as both a weapon of war and a tool of a dystopian national-global economic future marked by technoscientific advances and extreme inequality. The short story "Drone" by Hari Kunzru presents a science fiction account of the drone as a metaphor for abjected labor as well as a technology for surveillance and the extraction of profits that enable oligarchic power. *Grounded*, a prize-winning, internationally staged play written by George Brant, focuses on an American female drone operator for whom the remote bombing of children produces anxiety, trauma, and posttraumatic stress disorder, or PTSD. Fears of robotic labor as drones, drone warfare, and surveillance capture both the particularity of American anxieties regarding the recent wars as well as the violence generated by India's

[4] Schmidt, "Secret Service Arrests Man"; Sengupta, "Rise of Drones in U.S."

[5] Hansen and Stepputat, *Sovereign Bodies*; Brown, "American Nightmare."

[6] Drone Tech Report, "News and Product Reviews of Personal Drones and uavs," http://www.dronetechreport.com.

contemporary economic policies. Although these texts differ in numerous ways, including in their genre and form, both emerge from U.S. contexts of war, globalization, and technoscientific changes. Brant and Kunzru try to capture the intensive political and aesthetic disruptions caused by the advent of drones, which they imagine as the extreme privatization, banalization, and commodification of the new technology of aeromobility. While they focus on different temporalities, one focusing on contemporary wars and the other on a dystopic future, both examine the visuality of the drone as violent and disruptive.

Hari Kunzru, the author of "Drone," is a well-known fiction writer and commentator on postcolonial politics, technology, race, and literature. The author of several highly regarded novels that focus on colonialism, race, identity, technology, and new digital worlds, he has been an editor at *Wired UK* magazine and currently contributes to the online leftist British magazine *Mute*, which takes as its object of analysis the structures and impacts of neoliberalism.[7] Kunzru lives in the United States, though he was born in Great Britain to a South Asian Muslim father and white English mother; he is often compared to Salman Rushdie and Zadie Smith. In interviews and writings, Kunzru speaks of his focus on the new worlds and subjectivities—cyborgian, algorithmic-controlled, and intensely and competitively individualist—being created by the emergence and circulation of new technologies through neoliberal capitalist globalization.[8] His novels and writings reveal the influence of science fiction, science and technology studies, and postcolonial and Marxist theory; Donna Haraway is clearly an influence, as are writers such as William Gibson and Michael Moorcock.

"Drone" captures some of Kunzru's politics of protest against the technologized subjects and regimes that are imbricated in globalized neoliberal capitalism. In novels such as *Transmission*, he focuses on the difference between the cosmopolitan elites who profit from the labor of new technologies and the noncosmopolitan but mobile subordinate classes, seeking to expose the contagion of capital by tracing the lives of those who subvert it.[9] In critiquing what he considers to be an outmoded politics

[7] Kunzru, *Transmission*; Kunzru, *The Impressionist*; Kunzru, *Memory Palace*; Kun-zru, *Gods without Men*; Kunzru, *My Revolutions: A Novel*; see also the website for *Mute*, www.metamute.org.

[8] Haiven, "An Interview with Hari Kunzru."

[9] Leonard, "'A Revolution in Code'?"

that addresses liberal subjects and a liberal politics that cannot encompass both the migrants of the world and the viruses and contagions of techno-scientific change as it is harnessed by capital and postcolony, Kunzru does not disavow history. Rather, he sees sedimented pasts being used and circulated by powerful men to create even greater inequalities across race, class, gender, sexuality, and religion.[10] Postcolonial difference remains important to understand which groups are abjected as labor and which use cultural power to become global oligarchs. The drone is, for Kunzru, an example of visuality being captured by power and violence, and there is no countervisuality that can escape this power.

George Brant's widely acclaimed and frequently staged plays concern social and political issues in the United States.[11] Grounded has become one of his most celebrated plays, creating a buzz not only because of its focus on the moral and ethical problems posed by drones and drone warfare but also due to his creation of a strong and powerful female figure as the main character of the play. In an interview, Brant has revealed that the character of the pilot (who is nameless and always referred to as "the Pilot") is based on a report he found about the first female pilot in the Air National Guard, Jackie Parker. In adopting Parker's "fierce independence" for his main character, Brant created a woman who signals her freedom and empowerment through her love of flying F-16 jets.[12] Brant recalls that Parker recounted that she had more in common with male pilots than with women, and his play references this female desire for the imagined fraternal camaraderie of the US Air Force. Pilot is yet another figure in a long line of militant women who have appeared in popular media combining messages of female empowerment, equal rights, and national security. While many of these figures, such as the female protagonists of the television series *Homeland* or the film *Zero Dark Thirty*, are shown to be powerful and effective, they are, like Pilot, also represented as anguished and traumatized subjects. Their obvious lack of femininity or proper heterosexuality—indeed, their queerness—is often shown to be tragic yet necessary for national security.[13] Pilot's trajectory highlights the liberal feminist

[10] Haiven, "An Interview with Hari Kunzru."

[11] A full list of George Brant's plays and their staging appears on his website, http://www.georgebrant.net/plays.html.

[12] Simakis, "WriterGeorgeBrant."

[13] For an extended discussion of these figures in popular culture, see my forthcoming book *Saving the Security State: Exceptional Citizens in Twenty-First Century America*, Duke University Press, 2017.

equity discourse that draws in her audience, as does her traumatic relation to her job that is troubled by her maternal feelings.

Both "Drone" and *Grounded* direct their critiques not only at the violence of surveillance and war but also at economic policies—although each of these texts addresses the politics of U.S. empire and India as postcolony in quite different ways. *Grounded* focuses on the inequalities engendered by neoliberal economic arrangements that reduce the job of Pilot to that of a "drone operator." Moreover, the play suggests that even for the empire that deploys them, drones are dangerous; they not only enact surveillance of the enemy but also spy on their own citizens. The technology's visual power is double-edged since the drone monitors bring distant targets into close view even as that view has the ability to traumatize drone operators. In this play, the only innocent victims of drone attacks in distant regions of the Middle East and South Asia must be figured as children since only the very young can be unambiguously designated as innocent noncombatants. Even though accountability for these deaths is presumably dispersed across the drone's military and technology structure, Pilot comes to see herself as responsible. As the play unfolds, her maternal empathy for the children she has killed traumatizes her, and she ends up in military detention.[14]

Hari Kunzru's "Drone" also critiques the emergence of neoliberalism, but with an Indian specificity connected to the neocolonial and nationalist spread of global capitalism. The short story depicts a dystopian future where the immense wealth of a few is figured through one high-caste male oligarch who deploys Hindu nationalism as religion and tradition to capture labor and global capital through participation in the global economy and its designated economic zones that suggest Giorgio Agamben's camp.[15] While it may be tempting to contrast *Grounded* and "Drone" as completely divergent texts, they both critique global capitalism in the context of a neoliberal present. Their aesthetics reflect and engage the constant struggle, protests, and wars that have erupted in many nations and dispersed locations in recent years. At the same time, these texts articulate the violence of technoscientific advancement in quite different ways. "Drone" eschews a liberal politics for a cyborgian and dystopian future in which neoliberal capitalism's emphasis on the entrepreneurial individual

[14] For more on the relationship between war and medicine, see Terry, "Significant Injury" and *Attachments to war*.

[15] Agamben, *Homo Sacer*.

has dissolved ties of community and polity. There is not even liberal empire, since colonial power has been replaced by postcolonial, oligarchic power that uses caste and religion (particularly an authoritarian and homogenous version of Hinduism) as tools of control. The state is subject to such capital, as the market is unregulated and unbounded. A dystopic future is depicted as the result of territorially unbounded capital that creates profits from the "special economic zones" that are essentially labor camps. These zones, as spaces apart, are where the politics of visibility and visuality have been exhausted by the ubiquity of drones. Witnessing has been replaced by viewing and surveilling in a context absent of law and rights. Kunzru turns to a politics of a different sensorium, describing haptic effects that might better capture the violence of state and capital.

While "Drone" suggests liberal subjects are anachronistic to a new techno-security capitalism, *Grounded* connects the subjects of empire and its targets to produce an American liberal subject. This new kind of subjectivity recognizes that both soldier and victim are traumatized by U.S. empire's lethal military and policing power. Yet this flattening of the violence of empire erases differentials and the arbitrage of global insecurity, resulting in a uniform and homogenized concept of neoliberalism and global war. Both texts, nonetheless, help us to critically understand the ways in which the drone as weapon and commodity has come to articulate emergent fears of a technoscience that has been captured by empire, postcolony, and neoliberal capital.

Grounded: PTSD in the Empire

As many neoliberal ideas have become policy in the United States, and as the imperial wars in the Middle East have drained U.S. resources, the resulting effects at "home" have become visible through inequalities based on gender, class, and race. Movements such as Occupy and Black Lives Matter have made these inequalities visible in public discourse. We have also witnessed a struggle in geopolitical arenas over the image of the United States as a superpower and as an exceptional nation, since the wars that have depleted the U.S. economy have produced inequalities similar to many other (even non-Western) nations across the globe. While the United States continues to assert global superiority in geopolitics, global financial markets, militarization at home, and wars abroad, there are still concerns about the waning of American power from the Cold War period.[16] It is not so much that the United States is no longer powerful militarily, since it has the lethal weaponry and the ability to kill or to allow the killing of many in distant regions, but its logic of insecurity and fear has come to pervade the culture of its empire, proposing it is less powerful than in the past. Not surprisingly, this insecurity is also now a project of transnational capital that both contributes to and benefits from precarity and surveillance.

Grounded captures the anxieties of this waning empire in a number of ways, from the bleak landscape of the Nevada location where the U.S. military's drone program is featured to the breakdown of Pilot, whose tedious exertions at the screen are seen as traumatizing. A staging of the play in 2015 in New York City starring Anne Hathaway and directed by Julie Taymor (who has had many successes on Broadway), though presented at the very small theater The Public, was a hit, with a sold-out house for most of the shows (echoing its success in many other theaters where it was previously staged). Audiences at The Public responded to the one-woman play with admiration for Hathaway's performance and for the effective staging and directing.

In the play, Hathaway's character, called simply "the Pilot," is a nameless woman who aspires to be a Top Gun–type air force pilot who revels in flying F-16s in what she calls the "blue." She has to become a drone operator once she becomes pregnant, is no longer allowed to pilot fighter planes, and needs a job. With her husband and child she moves to Nevada, where she is charged with monitoring and bombing so-called terrorists in Pakistan and Afghanistan. The constant attentiveness demanded for the job—and we are told she has to be working long hours at the screen every day—begins to cause her to unravel psychologically. The discrimination against a woman pilot demoted to remote drone operation is foregrounded as Pilot expresses her frustration and anger that she cannot remain flying in the sky—in the "blue." This loss renders her immobile and grounded. Because she has to carry out close surveillance for many hours each day of people in distant regions imagined as targets, she comes to believe someone is watching her everywhere and that there are cameras all around her. Even while shopping at the local mall with her child, she becomes concerned about surveillance: "But there's always a camera, right? / J.C. Penney or Afghanistan / Everything is witnessed".[17] She imagines

[16] Nye, "The Future of American Power"; Wallerstein, *The Decline of American Power*.
[17] Brant, *Grounded*, 47.

those watching her to be like the nineteen-year-old (males, presumably) she works with or workers in India to whom surveillance has been outsourced; her disintegration is compounded by the thought of being watched by foreign brown men just as she has watched them through her monitor. As the play closes, she tells the audience that they are all being watched too, thus drawing her audience into both her psychic breakdown and the realization of the violence of this regime of war.

The play suggests that it is not family or husband that "ground" her; it is the U.S. military that is responsible for her situation. The tedium of commuting to and from work through a bleak desert, along with the long hours of looking at the screen, contrast intensely with the life of a pilot flying a fighter jet. As the character realizes that she has lost the excitement, pleasure, and sociality in being with other pilots, she loses her ambition and desire to work. Her achievement in becoming an air force pilot, the result of "sweat and brains and guts," signified by her flight suit, allowed her the thrill and empowerment of control of the "blue" sky:

> I'm in the blue for a reason I have missiles to launch
> I have Sidewinders
> I have Mavericks
> I rain them down on the minarets and concrete below me
> The structures that break up the sand
> I break them back down
> Return them to desert
>
> To particles
> Sand
> At least I think I do
> I'm long gone by the time the boom happens.[18]

The play suggests that it is not simply the thrill of flight that is exciting to Pilot but also her ability to rain down destruction from an F-16, especially in a Muslim country ("on the minarets"), without staying to see the destructive impact and deaths she causes on the ground.

While the play focuses on the trauma of viewing the results of "unmanned" missile attacks close up on the screen, the narrative moves too quickly over the violence of "manned" air attacks. While the monologue does mention the destruction caused by airpower, these violent acts

[18] Brant, *Grounded*, 9–10.

of aerial bombing become imbued with Pilot's nostalgia for the joy and pleasure of flying. What further unhinges Pilot—"unmanning" her in a gendered sense because she no longer works among male pilots in the air force—is that she is presumably able to see the impact of the bombs more clearly than she might have from a fighter jet or a piloted bombing run. Once she sees that one of the missiles she releases has killed a child, she has a nervous breakdown. In this key moment, the play asks us to critique the use of drones as a weapon of war. At the same time, however, we come to realize the power of drone technology and its visual capabilities. Military technology's success, paradoxically, is that it can seemingly make us look more closely at the violence in which we share responsibility.

Many analysts of visual culture have critiqued the idea that only proximity will bring about empathy and identification with the victims and the targets of drone attacks.[19] Some scholars of visual culture also have argued for the particularity of "drone vision" as an emergent and important aspect of militarization of everyday life.[20] While the play suggests that remote vision, or what Caren Kaplan has called "remote sensing,"[21] does not simply distance us from the violence of war, it also signals that distance and proximity matter for visual politics. If drone vision creates proximity to the violence it causes, aerial war allows separation from the carnage: Pilot in her military aircraft can be "long gone by the time the boom happens."

Not only are distance or proximity foregrounded by drone warfare but also the greater capacities of the screen, cameras, and the hardware and software that traumatize those viewing the monitors. While suggesting that the military's technological and intelligence failure to distinguish between child and terrorist is responsible for Pilot's traumatic breakdown, it is also Pilot's ability to see the missile strike the child, a sight compounded by her maternal feelings, that is to blame. Yet such a logic of technologically proximate visibility—both triumphant and tragic—ignores the deaths of civilians and the foundational assumptions of contemporary wars in the Middle East and South Asia through which all Muslims have come to be seen as threatening.[22]

As much as the play suggests that it is the viewing of harm to the child that undoes the imperial subject, war's spectacle has other effects. As

[19] Boltanski, *Distant Suffering*; Mirzoeff, *Watching Babylon*.

[20] Stahl, "What the Drone Saw."

[21] Kaplan, "Sensing Distance."

[22] Rana, *Terrifying Muslims*; Razack, *Casting Out*; McAlister, *Epic Encounters*.

Thomas Blom Hansen and Finn Stepputat argue, empire has to stage spectacles of violence, and the effective spectacle of violence on itself makes its sovereignty even more powerful.[23] Pilot's breakdown marks the power of empire over its subjects. Empire's move between spectacular and hidden violence is visible through its traumatic effect on the white, female, and American body of the drone operator.

Elise Morrison suggests that the staging of the play positions its audience as surveilling the action while also learning to be empathetic to the effects of such surveillance and bombing.[24] In this reading, empathy and humanity are the universals of the play, shared by Pilot and extended to Pakistani, Yemeni, and Afghan children. However, this moral logic remains a limited critique because empathy can only be directed at particular subjects, such as children, rather than adults who may not elicit similar empathy or presumptions of innocence.[25]

The play's staging at The Public also suggested more than simply the production of empathy. The minimal stage, with only sand on the ground, the action occurring below and in the center of the circle of rows of seats, enable the action to focus on the breakdown of Pilot rather than the violence that Pilot has both seen and rained down on targets far away. The play's directions state that "the audience is The Pilot's confidante, to varying degrees of familiarity, until perhaps the final pages." Julie Taymor, the director at The Public, interpreted the audience as both confidante and witness for Pilot. Seated in a circle around her, the audience becomes protector and witness as they watch her disintegration. To the extent that some of the activism against the use of drones for bombing has come from charging the United States with human rights abuses and extrajudicial killings of its own citizens and of distant Others, the play's moral trajectory emphasizes the power of witnessing and visuality. Yet if the audience is both witness and court of justice, the spectators come to understand the violence of U.S. war through its effect on a figure who shares some

[23] Hansen and Stepputat, introduction to *Sovereign Bodies.*

[24] Morrison, "Ambushed by Empathy."

[25] From scholarly studies of emotion and affect, we know that empathy is a historical project that has now become intricately configured into new, more "realistic" digital games in order to produce particular affects. As video game cultures are imbricated in military projects, and because games elicit feelings that are part of game design, who or what can elicit empathy is also a question of the power of militarized image-making. The production of affect from the visual is both critique and mastery of a technology that shared much with the culture of virtual games; Moore, "Invigorating Play."

responsibility for that violence. The play asks that only the distant child and Pilot be mourned.[26] In this way, the play enacts the limits of visibility that have become part of militarized vision in the United States, allowing us to see only certain kinds of violence on specific bodies, and to mourn only that which can be seen; in this case, the violence is perpetrated on the drone operator rather than on those being bombed in South Asia and the Middle East. This is the limited vision of the technopolitics of violence of drone warfare.

Thus, even as some of the violence of drone warfare is made visible, so much remains hidden. Drone missiles often kill within buildings, and their effects remain secret. It is only in sporadic cases that we hear about the effects of bombings. Because the regions where such drones operate are what Eyal Weizman calls "frontier" zones where researchers and reporters often cannot enter, it might be reasonable to believe that Pilot is the best witness to the deaths caused by drone war. Yet such witnessing limits empathy while it distributes blame. Weizman has argued that drone warfare, like many other forms of contemporary war, requires witnessing and accountability that have to come from a shift from testimony to "forensics."[27] This term designates both the use of technology to uncover the harm of military technologies and the "forum" that reveals evidence of violence via the use of digital technology. The art of the forum, according to Weizman, needs a triangulation of testimony between technology (satellite, digital architecture, and remapping) that uncovers the destruction, the human witness who has suffered the violence and who comes from the targeted regions, and the expert or translator who can bring these narratives together to reveal the complex causality of war. If one follows Weizman to analyze *Grounded,* neither Pilot as witness nor the audience as the court of justice who sees only the trauma of Pilot can adequately testify to either the visible or the hidden and extensive violence of military drones. The play does not reveal the pervasive and unseen violence of drone wars or the multiple ways that technoscience and the imperial state formulate its human and nonhuman targets and weapons. It cannot, crucially, reveal why some regions can be subject to drone attacks. As Jacob Burns argues, it is the long history of colonial law in South Asia through which such "frontier" and tribal zones are produced as places where

[26] Butler, *Precarious Life.*
[27] Weizman, *Forensic Architecture.*

sovereignty is left as a "politically productive zone of exception."[28] The history of colonial and nationalist powers that created these "frontier" zones suggests that designations of targets, subjectivity, and sovereignty are palimpsestic, while their designation is designed to defeat both distant and proximate seeing.

In addition, as so much of recent war involves "boots on the ground," from both U.S. military and private security companies who have killed civilians and others with impunity, the play is unable to move beyond a liberal critique of war to examine the imbrication between and co-construction of war machines, capitalism, and imperial histories. That the drone is imagined as a new technology that creates new fears for humans and humanity means that every iteration of its technological power and novelty can disguise the longue durée of technologized war and its lethal consequences as well as the multiple means—legal, geopolitical, economic—through which new technologies and their targets come into existence.

Pilot's nostalgia for manned, aerial war serves to make that earlier form of warfare more human, less distancing, and more intimate, evoking the nostalgia for lost community—gendered as a fraternity—that seems to accompany each new technology. The humanity of manned warfare is conveyed through Pilot's memories of the fraternal camaraderie between military pilots flying planes in war and her desire to recapture the thrill of flying F-16s. In this way, the play erases the violence of a history of empire and aerial bombardment.[29] Its reliance on empathy as the powerful ethic to resist new wars remains limited by a refusal to address any difference between the history of empire and its historical targets, even as it cannot but exhibit the power of imperial war and violence. Human witnessing and human embodiment by Americans become the play's tools for resistance. The power and limit of this embodied witnessing emerges via the white body of Pilot, who is brought down by the empire for whom she has become an insignificant, easily replaceable operative. Here, even the impact of neoliberal politics remains confined to an American subject, rather than to its broader, global effects.

[28] Burns, "Persistent Exception," 400.

[29] Kaplan, Loyer, and Daniels, "Precision Targets."

There is little doubt that *Grounded* was inspired by reports that drone operators were found to be suffering from PTSD.[30] Peter Asaro has examined drone operators as new subjectivities constructed through surveillance and remote agency combined with post-Fordist labor practices that distribute agency and responsibility across technology and its multiple producers and consumers. Reports and research have shown that the stress, long hours, and horrors of war seen "close-up," in tandem with the scorn with which drone operators are treated by others in the air force, have contributed to considerable turnover. The play also draws on news reports on gender equity issues in the military as the protagonist sees herself demeaned by being relegated, because of her pregnancy, from the position of jet pilot to what she calls the "Chairforce." The issue of gendered equality and discrimination is then factored into neoliberal working conditions and the realization of pervasive surveillance that leads to her traumatic breakdown. In addition, because she is a mother of a little girl, the killing of a child by a missile from the drone in a remote location is shown to be even more affecting. Finally, it is only Pilot's traumatized self who can warn the audience of the ubiquitous surveillance that surrounds us, thereby aligning, quite problematically, this surveillance of an American audience with those who live in the particular areas that are considered available for bombardment and who endure the constant hum and shadow of death by drones in the "frontier" zones of South Asia and the Middle East.

"Drone": Labor and Oligarchs in the Postcolony

If *Grounded* produces a critique of drone war and surveillance by revealing the harm these technologies cause to an American white woman in the military, Hari Kunzru's "Drone" takes us to a dystopic future set somewhere in South Asia in a "special economic zone," where drones carry out surveillance over labor camps that enrich wealthy oligarchs. If the global economy can be critiqued for the inequality that it produces, and the ways that neoliberal capitalism has empowered corporate and oligarchic sovereignties that have undermined the state, including U.S. empire, "Drone" pushes this critique further. It does so by suggesting that neoliberalism's

[30] Chappelle, Salinas, and McDonald, "PsychologicalHealthScreening"; Bumiller, "Air Force Drone Operators"; R. Martin, "Report"; Trimble, "Study"; Kaag, "Drones, Ethics and the Armchair Soldier"; Gettinger, "Burdens of War."

future is the production of hypercompetitive individuals that include both oligarch and various classes of workers. Postcolonial nationalism has disappeared, replaced by oligarchic power. In this context, the oligarch can be both global and postcolonial, Hindu and Indian. This is a postliberal dystopia where witnessing seems redundant because there is no legal redress or remedy to exploitation. In the locale of Kunzru's story, colonial, national, and international laws have designated some regions as zones without laws or government, giving them over to unregulated capital. Thus, drones operate outside community; anyone who can afford a drone can use it to look anywhere, but looking is not about witnessing. Drones are operated by so many heterogeneous entities that neither spectacle nor its counter is able to produce either justice or empathy. If the narrator shows us that the witnessing gaze is disinterested, what emerges is a different kind of political understanding: one that must be more broadly sensorial, both haptic and sonic. It is only by descriptions of the sensoria of the "special economic zone," which is the mining camp, that one can know the postcolony's banal necropolitics. But even that knowing is without a goal, without any futurity. Such a failure of sight, then, and the excess of the sensorium mark the divergent aesthetics of the postcolony's drone economy.

In Kunzru's text, Indian nationalism has disappeared to be replaced by a Hindu nationalism that is subservient to capital. Inequalities flourish, depending on primitive accumulation from histories of race, caste, and class. In the story, postcolonial elites are both cyborg and genetically enhanced to be as superior as possible, their bodies inscribed with Hindu caste and religious hierarchies and symbols. The oligarch controls all natural resources, ensuring that whatever is "natural" or "pure" is kept for the enjoyment and use of a select few. All others compete with each other at various levels of the economy. While all the bodies in this story are either genetically engineered or cyborgs, only the oligarch claims humanness, perfecting himself to be as handsome as the local ideal of masculinity might imagine. While Kunzru offers neoliberal empire as global and postcolonial, differences based on caste and religion are important because they are used to produce power and to exploit. Yet Kunzru does not offer a project of reclaiming humanity in the name of universals, nor is his story a project of cultural or civilizational difference. In "Drone," postcolonial elites rule by controlling capital and culture on national and global scales. There is no possibility of being external to this power, and no depiction of anything outside the dystopia of the economic zones.

The use of security forces to protect the expansion of capital has become an important aspect of contemporary Indian neoliberalism. It is well known by now that the Indian state has recently been buying drones for military use from Israel and is also developing its own drones, but little attention has been paid to this program in the Indian news media (much of which is also under corporate control). The digital economy has received much greater attention in the news, as its development and growth continue to be most important for politicians, businesspeople, and journalists. Neoliberal economic policies have become powerful due to the importance given to the private and corporate sectors as engines of development,[31] even though there is some continued emphasis on distribution of resources and welfare. This focus on economic growth means that corporations are seen as corrupt only if they collude with politicians or the state to amass wealth. With the rise of Hindu nationalism and the coming to power of Narendra Modi as prime minister with a history of pogroms against Muslims, there is continued disenfranchisement of religious minorities, Dalits, and the poor through neoliberal privatization on multiple scales. Modi's political party, the Bharatiya Janata Party, has continued the policy of the previous administration of appropriating the lands of indigenous peoples for mining corporations. Its goal is to control knowledge production through disenfranchising religious minorities. Tools of biometric identification are being sold as essential to development and poverty reduction, giving rise to fears among minorities, indigenous groups, and Dalits that new forms of uppercaste control are emerging. Given such conditions, it is not surprising that Kunzru's short story suggests that economic globalization has produced oligarchs who rely on right-wing Hindu nationalism to control economy and state, further disenfranchising labor.

By locating his short story in a postcolony and in a "camp" that is a "special economic zone" where rare minerals for the new economies are mined, Kunzru's story takes us to another space of exception than that in *Grounded*, but it is one that cannot be targeted by bombing because its condition of entropy enables exploitation. This entropy makes it possible for necropolitics to flourish. In Kunzru's story, the capitalist is called "the Seth" (a term that translates as "merchant," "banker," or "trader"), who is also a high-caste Hindu. Seth lives in an apartment building that towers over the slums below. Here "tower" is a reference to the house built by

[31] Shah, *In the Shadows of the State*.

one of the richest men in contemporary India, the Mumbai-based billionaire Mukesh Ambani. Ambani's house, Antilia, is a twenty-seven-story building with helipads, floating gardens, and swimming pools built at the reported cost of a billion dollars, and it towers over other apartment buildings and the slums of Mumbai. Kunzru incorporates this building into his story with an additional fictional twist: the owner has also purchased the air rights around it so that nothing can intrude on his privacy. While Seth initially designed the tower as a Tuscan fantasy, he has turned it into a "Hindu" version in order to be seen as a true patriot and to use religion to control the state and the population.

As the story begins, there are crowds at the temple in the courtyard of the tower. Men claiming to be gurus (popularly known as "godmen" in India), priests of "every orthodox sect," rub shoulders with businessmen and bureaucrats. All those present are high-caste men, all genetically augmented with legally mandated religious and caste marks on their bodies; these marks are not just inscribed but have become genetically incorporated into the bodies themselves. Since every person with money can be modified to become attractive, these men are all "generically handsome." They all look up to the oligarch with slavish attention, aspiring to become oligarchs themselves. As this large group gathers to participate in a religious ceremony in the courtyard, the police chief monitors the crowds below him while the state bureaucrats "inhale the scent of burning sandalwood, their noses twitching with jealousy and awe" (17).[32] The sandalwood is not a virtual or genetically modified product but comes from the last groves of the trees existing in the world, which are owned by Seth, who "controls everything from raw materials to staggeringly abstract forms of intellectual property" (17). Seth is part of a system that seems to be so powerful that it appears immune to resistance. Thus, the narrator says of Seth: "So entangled is he in the global economy that it is impossible to imagine how he could be excised" (17).

The inequality of this economy is conveyed through the narrator's emphasis on jostling bodies, their proximity to power, and the smell of sandalwood that evokes pleasures and desires that are unattainable for many in this world. Seth and his cronies designate this exploitative and unequal context as "Ramrajya," the mythical kingdom of God defined in the epic Ramayana as the most ethical state.

[32] All parenthetical page numbers refer to Kunzru, "Drone."

Unlike everyone else, however, Seth is an ascetic, and he is kept in that state by vast sums of money. The narrator compares him to Mahatma Gandhi in this regard, linking anticolonial nationalism's cultural politics to their more recent capture by capital. Seth eats only the freshest food, the most natural, nonsynthetic products, and the last wild animals and fishes left on earth. He relies on what are called "Vedic" principles to structure his life and work. In this, the narrator references Indian Prime Minister Narendra Modi and the Hindu nationalists who are now claiming to run the government and to conduct science on neo-Vedic principles, constructing a theology of profit-making and exploitation. The narrator tells us that even Seth's seventh wife is "headhunted from an isolated rural community" and becomes a "vessel" after "compliance with stringent genetic and astrological tests" (18). In this story, the combination of oligarchic masculinity and control over women, decontextualized theology and science, and invented tradition is deliberately staged as the source of the oligarch's wealth and power. Seth's daughter from this wife is similarly eugenically designed since the "biological matter that makes up her body has flowed in from the purest sources" (18). She is designed to be beautiful and trained to be obedient, since Seth is "molding a family aesthetic, a brand that can be passed on," an aesthetic that is both visual and material (19). She lives with constant surveillance and monitoring, with care offered by the "warm nebulous presence" of an entity that is both servant and dog that "exists in her sensorium as a repertoire of gestures, a nuzzling, a pleading, the scrabble of tiny paws on her skin" (19).

Despite his power, however, Seth is worried that his daughter, whom he surveils obsessively by watching her every move, seems to be interested in something outside his house. His surveillance mechanisms show that she is spending time, via a drone, in the networks of one of his mining companies. What Seth's daughter looks at is the benighted landscape of a mine, one of the last ones in the world where rare minerals are to be found, and she is taking an interest in Jai, one of the miners. This is a "special economic zone," which is "in a state of continual, undeclared war, the war of each against each" (23). It is designated to be outside any government or rule of law, and it exemplifies the kind of location where Seth is able to extract profits. The zone is called a "camp," and it is a location where bodies, all "blue-black" (21) and thus racially differentiated from anyone outside the camp, are constantly mutating, created by jumbled-up "organic and inorganic" fragments that rise up and disappear (22). "Teeming, swarming," the camp is a "mess of sensory fragments," where poor miners "know what it means to be exhausted, to lie down at the top of the pit, gasping through their masks"; they know "the feel of mud cakes on skin," and the mud waits for their bodies when they die (22). Those in power wear hazmat suits and have ventilators to protect themselves from the mud.

In this camp, the miners labor endlessly while "drones and chakras" enforce their labor. Chakras, based on Hindu and Buddhist religious concepts, are rotating wheels that reference the energy swirling in bodies. Along with drones, chakras enact surveillance on the miners. The numerous chakras are everywhere, producing a constant hum, a sonic reverberation that never ceases. "After a storm," we learn, "the ground is crunchy underfoot with little electronic corpses" (23). The miners are all seen as a security risk and "must participate in network identification and trust protocols to demonstrate they are not a threat" (23). They take the "precious dust" they have mined to dealers who are women—"fat and glossy"—working for governments or "any of the dozen other factions that depend on mining revenue to continue their obscure insurgencies" (23). The division of labor here positions miners as far more subject to necropolitical power than the women dealers who work behind shields that protect them from the miners and the noxious air of the camp.

Within the camp, there are other zones that are even more highly entropic. One of these is the "red-light district known as the Cages" (27), where the miners can go for sexual gratification. Here, the "process" offers "every type and quality of peak, dip, spread and intensification" (27). The narrator tells us that "whores" are "grafted onto walls [that] display available orifices or scroll out stims that grab the crotch"; there is a confusion of "tacky skins and feelies" (27). When one of the miners, Jai, ventures into this zone, semen "spatters the optics of his sensorium," and he is "brushed by nipples, hair, lubricated hands" (27). Women disappeared even as sex workers; only female body parts and genitals remain. Necropolitics produces the abject male as labor and fragmented women into sexual fragments or figures who profit from their place on the border of the economic zone. Only the haptic captures the abjection of labor; the miners, we are told by the narrator, "want the hard stuff" (27).

The only other female figure in "Drone" is Seth's daughter, who is seemingly outside the power of capital while being created by it. She watches Jai, a nineteen-year-old "human, a man," described as "beautiful" with "blue-black skin" and a "high strong voice" (25).[33] He is alone, "part of no tribe or community that he can remember," and finds "unremarkable" the horrors he has seen in his short life. Unlike the other miners, he is not covered with mud and dust, and wherever he moves, he is accompanied by "tiny drones and flyers" (25). Yet it is not clear who sends these machines, and the other miners wonder at the swarm of drones around Jai. The drones are described as "low grade personal devices" that "come from far away, carried on the wind" (25). These devices also see and feel, because they have "optics and sometimes haptics, but there may not be anyone watching or feeling." Every person, we learn, knows that they are being watched, if not by humans then by "some algorithm trained to sift through the feeds for porn or lulz or evidence of crime" (25). Drones are owned by numerous people and groups who send them to watch anyone they wish, so that "privacy is a quaint word, like chivalry, or superego" (26). People all over the world send these drones to look at things: "Go find something to look at. Not that, this. Not this, that. Floating about on solar-cell gossamer. Some are directed, others almost completely autonomous, trained to go in search of a particular kink of flavor. The famous put up security; otherwise they'd live in a swarm of angry voyeuristic bees" (25).

In this story, drones are manifestations of hyperindividualization and hypersurveillance; anyone can surveil anyone if they can purchase a drone. As well as surveilling, they offer commodities and services for purchase. But none of these drones surveil the mine in order to help the miners. No drone appears to protect Jai or any of the other miners from their miserable lives, and there is no other authority or power to turn to in this special economic zone. Jai dies after he buys a robotic arm; it is supposed to help him work better in the mine, but it infects him. Seriously ill, he has no money to take advantage of the numerous offers from the buzzing drones to protect him from the viruses that are replicating in his body. As he dies, offers come to him for his organs: "offers run right through him, subprime bids for his organs, corporate indentures. Your fatal condition cured in return for ten years' labour: new life just a click away" (30). He cannot take the offers and is too weak to do anything but die at the door of his hut, as the drones watch: "Overhead the plume swarms and wheels, eyes trained down on him" (31).

[33] *Jai* is a diasporic and popular name—easily pronounced globally. It translates into victory and is thus ironic because the dystopia does not allow any victory for workers like Jai.

While Seth's daughter has sent her drone to look at Jai, and perhaps she is the agent for the drone buzzing over Jai at the end, she does not come to his rescue. Although she makes Seth worried and anxious about her desires, she cannot reduce the entropy in the Cages. She is, however, a female cyborg who desires something else. What to make of her remains unclear; it seems that postliberal and postcolonial politics have unclear and heterosexual desires, although their rupture is promising. The narrator cannot tell us what she wants or why she looks at Jai. Her desires, in effect, defeat the narrator's ability to survey the scene.

In Kunzru's short story, the drone is both the embodiment of human labor available for expropriation and a technology produced by economic regimes that have come to reduce everyone to a competitive individualism. While the oligarch ruthlessly extracts and uses resources for himself, state bureaucrats, priests and godmen, dealers, and traders all compete against each other by becoming various types of cyborgs. Even workers work obsessively to improve their productivity. No collaborations are possible that may resist this structure; the power of sight does not produce community. The drones are commodities, deployed by numerous nameless and unknown people and machines; these drones fly and buzz around looking around for pleasure or for surveillance. Visuality has lost the ability to shock or elicit emotion. There are so many drones that privacy has become "a quaint word," an "evolutionary relic, a kink that is being ironed out by the forces of order" (26). There are no futures possible, as is the case with most dystopias, only extraction, exploitation, surveillance, and death allied to a hyperindividualized culture of both unbounded and deterritorialized capitalism that instrumentalizes Hindu nationalism for profit. In this text, drones are not there to kill as they are in *Grounded*, nor are they assigned to an agency separate from that of the cyborg whose commands they carry out. They are simply instruments of various desires and powers, many violent and many who just want to look, though their looking does not help reduce the violence. While nameless and countless consumers use drones to look at others without offering connection or community, the capitalists use them for control over the camp.

Conclusion

In these texts, as the latest avatars of technoscientific progress allied to neoliberal capital and militarized empire, drones evoke insecurity and exploitation. Whereas *Grounded* blames the state and the empire for this exploitation precisely because its violence has now "come home" to the empire, "Drone" sees the state and the empire at the service of capital that is in the hands of postcolonial oligarchs and cannot offer any visual counterpolitics. If, at the end of *Grounded*, Pilot exhorts the audience in the empire to remember that they are all being surveilled, in order to produce a politics of resistance to empire through visual witnessing and recognition of the insecurity produced within it, the postcolonial dystopia in "Drone" provides no such possibility. There is no emergent force of resistance by the cyborg,[34] and resistance is foreclosed because individuals, as securitized and militarized consumers, are no longer capable of being in community, nor can they defeat the powers of capital. Although there are ruptures to this power from unexpected entities, their direction and intent remain unclear.

By collapsing the meaning of drone as abjected labor and military and consumer technology, Kunzru's postcolonial critique, then, turns to production and labor in those economic zones to understand the effects of unregulated global capital as a totalizing power. If visuality produces no recourse from violence, and individual use of drones cannot be witness to violence, descriptions of the haptic also continue to reveal immiseration without any possibility of ending it. While visuality is clearly unable to turn to witnessing, the haptic dwells in the violence of abjection in the postcolony. While the haptic does more than the visual, its goals are not about rights or solidarity or interruptions to dystopia. Postcolonial politics then concerns more than that which can be seen, since it is the scale of the widespread and dispersed violence of empire, capital, and postcolony that cannot be captured by the visual. Even as researchers such as Eyal Weizman produce visual evidence as central to claims made at the United Nations, or at other national and international courts, or even in transnational news media or social media, the fate and uses of such evidence are limited to particular cases rather than the broader structural violence of contemporary capitalism and imperialism. We know that while the U.S. government has provided small sums as reparation for civilian deaths in Pakistan and Afghanistan, and that such sums can help in individual and limited cases, minimal reparation has not stopped the war, the bombing, or the destruction of ways of living.[35] Given the massive outpouring of images from all sorts of entities and all kinds of groups, as well as the control of media by

[34] Haraway, "A Cyborg Manifesto."

[35] See, for instance, Chakrabarty, "The Climate of History."

transnational corporations, there are limits to what sort of images can be seen, stored or circulated, or used for reparation or redress. If international law designates spaces of expropriation as outside law, then the history of looking is of limited use. For critical media activists such as Kunzru, the new modes of exploitation and violence are to be understood by other sensorial means, such as touch. Yet even as Kunzru's critique gestures to the widespread violence and the unnamed numbers who suffer it, it is unable to grasp the many ruptures, resistances, and movements that disrupt power and its effects. As much as visuality cannot grasp the extent of violence, Kunzru's postcolonial politics, confined to its dystopic sensorium, cannot capture how the violence is lived in complex, heterogenous ways that are not only necropolitical.

Postcolonial theorists have come to see the politics of representation as limited in its remit. While scholars debate the Anthropocene as demanding a new politics that is both planetary and regionally and locally accountable,[36] they turn to the many protests and migrations of the new century as evidence of the failure of nationalism's cultures to control the excesses of capital and the inability of either humanism or capitalist democracy to change the inequalities and hierarchies of the emergent order. Yet postcolonial politics still offers compelling approaches to understand these inequalities within historical and emergent cultures in the Global South, the logics of hierarchy and difference based on articulations and intersections of caste, race, gender, nation, and religion that enable accumulation by dispossession.

Notes

I dedicate this chapter to my late colleague Mark Poster. Mark's research inaugurated a whole new field of historical cultural theory on digital media, and his work has long been a great inspiration for many, especially in paying attention to the complexities of technology and the history of the relation between technology and culture. He read Kunzru's work long before I did and gave me his copy of Kunzru's first novel. I am indebted to him for many kindnesses and comradeship. My thanks also go to Laura Wexler, my good friend and colleague, who found the *Granta* issue and, purchased it for me, the Theory and Media Studies Colloquium in the Yale Department of English, especially to Julia Chan for her comments on this chapter that came from her brilliant research on dystopic fiction, and

[36] See, for instance, Chakrabarty, "The Climate of History."

to Peter Raccuglia and Anna Shechtman for inviting me to share this work. I also thank Caren Kaplan and Lisa Parks for their patience, encouragement, and excellent comments.

Bibliography

Agamben, Giorgio. 1998. *Homo Sacer: Sovereign Power and Bare Life*. Translated by Daniel Heller-Roazen. Stanford, CA: Stanford University Press.

Bashir, Shahzad, and Robert D. Crews. 2012. In *Introduction to Under the Drones: Modern Lives in the Afghanistan-Pakistan Borderlands*, ed. Shahzad Bashir and Robert D. Crews, 1–16. Cambridge, MA: Harvard University Press.

Benjamin, Medea. 2012. *Drone Warfare: Killing by Remote Control*. New York: OR Books.

Boltanski, Luc. 1999. *Distant Suffering: Morality, Media and Politics*. Cambridge: Cambridge University Press.

Brant, George. 2013. *Grounded*. London: Oberon Books.

Bumiller, Elisabeth. 2011. Air Force Drone Operators Show High Levels of Stress. *New York Times*, December 18, 2011.

Burns, Jacob. 2014. Persistent Exception: Pakistani Law and the Drone War. In *Forensis: The Architecture of Public Truth*, ed. Forensic Architecture, 400–408. Berlin: Sternberg Press.

Butler, Judith. 2006. *Precarious Life: The Powers of Mourning and Violence*. London: Verso.

Chakrabarty, Dipesh. 2009. The Climate of History: Four Theses. *Critical Inquiry* 35 (2): 197–222.

Chappelle, Wayne, Amber Salinas, and Kent McDonald. 2011. *Psychological Health Screening of Remotely Piloted Aircraft (RPA) Operators and Supporting Units*. Paper presented at the Symposium on Mental Health and Well-Being across the Military Spectrum, Bergen, Norway, April 12, 2011.

Evangelista, Matthew, and Henry Shue, eds. 2014. *The American Way of Bombing: Changing Ethical and Legal Norms, from Flying Fortresses to Drones*. Ithaca, NY: Cornell University Press.

Gettinger, Dan. 2014. *Burdens of War: PTSD and Drone Crews*. Center for the Study of the Drone, April 21, 2014. http://dronecenter.bard.edu/burdens-war-crews-drone-aircraft/.

Haiven, Max. 2014. An Interview with Hari Kunzru: Networks, Finance Capital and the Fate of the Novel. *Wasafiri* 28 (3): 8–23.

Hansen, Thomas Blom, and Finn Stepputat, eds. 2005. *Sovereign Bodies: Citizens, Migrants, and States in the Postcolonial World*. Princeton, NJ: Princeton University Press.

Haraway, Donna. 1991. A Cyborg Manifesto: Science, Technology, and Socialist-Feminism in the Late Twentieth Century. In *Simians, Cyborgs, and Women*, 149–181. New York: Routledge.

Kaag, John, and Sarah Kreps. 2014. *Drone Warfare*. Cambridge: Polity Press.

Kaplan, Caren. 2013. Sensing Distance: The Time and Space of Contemporary War. *Social Text*, June 17, 2013. http://socialtextjournal.org/periscope_article/sensing-distance-the-time-and-space-of-contemporary-war/.

Kaplan, Caren, Erik Loyer, and Ezra Claytan Daniels. 2013. Precision Targets: GPS and the Militarization of Everyday Life. *Canadian Journal of Communication* 38 (3): 397–420.

Kunzru, Hari. 2003. *The Impressionist*. [2002]. New York: Plume.

Kunzru, Hari. 2005. *Transmission*. [2004]. New York: Plume.

Kunzru, Hari. 2008. *My Revolutions: A Novel.* [2007]. New York: Plume.

Kunzru, Hari. 2013a. *Gods without Men*. New York: Vintage.

Kunzru, Hari. 2013b. In *Memory Palace*, ed. Laurie Britton Newell and Ligaya Salazar. London: V and A.

Kunzru, Hari. 2015. Drone. *Granta* 130:15–31.

Leonard, Philip. 2014. 'A Revolution in Code'? Hari Kunzru's *Transmission* and the Cultural Politics of Hacking. *Textual Practice* 28 (2): 267–287.

Martin, Rachel. 2011. Report: High Levels of 'Burnout' in U.S. Drone Pilots. *NPR*, December 19, 2011. http://www.npr.org/2011/12/19/143926857/report-high-levels-of-burnout-in-u-s-drone-pilots.

Moore, Christopher. 2012. Invigorating Play: The Role of Affect in Online Multiplayer FPS Games. In *Guns, Grenades and Grunts: First Person Shooter Games*, ed. Gerald A. Voorhees, Joshua Call, and Katie Whitlock, 341–364. London: Continuum Books.

Morrison, Elise. 2014. Ambushed by Empathy: George Brant's *Grounded. TDR/The Drama Review* 58 (4): 163–169.

Naylor, Brian. 2011. Look, Up in The Sky! It's a Drone, Looking at You. *NPR*, December 5, 2011. http://www.npr.org/2011/12/05/143144146/drone-technology-finding-its-way-to-american-skies.

Nye, Joseph S. 2010. The Future of American Power. *Foreign Affairs*, November 1, 2010. https://www.foreignaffairs.com/articles/2010-11-01/future-american-power.

Rana, Junaid. 2011. *Terrifying Muslims: Race and Labor in the South Asian Diaspora*. Durham, NC: Duke University Press.

Schmidt, Michael S. 2015. Secret Service Arrests Man after Drone Flies Near White House. *New York Times*, May 14, 2015.

Sengupta, Somini. 2013. Rise of Drones in U.S. Spurs Efforts to Limit Uses. *New York Times*, February 15, 2013.

Shah, Alpa. 2010. *In the Shadows of the State: Indigenous Politics, Environmentalism, and Insurgency in Jharkhand, India*. Durham, NC: Duke University Press.

Simakis, Andrea. 2014. Writer George Brant and the Star of 'Grounded' at the Cleveland Play House Talk Sexy Fighter Pilots, Drones and Why We Love Dark, Complicated Characters (Preview). *Plain Dealer*, May 8, 2014.

Stahl, Roger. 2013. What the Drone Saw: The Cultural Optics of the Unmanned War. *Australian Journal of International Affairs* 67 (5): 659–674.

Trimble, Stephen. 2008. Study: Flying Predators Bad for Pilot's Health, Family Life. Dew *Line*, April 2008. http://flightglobal.rbiblogs.co.uk/the-dewline/2008/04/study-flying-predators-bad-for/?replytocom=19989.

Weizman, Eyal. *Forensic Architecture: Notes from Fields and Forums*. Documenta 13.

CHAPTER 3

The Superfluity of Imperial Guilt: Drones and Civilian Casualties in Showtime's *Homeland* Season 4

Lopamudra Basu

The Showtime series *Homeland* can be interpreted as conducting the work of cultural acceptance and normalization of drone warfare in the global War on Terror and ostensibly an attempt to convince the American viewership of the merits of this technology with its advantages of limited loss of American military lives. The overt narrative of American humaneness and empathy unravels when this series is juxtaposed against the history of the tribal region in the Pakistan-Afghanistan border and its turbulent history since the Cold War. Moreover, the TV series, in spite of its attempt to render a heroic presentation of the CIA, provides many instances of its own collusion with militants. American diplomats represented in the series are also revealed to be corrupt and self-serving. In addition, both diplomats and the CIA officers are embroiled in many internecine rivalries that

L. Basu (✉)
Department of English, Philosophy and Communication Studies,
University of Wisconsin-Stout, Menomonie, WI, USA
e-mail: basul@uwstout.edu

M. W. Azeem (ed.), *Human Rights in the Age of Drones*, Palgrave Studies in Literature, Culture and Human Rights,
https://doi.org/10.1007/978-3-032-08191-9_3

mimic the blood feuds of the tribal militants they are trying to subdue. Thus, even though *Homeland* is mass entertainment designed to indoctrinate viewers into the ideology of the Homeland Security State[1] and the creation of spaces of immunity at the cost of relinquishment of civil liberties and rights to privacy, it is capable of offering a complex glimpse of the realities of the War on Terror which fail to exonerate and justify the brutalities of American imperialism and the work done by its intelligence agencies.

The show offers powerful debates about a variety of human rights issues. Two of the most significant are questions about rights of citizens to privacy versus the rights of the Homeland Security State to surveil all citizens for the purpose of preventing future acts of terrorism. This debate gets extended to the drone debate, the question of deploying small planes to surveil people in countries thought to be harboring terrorists and also deploying these planes to bomb strategic targets, violating the sovereignty of these nations by infiltrating their air space. However, unlike the genre of human rights films studied by scholars like Sonia Tascon (2012), *Homeland's* primary purpose is not to advocate for human rights. It is very different from human rights documentary films that Tascon discusses which present a human face of aboriginals, as in her study of Australian aboriginal films. While the visual form of *Homeland* allows for an immediate sense of verisimilitude or the aura of reality, the intention of the series is not to produce genuine empathy for those whose human rights have been violated. Even though Pakistani characters are presented as victims in *Homeland*, viewers are never offered a full opportunity to empathize with the face of the "other," in the sense articulated by Emmanuel Levinas. The idea of the face as invoked by Levinas is referenced by Tascon and also by Judith Butler in *Precarious Life* (2004), where she discusses Levinas's idea

[1] This is a term which has been used by Donald E. Pease in his book *The New American Exceptionalism*. Pease argues that 9/11 marked the transition from the National Security State of the Cold War era to the Homeland Security State, with a transformation of the enemy from Communist states to radical Islam. The concept of the Homeland Security State was based on ideas of American innocence and exceptionalism against the construction of an external enemy. Citizens of the Homeland Security State were promised protection against the threat of terrorism in exchange for relinquishing their civil liberties and consenting to indefinite detention of suspects without trial, searches without warrants, and other mechanisms of a state of emergency or exception. Pease argues that the consent of American people toward this logic of the Homeland Security State is disrupted with the breaking of the images of inhumanity and torture in Abu Ghraib.

of the face as a mode by which the other makes claims on our shared humanity (*Precarious Life* 2004: 130–135). Instead of the face of victims of drone strikes, the face we see most often is the tortured face of Carrie Mathieson, the CIA detective who is emotionally unstable due to her bipolar diagnosis. According to Lindsey Steenberg and Yvonne Tasker (2015: 133) "Homeland intervenes in a representational landscape in which moral legitimacy of (political) violence is debated with intensity and regularity." This is to reiterate that these actions are not undertaken lightly, and CIA officers like Carrie are traumatized by their decisions. However, as Steenberg and Tasker note the purpose of the drama is to legitimize "the surveillance of civil society" as "responsibly managed and absolutely necessary" (Steenberg and Tasker 2015: 132). *Homeland* dabbles in debates about human rights of private citizens and civilians in foreign countries. However, its aim is television entertainment and therefore it does not go far enough in these discussions. What is more interesting is that its legitimation of organizations like the CIA fail due to internal contradictions that I outline later in the essay.

Moustafa Bayoumi, in his book *This Muslim American Life: Dispatches from the War on Terror* (2015), highlights the paradigmatic shift from the depiction of terror in an earlier show *24*, shortly after the events of 9/11, to the representation of terror in *Homeland*, more than a decade after 9/11. Bayoumi argues that *Homeland* establishes the ubiquity of surveillance in a later phase of the War on Terror and deep-seated Islamophobia, which is seen as capable of transforming patriotic American soldiers like the protagonist of the first three seasons, Brody, into a secret terrorist. The potential for radicalization for all citizens becomes the rationale for suspending rights to privacy. This becomes the rationale for the new normalization of surveillance and the concurrent loss of privacy in the Homeland Security State.

Drone warfare represented in this television series is an extension of this panopticon-like global surveillance. In the fourth season, first televised by Showtime in 2014, the location of the show moves to Kabul, where Carrie, the protagonist CIA officer, who also suffers from bipolar disorder, is appointed head of the Kabul station. In the course of her posting, Carrie conducts operations to capture the leader of the Haqanni network Haissam Haqanni. The drone is deployed in Pakistan, where it becomes the weapon of destruction of a civilian target. Carrie's gamble of capturing Haissam at a wedding ceremony backfires when it in fact kills many innocent wedding guests and does not destroy the terrorist leader. For the rest of the season,

Carrie recruits Ayaan, a survivor of the drone strike and a nephew of Haissam, as a CIA asset, using her romantic and sexual influence to secure the loyalty of the young man. Her hope of capturing Haqanni is thwarted when ISI agent Tasneem is shown to be receiving intelligence from the husband of the American ambassador and feeding it to Haqanni. Even though Carrie is able to use drone surveillance on Ayaan to reach Haissam, Haissam ultimately kills his nephew for allowing himself to be tracked to his uncle.

The series does offer a glimpse of remorse on the part of Carrie for the loss of civilian lives and the death of young Ayaan; however, the critical debate about the ethics of drone strikes on civilian targets is quickly elided in the presentation of terrorists as ruthless and manipulative agents. Even though some Americans are shown to be corrupt, Pakistan is presented as an unreliable ally in the War on Terror, consumed by its corrupt nexus between intelligence officers and terrorist groups. This presentation then becomes a covert justification for the use of drones in the War on Terror and protection of a post-9/11 American homeland security state. Carrie is given the title of the Drone Queen after she orders the strike, and the show highlights the lure of drone technology, its illusion of absolute control, and its devastating potential for dehumanizing lives not deemed grievable.

A significant critique that Bayoumi levels at *Homeland* is that the show received regular input from the CIA. Citing the research of Tricia Jenkins, Bayoumi claims that "the office has been directly involved with *24*, *Argo*, *Zero Dark Thirty*, and *Homeland*" (Bayoumi 2015). Bayoumi argues that since the Cold War, the CIA has been working in conjunction with Hollywood to propagate a better image of itself. It has refused to advise on scripts such as *The Bourne Identity*, which depicts CIA assassinations, but has been forthcoming in providing advice to *Homeland* and *Zero Dark Thirty*, which focus on its meticulous attention to tracing and capturing terrorists. Bayoumi has argued that the series consults directly with the CIA and can be seen as engaged in an attempt to improve the image of this controversial intelligence agency linked with many extra constitutional assassinations and coups in its long history, particularly during the Cold War. In presenting a contrast between Carrie, the CIA agent who is introspective and traumatized by the human costs of her decisions to use drones, and the cold and calculated machinations of the Pakistani ISI officer Tasneem, the television show overtly attempts to present a moral binary between the humane American and the inhumane and unethical

Pakistani intelligence services. I argue that this schematic presentation of two strong female characters revives old stereotypes of Orientalist immorality versus norms of American righteousness. This ideological schematization obfuscates the deeper injustice of drone warfare on unarmed and unprepared civilian populations by the full force of the American "Predator Empire," a term used by Ian G. R. Shaw in his book titled *Predator Empire: Drone Warfare and Full Spectrum Dominance* (2016). Although the series presents Haqqani and Tasneem as the Pakistani villains responsible for the death of innocent wedding guests and, ultimately, Ayaan, the series does not entirely succeed with this rhetorical presentation. In the following sections, I trace how *Homeland* normalizes the culture of domestic surveillance in post-9/11 America and how the logical extension of that surveillance leads to drone strikes in the tribal areas of Pakistan in Season 4. Even though *Homeland* Season 1 alluded to drone strikes as being the cause of an American protagonist Brody's induction into radical Islam, Season 4 comes full circle with Carrie continuing this cycle of drone violence. Thus, *Homeland* inaugurates on television an era of perpetual war, where geographies and characters may change but the cycle of revenge, terrorism, and the targeted killing of potential terrorists is unending.

Surveillance and Drones

Showtime's series *Homeland* powerfully explores the connection between surveillance and drone warfare. While the initial seasons of *Homeland* detail the role of drones and torture as two powerful causes of the rise of anti-American sentiment and the rise in terrorism against the United States, the fourth season paradoxically employs the same drone technology not only to surveil domestic and foreign terror suspects but also to assassinate them through extrajudicial means. While this technology seems to be tremendously advantageous to the United States in reducing the potential loss of American lives, it not only produces tremendous collateral damage for foreign civilians but also perpetuates the cycle of war.

In the opening season of *Homeland*, Nicholas Brody, the protagonist of the show, returns to the United States after eight years of captivity and ostensibly readjusts to civilian life. He runs for political office and becomes a congressman and potential vice-presidential candidate, all the while concealing his secret identity as a terrorist and working in close conjunction with the terrorist leader Abu Nazir, who was instrumental both in his torture and subsequent radicalization. We witness a strong homoerotic dynamic between Brody and Abu Nazir. In one scene, Abu Nazir confesses to Carrie, Brody's CIA case officer and eventual love interest, that he, like Carrie, loves Brody. Brody's relationship with Abu Nazir is cemented by their shared love and grief over the death of Issa, Nazir's son, in an illegal drone strike on a civilian target in Abu Nazir's Middle Eastern country. Thus, it is the primal wound of the death of an innocent through drone warfare that acts as the stimulus for the growth of Islamic radicalism and its capacity to seduce even an American soldier.

Along with this insight into the causes of radicalization, the show proposes that the best way to protect American citizens in the course of the War on Terror is to engage in mass surveillance. In the world of the television show, we are completely immersed in the post-PATRIOT Act world, where Americans have willingly given up their civil liberties, including the right to question the policies of the government for the sake of protection against the threat of terror. Donald E. Pease describes this condition as follows:

> Rather than sharing sovereignty with the state, U.S. citizens were treated as denizens of a protectorate that the State of Exception defended rather than answered to. This new protectorate or consumer compound was composed of passive consumers who understood good citizenship to entail the practice and consumption of the American way of life. (Pease 2009: 169)

When Carrie illegally installs surveillance cameras on Brody in the hope of discovering implicating evidence against him, we see an extension of the logic of the "Predator Empire" that has been theorized by Ian G. R. Shaw (2016). Shaw argues that drones extend the logic of Foucault's panopticon, the formation in prison that enabled the surveillance of an incarcerated population. Drones are spying and surveillance machines that also have the capacity to bomb. In the first season of the show, we witness domestic surveillance. It is not a drone that is surveilling Brody; Carrie has installed hidden cameras. However, the logic of surveilling external threats has also been applied on American civilian populations. Caren Kaplan has noted that most Americans express a duality in their approach to surveillance. For the most part, they accept the surveillance of foreigners abroad but rush to defend the privacy of their own citizens. This binary is also complicated by the racialization of surveillance options. Communities of color are surveilled far more aggressively than white communities. Caren

Kaplan has pointed to the increasing militarization of the police force, with war weapons, automatic rifles and tanks finding their way to inner city police departments that surveil and kill minority populations. Kaplan asserts:

> In practice, particularly following the violent response by the state in 2014 to demonstrations protesting police brutality directed disproportionately against young African American men, we know that unarmed populations are killed in battle zones while 'at home' racial profiling and other practices lead to many instances of summary judgement and even execution by police or citizen proxies, blurring the boundaries between battlefield and home as well as between military and police power. (Kaplan in Parks and Kaplan 2017: 174)

Overall, the show does not register much of a protest against Carrie's actions of surveilling a U.S. citizen, a returning war veteran. Moustafa Bayoumi has noted that the representation of torture in post 9/11 television shows went from its presentation as "extrajudicial but necessary in *24* to routine and procedural in *Homeland*" (Bayoumi 2015: 224). Even though the status of surveillance may be questionable in its legality, it is something that is inevitable in the current climate, and the show normalizes the everyday nature of the invasion of personal privacy. It is even morally justified when Brody is indeed revealed to be a radical.

In the early seasons, Brody enters into a romantic heterosexual relationship with Carrie, the CIA officer assigned to his case, and this relationship marks a predictable return to his American patriotic affiliations at the expense of his newer identification with the terrorists. Even though the reform and rehabilitation of terrorists is offered as a passing fantasy, the show does not deliver on this promise. In the shocking finale of season 3, when Brody is recruited by Carrie into the CIA, he carries out his assignment with the CIA but is abandoned in Iran and left to be executed as a prisoner of the Islamic Republic. It is almost as if a Marine who has succumbed to the radical ideology of Islamic fundamentalists cannot be accommodated into the national imaginary again. Even if he becomes a CIA agent and fulfills a dangerous mission, his former decision to wear a suicide vest bars his reintegration into the American nation. Brody is treated as "spoiled goods," almost a feminine victim of rape and ethnic violence who is symbolic of national and communal dishonor and is, therefore, shunned by the community. However, this lack of accommodation of Brody is deflected as an atrocity committed by a fanatical Islamic regime. They are the horrific executors of Brody. The execution is spectacularly sensational in the form of a public hanging, cheered by an Iranian crowd, and the billboard of Khomeini framing the scene visually transfers the burden of guilt on Iran, even though it is the CIA who have ultimately reneged on its commitment to get Brody out of Iran. Brody is also denied the rites of memorialization. His reputation as a terrorist is not cleared, and Carrie does not succeed in lobbying for a star for him on the CIA wall of remembrance. Thus, even though Brody's association with Carrie represents a re-establishment of a heterosexual and nationalist paradigm, his reintegration with the American nation is unfulfilled.

Another critique that Bayoumi offers about *Homeland* in *This Muslim American Life* (2015) is its deep-seated Islamophobia. This is also echoed by Akbar Ahmed in his brief remarks on the show in his book *The Thistle and the Drone* (2013). Bayoumi argues that all Muslim characters are depicted as potential terrorists, and the only way they can avoid this stigma is by colluding with the CIA. Bayoumi asserts that the thrill of the show lies in the uncertainty about whether Brody will fulfill his destiny of American hero or that of a secret terrorist: "the show feeds off the same presumption of future malfeasance that is the essence of today's anti-Muslim prejudice" (Bayoumi 2015: 10).

This latent prejudice against Muslims transfers to the fourth season, even when Muslims are presented as civilian victims of American imperial aggression through drone warfare. Even though there is no potential civilian who is a suspected terrorist and therefore needs to be surveilled, an entire region is being watched by drones because of the potential existence of militants and extremists in the area. An entire population rather than an individual is under continuous surveillance by the CIA in this season. A crucial difference in the shift from the domestic surveillance of Brody to the surveillance of the Haqqani network is that surveillance of a remote tribal region in Pakistan does not entail any judicial warrants. Unlike the previous season, when Carrie had to fight or break laws to secure permission to surveil Brody, the surveillance of Ayaan's family is completely extrajudicial. Moreover, unlike just the installation of cameras at Brody's home, we now witness surveillance by drones, which are not just machines for surveillance but machines that can transform quickly from cameras to bombs and killing machines.

Homeland Season 4 does not provide an unequivocal endorsement or celebration of drone technology. It dramatizes the limits and fallibility of this technology. In spite of the best intelligence about the probable presence of Haissam Haqqani, Carrie's decision to strike the target results in a tremendous number of civilian casualties attending a wedding. Ayaan, the young and innocent medical student who loses his family in this carnage, is the visible and empathetic reminder of the inhumaneness of this technology. However, the show deliberately complicates the seeming innocence of Ayaan by presenting him as nefariously connected by kinship ties to Hassim Haqqani, the wanted militant. Moreover, his innocence and vulnerability are further compromised when he is shown to be smuggling life-saving drugs to his uncle, Hassim Haqqani, from his medical school.

Instead of acknowledgement of the inherent power differentials of drone warfare, resulting from the complete vulnerability of the country being surveilled and the collateral damage of drone strikes and fear it has to live with compared to the relative freedom from any vulnerability and danger to the nations operating drones, *Homeland* seeks to subtly justify the necessity of constant surveillance by presenting the vulnerable population as unreliable and nurturing dubious ties with militants. Season 4 thus extends the logic of Islamophobia established in the opening season. All Muslims are potentially terrorist sympathizers whether they live in the United States or in Pakistan, and therefore civil rights of domestic U.S. citizens and the rights of sovereignty of Muslim countries, such as Pakistan, can be justifiably compromised.

Center and Periphery: The War on Terror and the Targeting of Tribal Areas

It is important to explore the history of the region and the people of the tribal areas of Pakistan bordering Afghanistan that have been the brutal target of massive American drone strikes. *Homeland* Season 4 refers to drone strikes against the Haqqani network. This tribal group is not a fictional construct but does have a historical presence in the Northwest Frontier province of Pakistan and in neighboring Afghanistan. Moreover, this group has had long-standing links with the Taliban, Al-Qaeda, and other militant groups, including militants being trained for the liberation of Kashmir and Uzbekistan and other Muslim minority struggles emerging from the former Soviet Union and China. *Homeland* is also accurate in depicting strong links between the Pakistani intelligence group ISI and the Haqqani network. Vahid Brown and Don Rassler's book *The Fountainhead of Jihad: The Haqqani Nexus* (2013) is a detailed account of the significance of the Haqqani group in the War on Terror being waged by the United States and NATO in Pakistan and Afghanistan.

In their introduction, Brown and Rassler trace the origins of the Haqqani network. The Haqqanis in their videos and other publications refer to themselves in Arabic as *Manba Al'Jihad,* which translates to a well spring of jihad. Based in north Waziristan in the FATA (Federally Administered Tribal Areas), the semi autonomous region of Pakistan, they emerged as a platform or space where various disenfranchised Muslim freedom fighters congregated. These included the Afghan soldiers fighting the Soviet invasion followed by Uighurs opposing Chinese rule and Uzbeks fighting Uzbekistan and, of course, militants fighting for the liberation of Kashmir. Since the Soviet invasion in 1979, the Haqqanis have acted as a funnel receiving money from various foreign sources, including the United States, Saudi Arabia, and Pakistan. Brown and Rassler point out that "Direct American support for the Haqqani network ended in the early 1990s; the Pakistani state relationship continues to this day" (Brown and Rassler 2013: 4).

Brown and Rassler argue that the state of Pakistan has been largely tolerant of the Haqqanis with Pakistani Intelligence Services cultivating and maintaining active relations with this group. The reason for this dependence, they argue, stems from the advantages the Pakistani state is able to wield as a result of this connection. The Haqqanis have served as peace brokers among different feuding tribes, and an association with them carries with it the promise of Pakistan's continued influence in Afghanistan in a post-NATO era. Brown and Rassler claim that India, Pakistan's long-standing political rival, has sought to have an active presence in contemporary Afghanistan. The targeted attack on the Indian Embassy in Kabul on July 7, 2008, by the Haqqani network was a not so subtle message to India that it should not try to extend its regional influence on the new regime in Afghanistan. Brown and Rassler suggest that the July 7, 2008 bombing of the Indian embassy in Kabul by Hamza Shahkoor, who was affiliated with Lashkar-e-Taiba, a group connected to the Haqqani network, was meant to send a message: "Islamabad viewed India's increasing influence inside Afghanistan as a threat. Its strong role in the country would not be tolerated" (Brown and Rassler 2013: 151). The Afghanistan government's defense ministry led by anti-Taliban/Northern Alliance coalition supporters was favored by India and distrusted by Pakistan. Brown and Rassler argue, "So long as Pakistan's army remains committed to unilaterally shaping the post-American future of Afghanistan in its perceived interests, the Haqqani network will continue to be a valuable asset to the military" (Brown and Rassler 2013: 10). Brown and Rassler argue that the "Haqqani network is not a rogue insurgent group, but rather is a fighting group that at times acts as a paramilitary and diplomatic arm of the Pakistani government" (Brown and Rassler 2013: 161). These authors offer examples of Haqqanis helping to build bridges and trust between the Taliban and the Pakistani government.

Although Brown and Rassler generally highlight the symbiotic association of the Pakistani military and the ISI with the Haqqani network, which helps to facilitate Pakistan's military and strategic interests in the region, the authors also point to sources of friction between them. They write that in the post 2001 period, "Haqqani and Taliban fighters resent the ISI's influence over them and they fear ISI harassment....... Frustration also appears to exist over the ISI's efforts to play militant groups off one another—to either shape their trajectories or make them more compliant, a tactic which has long been used by the ISI in Kashmir" (Brown and Rassler 2013: 156).

This contentious and difficult strategic relationship between the Haqqanis and the Pakistani military and intelligence wings is alluded to more directly in Akbar Ahmed's book *The Thistle and the Drone: How America's War on Terror Became a Global War on Tribal Islam* (2013). Unlike Brown and Rassler, Ahmed's book is more encyclopedic, covering a broad range of Islamic societies and tracing the essential center and periphery model that has shaped these societies. Ahmed argues that in many parts of the Muslim world, the primary component of identity is tribal rather than Islamic heritage; often tribal and Islamic values are not compatible. For example, Islam has a well-developed system of jurisprudence, whereas tribal societies rely on notions of honor and revenge. Revenge and murder are sins that are not acceptable by Islamic tenets. As a result of these differences, tribal societies have often been relegated to the margins of Islamic nations. They have also been largely excluded from the benefits of modernity and economic prosperity. Akbar Ahmed offers a multitude of examples of the marginal status of tribal societies in Islam, such as the Pashtun tribes in the FATA regions of Pakistan or the Yemeni tribes in the Arabian Peninsula. He also argues that in the post 9/11 context, these tribal regions have become identified as spaces associated with terrorist training grounds and have been disproportionately targeted for drone strikes, which have exacted large civilian tolls.

In Pakistan, the tribal regions were difficult to govern even under British rule. The tribes did not obey or accept British judicial codes. Therefore, the British followed a policy of allowing these tribal regions to govern themselves through councils called jirgas. After the creation of modern Pakistan, the first Governor General, Muhammed Ali Jinnah, also followed a policy of autonomy and noninterference for the tribal regions. According to Ahmed, this policy was essentially reversed by the Pakistani President Pervez Musharraf after the War on Terror and under pressure from the United States. Musharraf conducted military attacks in Waziristan, reversing decades-old policies of noninterference in tribal areas. According to Ahmed, there was a remarkable shift in U.S. relations with regions representing tribal Islam after 9/11. Akbar Ahmed summarizes this when he writes:

> Before 9/11, the United States intervened frequently to save thousands of Muslim tribesmen on the basis of its concern for human rights. It was this temperament and momentum to do something good and positive on the world stage that led Americans to help those being persecuted or in need. The Pukhtun of Afghanistan fighting Soviet forces in the 1980s, along with clansmen across the border in Pakistan, were grateful for American support in their war of liberation. President Ronald Reagan, who helped arm and train them, welcomed Pukhtun tribesmen to the White House and declared them "the moral equivalent of America's Founding Fathers."...... In Kosovo, American intervention halted the massacres in which Muslim tribesmen were the main victims. (Ahmed 2013: 257)

Ahmed maps the shift after 9/11, an event that he argues marks the beginning of the age of globalization and the entry of the United States into the lands of tribal Islam. Prior to 9/11, the tribes occupied a peripheral space with respect to the centers represented by Muslim nations, making their way into Western modernity. However, after 9/11, the United States has come to occupy the position of the center. This, according to Ahmed, has destabilized and created untold suffering for the tribal regions.

> The United States has thus slipped into the role of a global center in its confrontation with the Muslim periphery throughout the world....... No longer isolated as they once were, Muslims on the periphery moved to the eye of a global storm as the United States, allying with the central

> government, hunted for al Qaeda and its associates in the periphery's communities. The United States scoured the world for "terrorists" as if they were a malignant tumor that needed to be removed surgically, not quite realizing the trauma the operation was creating for the body. (Ahmed 2013: 259)

In this confrontation against tribal Islam, the United States was not fighting a traditional enemy with a military but striking at small groups and communities essentially to hunt for sheltered terrorists. As the War on Terror became "a global war on tribal Islam" (Ahmed 2013: 260), the "chosen weapon in the war was the drone" (Ahmed 2013: 260). Ahmed documents that the arrival of the United States in Afghanistan had many consequences for the region. Many refugees crossed the border to come to Waziristan to escape U.S. bombings. Pakistan was pressured by the United States to capture Taliban and Al-Qaeda members. According to Ahmed, this could only happen with consensus from the tribes through a tribal council or jirga. Under U.S. pressure, Pakistan broke its agreement with the tribes and "launched large scale military operations in Waziristan for the first time in Pakistan's history. In October 2003, 2500 commandos were airlifted into the village of Baghar, near Angoor Adda in South Waziristan, along with twelve helicopter gunships. Within a few months, Musharraf was the target of two assassination attempts" (Ahmed 2013: 69).

These accounts thus reveal the very complex position of Pakistan vis a vis the War on Terror. On the one hand, Pakistan is under pressure as an ally of the United States to take a tough stand on Al-Qaeda and its affiliates. This has brought a fair share of retaliation in the form of terror plots against its own leaders and its own urban populations. One of the recent episodes has been the attack of a suicide bomber on a mosque in Peshawar on January 30, 2023, which left more than a hundred dead (Goldbaum et al. 2023).

On the other hand, elements within Pakistan have traditionally relied on Haqqanis, friends of the Taliban, for their strategic interests in Afghanistan and need these allies in the face of quickly changing regimes in Afghanistan as well as the increasing influence of India in Afghanistan. Thus, the ISI and members of the Pakistani military have strategic ties with tribal groups such as the Haqqanis, but the relationship is not without contention. With military interventions in Waziristan, the Pakistani government has lost the trust of these groups, which had been carefully cultivated by founding leaders such as Jinnah. The tribal groups feel betrayed by the United States that had previously supported them only to abandon them after the defeat of the Soviet Union. They now feel targeted by U.S. drone strikes, aided by the Pakistani military.

In the representation of CIA drone strikes on members of the Haqqani network, in *Homeland*, many of these complexities have been elided. There is no acknowledgement of the long involvement of the U.S. military and the CIA in the fight to liberate Afghanistan against the Soviets. The long history of the Haqqanis' rise to prominence emerging from the era of the Afghan struggle against Soviet invasion is relegated to historical amnesia. There is also no discussion, for example, of the precarious nature of Pakistan and Afghanistan's sovereignty in the post 9/11 deployment of drones, which are essentially war machines on the remote tribal areas that belong to both these nations. What is highlighted is the mutual dependence of the ISI and the Haqqani network. The tensions within this alliance, resulting from Pakistan being forced to take military action in tribal areas under pressure from the United States, are not explored. Nor is there any hint of Pakistan's tenuous strategic position vis-a-vis India and its growing influence in Afghanistan. Thus, the narrative that emerges is a binaristic presentation of the ethical, empathetic, or at least conscientious CIA intelligence officer Carrie versus her Machiavellian ISI counterpart Tasneem. What this presentation elides is the more insidious nature of CIA's drone attacks on Waziristan and Carrie's ruthlessness in using seduction and manipulation to reach her terrorist target. Both at the personal and the public levels, Carrie's role in Afghanistan and Pakistan is more devastating to local populations than the ISI's, and even the official narrative of the TV show cannot alter that.

Differential Grievability/Vulnerability of Drone Victims and Pilots

Judith Butler in *Precarious Life* pointed out "the radically inequitable ways that corporeal vulnerability is distributed globally" (Butler 2004: 30). For Butler, the moment of 9/11 was a jolting awareness for Americans that they were no longer protected by their First World status. She calls this moment "a dislocation of First World safety" (Butler 2004: 30). She emphasizes that this moment of post 9/11 grieving, which the Bush administration wanted to hasten to a speedy conclusion, is actually the moment of recognizing grief as a resource "through which we develop a point of identification with suffering itself……. a point of departure for a new understanding of the narcissistic preoccupation with melancholia can be moved into a consideration of the vulnerability of others" (Butler 2004: 30). Butler's hope was that if we could work our way out of the self-preoccupation with our own grief, we could learn to understand and "oppose the conditions under which certain human lives are more vulnerable than others, and thus certain human lives are more grievable than others" (Butler 2004: 30).

However, in the real world, the aftermath of 9/11 ushered in the War on Terror with its increasing dependence on drone warfare. Gregoire Chamayou, in his influential book *The Theory of the Drone* (2013), notes that the drone eliminates "any immediate relationship of reciprocity". (Chamayou 2013: 14). Drones pose a constant threat to targeted and surveilled vulnerable populations, but unlike traditional warfare, drone operators are invisible and operate remotely, effectively eliminating any risk of exposure to retaliation. Drone warfare thus intensifies the differential corporeal vulnerability of differently positioned actors in the War on Terror. Chamayou illustrates this differential vulnerability in this description: "the fundamental structure of this type of warfare is no longer that of a duel, of two fighters facing each other. The paradigm is quite different: a hunter advancing on a prey that flees or hides from him" (Chamayou 2013: 33). Drone warfare, Chamayou goes on to argue, "turns against the guerillas their own long-established principle, namely, deprive the enemy of an enemy. An insurgent confronted by an army of drones no longer has any target to attack" (Chamayou 2013: 62). This creates a feeling of hopelessness to those subjected to drone strikes and arouses feelings of bitterness, feeding the desire for more revenge among civilian populations who feel targeted. Chamayou goes thus far in his critique of the differential vulnerability of bodies in drone warfare to state that "drone strikes are equivalent to bomb attacks. They constitute weapons of state terrorism" (Chamayou 2013: 63). Chamayou draws on the work of Talal Asad and others to argue that suicide bombers and drone operators are viewed as cowardly and "mirror images" of each other. While strategically favorable in terms of low costs to American armies and less risk of loss of American lives, drone warfare has caused a crisis of warrior ethos among many Air Force pilots for whom courage has now been redefined as doing the dirty work of Empire at minimal risk to their own bodies.

Chamayou discusses the debate over the psychic wounds of drone operators. He argues that in initial reports, many drone operators said that drone warfare felt like a video game. However, as public outrage against drone warfare began to grow, that position was retracted, and there was more talk in the media about the combat stress, emotional fatigue, and burnout of drone operators. Many American soldiers scoffed at the idea of drone operators who had never set foot in combat zones, experiencing battle fatigue. Chamayou argues that the emotional toll of drone operators and their empathy for the enemy, considered a deterrent in traditional warfare, changes when in the current situation, empathy "serves to apply a layer of humanity to an instrument of mechanized homicide" (Chamayou 2013: 108). For Chamayou, this pain and empathy of drone operators evokes the image of "the crocodile shedding tears, the better to devour its prey" (Chamayou 2013: 108).

Butler's theorization of differential vulnerability followed by Chamayou's theorization of drone warfare as exacerbating asymmetries of vulnerability undergird my reading of Carrie's role as CIA station chief ordering drone strikes in the tribal regions of Pakistan. Carrie is shown to be remorseful after the first drone-strike she orders causes heavy civilian casualties. Nevertheless, she does not relinquish drone technology as a resource to hunt down wanted terrorists. She recruits Ayaan, the young medical student who is a nephew of Haissam, by promising safe passage out of Pakistan. He is initially reluctant to speak to the CIA but succumbs to Carrie's personal requests, especially after she seduces him romantically. Carrie does not divulge that her ulterior motive for this intimacy is to establish contact with Haissam. She is therefore responsible for provoking Haissam's ire against Ayaan when he is made aware that Carrie is tracking him. In the end, Ayaan is murdered by his uncle. Carrie plays the role of the spy, who is not emotionally defunct, in contrast to Tasneem, who is shown to be coldly manipulating the husband of the American ambassador and others and exchanging state secrets with the Haqqani network. However, it is Carrie's and CIA's actions that have the most devastating effects on the innocent civilian populations in the tribal areas—not Tasneem's or the ISI's. This is true not only for the show but also in terms of actual statistics of civilian casualties caused by American drone strikes. According to a 2013 article by Craig Whitlock published in the *Washington Post*, information gathered by Amnesty International and the U.N. confirm that in the first decade of the War on Terror, about 2200 people were killed by drone strikes in Pakistan of which 400 were civilians and 200 were "probable noncombatants" (Whitlock 2013). What is pervasive is the reluctance of the U.S. government to release full counts of casualties.

Derek Gregory has described this phenomenon as the creation of states of exception within the FATA regions of Pakistan. Gregory uses Giorgio Agamben's theorization of the state of exception as a condition deriving from the suspension of laws in a Nazi concentration camp and extends it to describe the tribal regions of Pakistan and Afghanistan. Gregory argues, "The FATA has become a state of exception, I suggest, through its constitution as borderlands and battlefields" (Gregory in Parks and Kaplan 2017: 29).

In episodes 5 and 6 of *Homeland* (Season 4), titled "About a Boy" and "From A to B and Back Again", respectively, we witness Carrie's absolute ruthlessness in pursuing terrorists using drone and surveillance technology. These two episodes contrast Ayaan's status as a victim of drone warfare and a civilian caught between the deployment of drone surveillance and strikes by the CIA and the codes of tribal family ties and loyalties that involve association with terrorists that he cannot escape from. Ayaan is ultimately unable to extricate himself from these compelling forces that exert a stranglehold on his life. At the beginning of *Homeland* Season 4 Ayaan loses his immediate family in a drone attack ordered by Carrie as station chief. While the overt aim of this strike was to target Haissam Haqanni, Ayaan's uncle remains unharmed by this attack, while Ayaan's immediate family and many other civilians are killed.

Ayaan returns to the city to continue with his medical studies, but he comes to the attention of the CIA when his video footage of the drone attack is posted on the internet by a friend. This episode and his identity as a close relative of Haissam Haqanni make him desirable as a potential CIA recruit.

Meanwhile, Ayaan's situation becomes more precarious when he asks his girlfriend Kiran to store some of the medicines. Kiran's father discovers the medicines and accuses Ayaan of being a drug dealer, going so far as to report this incident to the medical college, which leads to his immediate expulsion. Even though Ayaan had resisted Fara and Carrie's attempts to recruit him, the urgency of recovering the lost medicines and the need for cash to procure new medicines leads him to seek Carrie's protection. Carrie delegates the operation of surveilling Ayaan to Fara, the young Iranian American who has recently joined the CIA. It is Fara's surveillance of Ayaan that reveals that he is collecting medicines from the hospital of his medical school and delivering them to his uncle. Fara's discovery of this secret meeting and photographic evidence establishes definitively for the CIA that Haissam is still alive. Carrie then decides to use Ayaan as a stalking horse that will lead the CIA to the elusive Haissam Haqanni. Her modus operandi includes false promises to Ayaan of a safe passage to England and admission to King's College, London. In addition, she offers him refuge in a CIA safehouse and makes romantic overtures at him to which he eventually succumbs.

Carrie then proceeds to make Ayaan believe that the ISI is aware of his plan to escape to England by having him follow on his brief visit back to his college and his last meeting with his former girlfriend, Kiran. Carrie arranges for some of her colleagues to break into the CIA safehouse and kidnap her while strategically allowing Ayaan to escape. This is engineered with the precise intention of propelling Ayaan to seek out his uncle since he has no other channel of support or escape. Carrie and the CIA have also craftily installed a GPS chip in Ayaan's new passport. Carrie and her colleagues proceed to surveil Ayaan as he moves north to a terrorist training camp that his uncle runs, intercepting his phone calls to his uncle on the way.

When Ayaan reaches the bus station close to the town where his uncle will meet him, he calls Carrie and tells him he loves her and thanks her for saving him. This message is heard by the entire CIA team; some of her colleagues, such as Quinn and Fara, have been critical of her seduction of someone so young. Fara, in particular, in an angry confrontation, wants to know how Ayaan will be protected when the CIA targets his uncle with a drone attack. Carrie attacks Fara for not being committed to the mission. Fara retaliates by reminding Carrie that she is the one who surveilled Ayaan and produced definitive proof of his uncle being alive. This is a clear instance of Fara, a nonwhite and apparently Muslim American CIA employee being treated as an outsider. Fara calls out Carrie on these double standards. However, even though the show incorporates these critiques of Carrie's actions, Carrie is unswerving in her single-minded determination to get to Haissam Haqanni and authorize a drone strike on him. When she is reminded by the drone pilots that they will not be able to protect her asset, Ayaan, she accepts this as collateral damage.

In the rest of episode 6 of *Homeland Season 4*, we follow Ayaan to the mountainous northern region. We see him sleeping peacefully under an open sky beside a clear stream. He is woken up by armed men and escorted to a place where several vehicles are gathered. Meanwhile, in Islamabad, Carrie and her team are waiting for Haissam Haqanni to arrive and preparing for the drones to strike. Haissam arrives and disembarks from his vehicle. He is not pleased to see Ayaan and speaks to him in Urdu, telling him he should not have come to this area. Ayaan protests that he was not left with any other option. Haissam kisses him on the cheek and says he is not ungrateful for Ayaan's help with medicines. However, he then reveals another figure getting off from his van. It is the ex-CIA director, Carrie's boss, Saul Berenson. Haqanni tells his nephew that he should not have allowed himself to believe that his new friend would have helped him. Because of Ayaan's naivete, there is a drone waiting to attack Haissam. This is immediately followed by a quick shot by Haissam directed at Ayaan at close range, which kills Ayaan instantly.

Carrie is shocked at this drama unraveling before her, and she is ready to order the drones to strike and finish Haissam. However, Quinn intervenes and stops the operation because he wants to protect Saul, who has devoted his life to the CIA. The episode ends with Carrie feeling a sense of extreme rage and throwing various articles from her desk. Thus, at this moment, we witness Carrie as someone who is driven by the dictates of CIA operations and someone who does not ponder the ethics of using certain kinds of unequal technologies of warfare. She does not hesitate to use lies and seduction to lure Ayaan, nor does she ever try to protect him from the danger of the drone strike she is planning on his uncle and all who surround him. She is very instrumentalist in her use of her assets, almost as clinical in her interactions with people as the drones she deploys. Her latent Islamophobia is also revealed when she questions Fara's loyalty to the mission.

The presentation of Ayaan by actor Suraj Sharma underscores the relative differences in youth and age, innocence, and experience between Ayaan and Carrie. In the literary archive of colonial narratives, there is no dearth of interracial romances. However, in the most popular framing of these romances that is part of our postcolonial inheritance, the white woman or memsahib is presented as an epitome of Victorian femininity, seduced by the unpredictable cultural landscape of India, often by a more experienced native man. This is the classical trope of E. M. Forster's *A Passage to India* (1924), which is repeated in romances of the late Empire, such as the British TV series *Jewel in the Crown* (1984), based on Paul Scott's novel of the same name. Another novel using this same framework is Ruth Prawer Jhabvala's *Heat and Dust* (1976). What is remarkable is that in Forster and others, these romances express the secret longings and fantasies of the white woman vis a vis the native man, which often had dangerous consequences for the native man. In *A Passage to India*, Dr. Aziz gets charged with the rape of Adela Quested after the two have an encounter in the Marabar Caves. The interracial romance does not turn out well for the Indian man and usually results in the loss of his reputation and social standing. In the imperial imaginary, it is impossible to accommodate an interracial romance between a brown man and a white woman because of powerful fears of miscegenation. This fear of rape or the tarnishing of the honor of white femininity is a trope that is also observed in other segregated and racially hierarchical societies, such as in the American South.

To an extent, *Homeland* seems to subvert the trope of the innocent white woman being seduced by the more experienced and sensual Oriental man. In the seduction of Ayaan, Carrie is presented as the initiator and the more sexually experienced partner. There is no concern about the sanctity of her chastity or fear of miscegenation in the presentation of this relationship in the early twenty-first century. To an extent, they seem to be in a cocoon in CIA safehouses, not under any kind of social scrutiny. However, the old trope of a romance between a South Asian man and a white woman having devastating consequences for the brown man is replayed in the conclusion of this affair. Although there are no rape charges against Ayaan, he arouses the ire of his kin group, chiefly his uncle, for allowing himself to become intimate with Carrie. Although it is unclear whether Ayaan's uncle, Haissam, knows of the romance, he is angry and wrathful of the fact that Ayaan has become a pawn in the hands of the CIA, thereby exposing himself to their surveillance. In the revenge and honor codes of tribal Islamic society, Ayaan has to pay for this with his life. The romance between Ayaan and Carrie thus extracts a heavy toll on Ayaan but leaves Carrie unscathed by any material loss. She is shown to be grieving, but this grief is a little disingenuous. She accepts the logic of Ayaan's death as collateral damage to drone warfare. The show seeks to justify it by revealing the nefarious connections between the ISI and Haqqani networks.

Ayaan's death by his uncle Haissam Haqqani as punishment for allowing the CIA to surveil him and trace him to the terrorist leader bring Season 4 of *Homeland* to a climax. This plot, preceded as it is by the death of Ayaan's immediate family by the drone strike ordered by Carrie, reveals the logic of differential vulnerability of different corporeal bodies in the show. There is no doubt that Ayaan and his family, as victims of drone strikes, face a far greater burden of corporeal vulnerability than Carrie and her colleagues, who order drone operations. Not only does this narrative emphasize the differences in physical vulnerability of different populations with respect to the positions they occupy in the new imperial landscape, but also drone technology showcased in the series is a reminder of differential vulnerability based on who uses drone technology and who is at the receiving end of it.

Carrie's relationship with Ayaan with its invitation to provide Ayaan with protection and safe passage to another country seem false lures to obtain her strategic goals. When Ayaan is killed by his uncle, his loss is accepted as collateral damage in the War on Terror in the same vein as the initial mistaken drone strike on a wedding party. The loss of Ayaan's life, like the loss of his Pakistani relatives at the wedding, does not truly register losses because of the differential value and grievability of their lives. In the overarching structure of the multiseason narrative of the show, Ayaan's death parallels Carrie's previous lover Brody's death. It is significant that both deaths can be conveniently attributed to terrorists or Islamic theocratic governments, leaving the CIA officer grieving but also absolved of direct moral responsibility for the deaths of these victims. Carrie's grief at both junctures is an attempt to shift the burden of moral responsibility for the innocent deaths to a purported external enemy in the War on Terror.

Although sympathetic in its presentation of Brody and Ayaan's ill-fated encounters with the CIA and depicting them as victims whose human rights are compromised by U.S. policies, *Homeland* accepts the status quo about the erosion of human rights as an expected outcome of the War on Terror. It endorses an inherent hierarchy of human lives, under which some lives are less grievable than others. Although it tries to show characters like Brody as complex, it still falls into the trap of presenting most Muslim characters as potentially susceptible to an ideology of terror. This scapegoating obfuscates fledgling attempts at self-reflection of the United States's own flawed record with human rights both domestic and abroad and the continuing refusal to reckon with the full costs of civilian lives lost in the War on Terror.

References

Ahmed, Akbar. 2013. *The Thistle and the Drone: How America's War on Terror Became a Global War on Tribal Islam*. Washington, DC: Brookings Institution Press.

Bayoumi, Moustafa. 2015. *This Muslim American Life: Dispatches from the War on Terror*. New York: NYU Press.

Brown, Vahid, and Don Rassler. 2013. *Fountainhead of Jihad: The Haqqani Nexus, 1973–2012*. New York: Columbia University Press.

Butler, Judith. 2004. *Precarious Life: The Powers of Morning and Violence.* New York: Verso.

Chamayou, Gregoire. 2013. *A Theory of the Drone.* Translated by Janet Llyod. New York: New Press.

Forster, E. M. 1924. *A Passage to India.* New York: Harcourt Brace.

Goldbaum, Christina, et al. 2023. In Pakistan, "Fears that Terrorism has Returned" After Bombing Kills 101. *The New York Times*, January 31.

Gregory, Derek. 2017. Drones and Death in the Borderlands. In *Life in the Age of Drone Warfare*, ed. Lisa Parks and Caren Kaplan, 25–58. Durham, NC: Duke University Press.

Homeland Season 1–4. 2011–2014. Dir. Alex Gansa. Perf. Claire Denis. Showtime, DVD.

Jewel in the Crown. 1984. Dir. Jim O' Brien. Perf. Peggy Ashcroft, Tim Pigott-Smith Granada Television.

Jhabvala, Ruth Prawer. 1976. *Heat and Dust.* New York: Harper and Row.

Kaplan, Caren. 2017. Drone-O-Rama: Troubling the Temporal and Spatial Logics of Distance Warfare. In *Life in the Age of Drone Warfare*, ed. Lisa Parks and Caren Kaplan, 161–177. Durham, NC: Duke University Press.

Pease, Donald E. 2009. *The New American Exceptionalism.* Minneapolis: University of Minnesota Press.

Shaw, Ian G. R. 2016. *Predator Empire: Drone Warfare and Full Spectrum Dominance.* Minneapolis: University of Minnesota Press.

Steenberg, Lyndsey, and Yvonne Tasker. 2015. "Pledge Allegiance": Gendered Surveillance, Crime Television, and Homeland. *Cinema Journal* 54 (4): 132–138.

Tascon, Sonia. 2012. Considering Human Rights Films, Representation, and Ethics: Whose Face? *Human Rights Quarterly* 34:864–883.

Whitlock, Craig. 2013. Drone Strikes Killing More Civilians than U.S. Admits, Human Rights Groups Say. *The Washington Post*, October 22.

CHAPTER 4

Imperial Arbitrage: Global Precaritization, Human Rights, and the Financial Logic of Risk Management in the United States Drone Program

Marcus Heiligenthal

> We live only by knowing *something* about the future; while the problems of life, or of conduct at least, arise from the fact that we know so little.
> —*Frank H. Knight,* Risk, Uncertain, and Profit

> It is as if, in the face of an increasingly uncertain future, a secure basis for making decisions now had to be found. All this meant a vast expansion in the scope and pretensions of capability...
> —*Niklas Luhman,* Risk: A Sociological Theory

When the Obama administration through the Director of National Intelligence (DNI) released its statistics on "U.S. Counterterrorism Strikes Outside of Areas of Active Hostilities" on July 1, 2016, it was met, broadly,

M. Heiligenthal (✉)
Binghamton University, Binghamton, NY, USA
e-mail: mheilig1@binghamton.edu

M. W. Azeem (ed.), *Human Rights in the Age of Drones*, Palgrave Studies in Literature, Culture and Human Rights,
https://doi.org/10.1007/978-3-032-08191-9_4

in the media by the striking discontinuity between the official record of "non-combatant" deaths and those of independent watchdog agencies: the official report from the DNI gives the range of non-combatant deaths as "64–116" yet, according to *The New York Times*, three watchdog organizations (the *Long War Journal*, *New America*, and the *Bureau for Investigative Journalism*) have the number of civilian deaths between "200 and 800" (Savage and Shane 2016). While the difference between these numbers is staggering, with Frederico Borello, executive director of the Center for Civilians in Conflict, going so far as to claim that the official numbers "do not add up," somewhat lost in the response to the long-awaited release of statistics on drone strikes was the ***amount*** of strikes and casualties that occurred "outside of areas of active hostilities" and the ***range*** of even the official number of civilian casualties. The United States has officially killed between 2372 and 2581 enemy combatants and from 64 to 116 non-combatants in 473 strikes outside of areas of active hostility since 2009—which represents a ***potential but unverifiable*** death-range of 209 enemy combatants and 52 non-combatants based on these numbers[1] (Savage and Shane 2016). While the document released by the DNI does respond to and qualify a series of methodological questions, including a clarification on the claim in the press that any male of military age is counted as an enemy combatant and several reasons for the differences between official numbers of non-combatants killed and unofficial numbers, the brief three page document covering over six years of drone strikes resoundingly proves the ***means*** of drone warfare valorizes the ***reduction*** of human life into a numerical register: any disagreement, as the document spends over two pages proving, is over categorization rather than the logic that justifies these bodies as imminently ***killable***—whether as regrettable-but-necessary non-combatant or an EKIA. While the official numbers have been released, the logic of preemptive strike that produces the conditions for the United States drone program continues to be normalized.

Since the release of the statistics by the Obama administration's DNI, the drone program under Trump has continued to expand in scope—with pushes to include lower-level terrorists "foot soldiers" as possible targets—and regularity—with the call to relax "high level vetting" and make the process of approval more bureaucratically efficient (Savage and Shane

[1] These numbers vary wildly in official sources, furthering the claim. For example, per the Bureau of Investigative Journalism the number of dead are instead 2525 to 3613 of which 407 to 926 were civilians (Abad-Santos 2013).

2016). While the deregulations do still maintain the standard of "near certainty" that no civilian bystanders will be killed in the strikes, looking at even the official numbers from the DNI shows that *neither* the validity of the numbers *nor* the actual number of non-combatants killed are "certain" or "near" it (Savage and Shane 2016). Yet, while it would be convenient to see these developments as the reserve of the Obama administration in its final year, looking closer at *means* of the drone strike for the *ends* of security *always already* includes growth as a constitutive aspect of its temporally-interventionist logic.

Through the vehicle of the "War on Terror," the United States has engaged in a global project of precaritization in the name of national security. Shifting the risks inherent to the US imperial project from the American center to the global periphery by privileging US rights to safety over global human rights, the "War on Terror" becomes the dehumanizing, justificatory discourse in which securitization—or the transferring and thus off-loading of risk—takes place. While the claim that the "War on Terror" is an effort to proactively secure American interests is well-tread intellectual territory, what remains underdetermined in this conversation is the relationship between the technology of the drone and, bearing in mind Randy Martin's *Empire of Indifference*, the "financial logic of risk management" constitutive of American preemptive warfare (Martin 2007). Reading the earlier formations of preemptive warfare through the lens of both economic theories of risk, this chapter makes three primary claims:

1. That through the logic of preemption, the United States *intervenes* into the uncertainty of the future, names these *imagined* dangers as not possible but probable, and—in a massive disregard of the right to life—"find[s], fix[es], and finish[es]" these conjured "potential threats" through assassination-by-drone.
2. The technology of the drone is the means par excellence facilitating a strategy I am naming "imperial arbitrage," one that creates a "zero-risk" scenario for the imperial center where no Americans bodies can be harmed (but any non-American body has *no* rights and can be killed without trial); US capital expenditures a relatively minimal; and political optics are largely controllable by obfuscating statistics and procedure via classification (for "national security reasons") and the discourse of "precision," sanitizing and rationalizing the brutal reality of hellfire missile strikes and disguising and con-

taining the global suspension of the right to life *merely* to the targets/threats (including "military age males geographically close to the suspect").

That the result of the logic of preemptive securitization through the *means* of the drone, or the "Hellfire Hedge," is a presumed, normative expansion of strikes ad infinitum as blowback only stabilizes when exponential expansion of interventions is presumed: not only does each strike potentially create *more* resistance to American empire but, to borrow Anne McClintock's phrasing, the "imperial paranoia" of the United States constructs an autopoetic and inexhaustible system of global precaritization in the name of rendering *conjured* nightmares of terrorism into *material* "touchdowns" and "bugsplats" (drone operator slang for the victims after a strike).

Paranoia, Pre-emption, and Rendering the Imaginary Assailable

Reports that say that something hasn't happened are always interesting to me, because as we know, there are known knowns; there are things we know we know. We also know there are known unknowns; that is to say we know there are some things we do not know. But there are also unknown unknowns – the ones we don't know we don't know. And if one looks throughout the history of our country and other free countries, it is the latter category that tend to be the difficult ones.
—Donald Rumsfeld 2002, "DoD News Briefing – Secretary Rumsfeld and Gen. Myers"

When Donald Rumsfeld gave his, now infamous, "Known Knowns, Known Unknowns, and Unknown Unknown" reply at the Department of Defense news briefing on February 12th, 2002, it was in response to a question about evidence.[2] While particularly questioning if evidence existed of either WMDs in Iraq or the intent to sell WMDs, the question

[2] The question that was asked that resulted in Rumsfeld "Known Knowns" answer was asked by Jim Miklaszewski and was: "In regard to Iraq weapons of mass destruction and terrorists, is there any evidence to indicate that Iraq has attempted to or is willing to supply terrorists with weapons of mass destruction? Because there are reports that there is no evidence of a direct link between Baghdad and some of these terrorist organizations?" (As quoted in Morris 2014).

was in the context of the other reports claiming of "no evidence" of either of these situations. Rumsfeld's response, which serves as the epigraph to this section and won him the Plain English Campaign's "Foot in Mouth" trophy, was read in a variety of ways—ranging from a non-answer, a gaffe, and as "a brilliant distillation of quite a complex matter" (Ezard 2003; Steyn 2013). Bearing in mind the context of the remarks, where the policy of preemption was still being formulated before being codified in the National Security Strategy published in September of that year, Rumsfeld's comments about the build up toward military action against Iraq—while the presences of WMDs were still, at best an "known unknown"—provides keen insight into how the policy later culminates in the United States Drone warfare campaign. Whether Rumsfeld was aware of it or not, his categorization of "knowns" is imbricated in economic theory, recalling a similar delineation made by the economist, Frank Knight, almost eighty years prior in his formulation of the theory of profit. Returning to Knight through Rumsfeld both discloses the logic separating the "known unknown" from the "unknown unknown"—or "risk" from "uncertainty" for Knight—and how discourses of economic profit merge with those of security in an age of preemption.

Frank Knight, a founding influence on what is referenced as "the Chicago school" of economics, wrote *Risk, Uncertainty, and Profit* to differentiate the concept of economic "profit" from that of common notions of "rent" and "wage." While the distinction of "profit" from "rent" or "wage" is not in the interests of this argument, Knight's articulation of "profit" lies at the center of Rumsfeld's logic surrounding the debate to launch preemptive war against Iraq. For Knight, the problem of profit is a result of "a confusion of ideas" and the "key to the whole tangle will be found to lie in the notion of risk or uncertainty and the ambiguities concealed therein" (Knight 2014: 19). Knight argues that the difference, which was absent in economic discussions up until that point, lies in quantifiability:

> Uncertainty must be taken in a sense radically distinct from the familiar notion of Risk, from which it has never been properly separated. The term "risk," as loosely used in everyday speech and in economic discussion, really covers two things.... "risk" means in some cases a quantity susceptible of measurement, while at other times it is something distinctly not of this character; and there are far-reaching and crucial differences in the bearings of the phenomenon depending on which of the two is really present and operat-

> ing.... It will appear that a *measurable* uncertainty, or "risk" proper, as we shall use the term, is so far different from an *unmeasurable* one that it is not in effect an uncertainty at all. We shall accordingly restrict the term "uncertainty" to cases of the non-quantitative type. (Knight 2014: 19–20)

According to Knight, "profit" is a result of an entrepreneur correctly measuring "risk" from the broader category of unmeasurable, unknown "uncertainty"—a distinction rendered meaningless if the terms are collapsed—in a competitive, market economy; risk is still quite indeterminate, but calculable based upon past data and research. Risk has odds, uncertainty is random; or, to borrow Rumsfeld's categories, in Knight's articulation "risk" is the thing "we *know* we do not know" quantified by probability where "uncertainty" is something "we don't know we don't know." Yet, in order to arrive at "profit" one cannot merely assess the risk, one must choose to *act*—whether by doing or not doing—within the market. It is at the cusp of profit in Knight's theorization, or the decision to do or not do based upon a calculation of the measured "risk" pulled from the chaos of uncertainty that is the future, that concerns this paper and the complications of preemption in national security policy.

Imbricated in Knight's theorization of "profit" as the successful calculation of risk from uncertainty is the temporal relationship between present and future that embodies capitalism. As Jens Beckert argues in *Imagined Futures: Fictional Expectations and Capitalist Dynamics*, "capitalism is an economic system in which the present is assessed principally through the lens of the future which is itself considered using imaginaries of future states in order to anticipate as yet unrealized profit and loss" (Beckert 2016: 22). Goods made today are sold in the market of tomorrow; as such, the amount and type of goods made today results from a *prediction* of what the market *will be* tomorrow. It is because of the temporal leap of present decisions that draw yield from imaginary futures that Knight arrives at "profit" being inherently errable:

> We must infer what the future situation would have been without interference, and what change will be wrought in it by our action. Fortunately or unfortunately, none of these processes is infallible, or indeed ever accurate and complete. We do not perceive the present as it is and in its totality, nor do we infer the future from the present with any degree of dependability, nor yet do we accurately know the consequences of our actions. In addi-

tion, ... we do not execute actions in the precise form in which they are imaged and willed. (Knight 2014: 202)

Knight, however, sees the fallibility of these inferences as beneficial, the reason why perfect competition in the market is impossible: people differ on their speculations of the future and, thusly, their measurements of risks and decisions to act will be wildly divergent. Niklas Luhmann argues in *Risk: A Sociological Theory* that "[Knight] explain[s] entrepreneurial profit in terms of the function of uncertainty absorption"—the entrepreneur only profits by successfully *mapping* the uncertainty of the future market through measuring its probabilities, or rendering it "risk," and finally *acting* based upon those calculations (Luhman 2008: 1). While this temporal gap in calculation serve as the conditions that make competition in the market possible, it becomes *increasingly* problematic when the logic of Knight's entrepreneurial uncertainty absorption is utilized for national security.

The connection between risk and security are at the heart of national security policy and the "War on Terror" as articulated by Rumsfeld in 2002. When risk management or aversion techniques become applicable outside of the market, it quickly becomes delineated by threshold concepts such as security, on one side, and danger, on the other. As such, bracketed on each side by security and danger, Luhmann notes "the risk form becomes a variation on the distinction between desirable/undesirable" (Luhman 2008: 19). In a shift, security is no longer a state free from harm but the effect of a risk management strategy. As Joseph Masco argues in *The Theater of Operations*: "the innovation of the War on Terror is that if formally rejects *deterrence*, with its focus on global stability, as an objective in favor of *preemption* – an unending manipulation of the future for national advantage" (Masco 2014: 15). When empowered to consider security from the lens of the future, the counterterror state becomes engrossed in the project of the entrepreneur, as Knight articulates her: as a technique to *absorb* uncertainty, *render* it calculable as "risk," and *intervene* to insure the "safe/secure" outcome. As Louise Amoore shows in *The Politics of Possibility*, when made active, "it is not strictly collected data on identifiable risks that become security interventions but a different kind of abstraction that is based precisely on an absence, on what is not known, on the very basis of uncertainty" (Amoore 2013: 58). Considering security through the policy of pre-emption, the role of Knight's entrepreneur to *predict* and *act upon* the future *in the present* becomes paramount.

Recoding from the economic register into one of *preemptive* "self-defense," security becomes a perpetual, contingent *goal* (we *will be* secure *if*) that is only achievable as comparative, retroactive nostalgia (we *were* secure *then*) rather than state of being one can possess without temporal disavowal (we *are* secure *now*)—with the "we," in this case, being US security interests *over* and *against* any other. As Masco argues, "security is thus constituted as both a necessity (to defend against catastrophic shock) and as an unachievable goal (*as the future is an inexhaustible source of unknowability*)" (Masco 2014: 17). When national security becomes a product of risk management it *must continually occur* to render future uncertainty as risk and, then, *intervene* to "secure" against any undesirable future outcome. Returning to Amoore, preemption is an "anticipatory logic: it acts not strictly to *prevent* the playing out of a particular course of events on the basis of past data tracked forward into probable futures but to *preempt* an unfolding and emergent event in relation to an array of possible projected futures" (Amoore 2013: 9). As such, the implications of securitization through preemption complicates a series of relationships between what Masco calls the "counterterror state" and human rights. The rights of US securitization render all other basic human rights striated by *national* delineations; furthermore, any preemptive intervention as a part of the US risk assessments is always already justified to *protect* and *secure* rights (for the US) in a predicted future—regardless of other's rights infringed in the real, material present.

When engaging with absorbing uncertainty and calculating risk, increasing information from which one can derive probabilities becomes both an imperative *to gather*—even if such data does not or cannot exist—and resource *to protect* from others. As Luhmann notes, "one demands more information, better information, complains about the information being withheld .... as though there *were* 'information' available that one could *have* or *not have* as the case may be" (Luhman 2008: 21). The disparity in information that is used to forecast probability, a competitive edge in Knight's market, becomes an impediment for critique.[3] With such information inaccessible to public verification, *any* bit of information can be deemed sensitive for such risk calculation and classified *from* public access; furthermore, the ability to justify *any* action taken or *any* violation of human rights—both domestically and globally—by the counterterror as

[3]To use the common tech parlance: for the US national security apparatus, this is "not a bug, it's a feature" – as will be shown.

necessary in the name of security becomes routine and beyond contestation. Masco shows how these two sides of the national security, classification and justification without proof, deter political resistance:

> When security state officials announce an imminent, existential threat based on classified material … citizens are left with only two options: acquiescence or denial.… it functions to disable political resistance and countermobilizations (easily dismissed by officials as uninformed about the true nature of risk in the world and working on vastly slower time scales). (Masco 2014: 21)

Yet, while the ability to resist broadly expanding means of surveillance and censorship to better predict potential threats is ever retreating, the cost of the *means* of preemption remained an important counterweight that eventually led to Rusmfeld's resignation.

Rumsfeld's resignation on November 6, 2006—just a day before the 2006 mid-term elections—disclose the limits of the early pre-emptive strategies prior to drone warfare: political pushback against the material cost of pre-emption *could outweigh* immaterial guarantees of securing against conjured dangers from an unrealized future. In focusing on the need to *act* and that *action* to be attributable to be politically advantageous (the counterterror state *made* us secure is a far better rallying cry for votes than being secure by happenstance), the counterweight of "means" is presented. While threats are "conjur[ed] up images of dangers from an unrealized future" by the counterterror state, they are met with *real* soldiers costing *real* capital and bleeding *real* blood—each representing a tangible, limited resource that is exposed to "danger" in preemptive action (Masco 2014: 15).[4] In the era of the drone, however, these financial, military, and political costs to interventions into the future are rendered moot. The technology of the unmanned aerial vehicle and the means of drone warfare are, for all of these purposes, politically "cost-free" while

[4] The quote continues: "In this way, imagined futures and the affects they produce have become institutionalized as national security policy, creating a form of expert judgment that is at war with its own apocalyptic imaginary before it meets the real world, creating a massively productive form of militarization that is easily delinked from evidence, facts, or the observable in the name of confronting and eliminating potentially cataclysmic future danger" (Masco 15). While the author agrees with Masco in these arguments, the focus on the global fear in tying the counterterror state to the nuclear anxiety of the Cold War underdetermines the role of the local – and thus disavowed – drone strike. While the fear is global, the missiles – couched in language of precision – are devastatingly local in their materialization of such policy.

precaritizing the rest of the world to a state where the "right to life" is secondary to US securitization.

Risk Transfer War and the Rise of the Tactics of Assassination-by-Drone

Trouin said, 'Today's affair – that is not the worst for someone like myself. Over the village they could have shot us down. Our risk was as great as theirs. *What I detest is napalm bombing. From 3,000 feet, in safety.' He made a hopeless gesture. 'You see the forest catching fire. God knows what you would see from the ground. The poor devils are burnt alive, the flames go over them like water. They are wet through with fire.'*

—Graham Green, *The Quiet American* (emphasis mine)

The real advantage of unmanned aerial systems is that they allow you to project power without projecting vulnerability.

—Air Force officer David Deptula (as qtd in Chamayou 12)

The counterforce to the extension of the "Global War on Terror" and its materialization as regime change in Iraq is the same that was deployed to justify the preemptive war in the first place: risk. The wars, in large part, became politically unpopular and strategically unviable toward the latter years of the Bush administration due to the materialization and perpetuation of risk to the United States: it is a "hard sell" to convince someone that engaging in and paying the cost of an on-going, actual war and nation-building project was better than the *chance* of a war on less advantageous terms. It is in the gap between the level of exposure and political cost that the technology of the unmanned aerial vehicle and the means of assassination-by-drone comes to occupy and thrive. A closer look at the work of Martin Shaw shows that the *means* of the drone, a style of warfare based upon the transfer of risk—as a method to limit exposure on the battlefield for *your* troops and capital by *transferring* it onto a civilian population as "collateral damage" or "acceptable casualties"—was present long before the technology of an armed, unmanned aerial vehicle epitomized its logics.[5]

[5]While Caren Kaplen's *Aerial Aftermaths* shows how the tactic of utilizing aerial vehicles traces farther back than is traditionally attributed, it is the argument of the author that the shift from aerial-as-survellience and the means of, what will be shortly expanded upon, risk transfer warfare (Kaplan 2018). While Kaplan's argument is convincing and foundational to this paper, the differentiation that is articulated here from that project to the arguments of this paper is focused on the utilization of air-as-unassailable but imprecise – as the Greene quote that serves as this section's epigraph voices – that is realized in risk transfer warfare.

The means of limiting exposure in warfare is not a revolutionary idea but, as Martin Shaw notes in *The New, Western Way of War*, there was a shift in the management of risk since Vietnam—after which a "new, western way" of risk-transfer warfare was developed. With "Western governments … profoundly sensitive to the potential political danger from losses of soldiers' lives," the military, financial, and political risks of warfare-as-policy begin to resonate into warfare-as-tactic. Shaw argues:

> The new Western way of war is ultimately about how risks are managed.… At the centre of the new way are the political risks that governments take: ultimately wars must not undermine, and should preferably strengthen, their domestic political and especially electoral situations. However, unlike other forms of policy-driven action, war mediates political risks via life-risks – to the West's own combatants, to enemy combatants, and to non-combatant civilians. In elaborating … that there are *systematic transfers of risk*. (Shaw 2005: 94)

For Shaw, risk-transfer is twofold: offshoring the political risks of engaging with warfare onto the battlefield as well as offloading risk from western soldiers onto enemy combatants and civilians. While Shaw's argument concludes with "Operation Desert Storm" in Iraq, extending the concept shows how the tactics of risk-transfer are materialized in the technology of the drone.

In weaponizing the unmanned aerial vehicle, the risk relationship removes the operator from harm; however, the "life risk"—to borrow Shaw's term—does not simply leave the battlefield but *transfers* as an effect of such departure through mechanization to non-combatant civilians and "collateral damage." As Shaw articulates, "in minimizing the risk to its own combatants, the West consistently adopts methods of war that effectively transfer risk from its own personnel to civilian non-combatants, so that far more civilians are killed, injured and otherwise harmed than Western military personnel" (Shaw 2005: 94). In risk-transfer warfare, "any situation where the question of priority arises, the West is likely to put its own soldiers' lives before those of civilians" (Shaw 2005: 94). Looking at the technology of the drone, the strategy is clearly seen. While "self-preservation by means of drones involves putting vulnerable bodies out of reach" as Gregoire Chamayou argues in *A Theory of the Drone*, its prerequisite is that all others in the field of deployment are less secure (Chamayou 2015: 12). Unlike a "boots on the ground" combatant, to use the adage of deploying soldiers in a combat zone, the drone operator is limited to only actively interacting via means available to a Raptor or Predator drone. As such, removing risk to the operator *always already* accepts the costs of that removal in reducing a litany of engagement strategies to two: surveillance or death by Hellfire missile. "Collateral damage," both as term and as a perpetual result of drone warfare, discloses the commonplace result of risk-transfer tactics. Looking at risk-transfer from the perspective of political risk discloses how the combination of the goals of protecting US military personnel, low-cost financial expenditure, and electoral viability—in no small part shaped by the former two—all cohere into the technology and usage of drones.

Shaw describes the logic of risk-transfer as a move to minimize Western causalities not only to protect Western lives, but to shape political opinions. By privileging those tactics that shift risk from western troops to non-western innocents, the *framing* of such a horrifying approach to war *must also* justify the transfer of "life risk" and limit potential avenues of critique. Shaw states:

> Given the central priority of minimizing Western causalities, which in turn derives from the core media-political context within which governments fight war, these transfers are a large part of what the Western way of warfighting is now *about*.... These transfers bare a fundamental contradiction between the norm of civilian protection and the reality of Western warfighting, and so make the *legitimacy* of this way of war fundamentally problematic.... It is precisely because minimizing Western casualties is considered the bottom line of domestic political support that it becomes the *modus operandi* of war itself. *Risk-transfer militarism operates throughout the media to neutralize electoral and other forms of surveillance that highlight the realities of death and suffering in Western wars.* (Shaw 2005: 95, emphasis mine)

The tactics of risk-transfer warfare must resonate throughout the media to frame the unilateral violence and sanitize the realities of the "collateral damage" that each presumes—lest popular, political support is lost. Part of the tactics of risk-transfer is framing the offloading of risk as both necessary *and* benevolent. If, as Chamayou notes, "judg[ing] by the yardstick of such classical categories" of warfare the "drone looks *like* the weapon of a coward" and "transforms not only the material conduct of armed violence ... but also the traditional principles of a military ethos officially based on bravery and sense of sacrifice"; then, the role of risk-transfer militarism is to render drone warfare as Michael W. Lewis does in *The Atlantic*, "the most humane form of warfare ever" (Chamayou 2015: 17; Lewis 2013). The result of these attempts to frame risk-transfer positively are seen in the discourse of "precision" and the secrecy surrounding casualties—both of which, while predating the US drone program, embody policies and rhetoric around it.

While the practice of reporting a "body count" was prevalent as a measure of success in the Vietnam war, it was neither necessary nor thought relevant by 2003 when General Tommy Franks declared "we don't do body counts" in response to question regarding causalities in Operation Anaconda in Afghanistan (Broder 2003). Following Franks, the release of drone strike statistics from the DNI on July 1, 2016 discloses the continuance of risk-transfer in drone warfare: even when numbers are eventually released after longstanding pressure from news outlets, they are uncontestable through official channels, determined inaccurate by journalists, and can still only amount of dead in a "range." The non-reporting of "body counts" by Frank and the mis-reporting or under-reporting of the deaths by drone strike—both civilian and combatant—both serve a similar function in framing the war effort: obfuscating the reality of death and destruction caused by the war and neutralizing such an avenue of critique. These tactics render the result of the transfer of risk, the "collateral damage" resulting from the removal of operators—or embedded journalists—from the battlefield while still engaging in combat, illegible.[6] Distance from combat, then, produces the validation for the sanitizing frame of unknowability.

While obfuscating the casualties of risk-transfer warfare is an important aspect of Shaw's claim, framing the technology as "surgical" and "precise" preempts and minimizes claims of collateral damage. Through this interpretative lens, the importance of "precision" and "smart weapons" in American warfare and, more in-line with the goals of this essay, surrounding discussions of drone technology becomes less about technological limitations and more about retroactively justifying the tactics of "risk transfer." Shaw outlines how far the term resonates through understanding modern combat:

[6]This process is then reaffirmed by memorializing the deaths of U.S. soldiers, as any risk or cost serves as a justification to double down on risk transfer to reinforcing only certain lives matter and only certain lives have the *right* to matter.

> Precision *defines* war, narrows it down, and makes it a discrete and manageable business. Precision makes war seem efficient in achieving delimited political goals, so that it does not intrude more than marginally and temporarily into Western society. Precision makes war *calculable*: it confirms that it is possible to weigh the political, military and human risks, produce a rational assessment, and act accordingly, with a realistic hope of agreement between project and outcome. Precision promises to make war like any other political, economic or social project. Precision subsumes the violence of war under its rational schema: it contains the bloody mess. The use of force is 'clean' and 'surgical'; only a few 'unfortunate' soldiers dies; civilian victims are 'accidental'; and the enemy is 'defeated', its deaths hardly observed. (Shaw 2005: 88)

The narrative of precision that Shaw articulates allows for a series of a priori disavowals regarding the use of violence while also making the violences of combat legible through a framework of rational and purposeful decisions. While "mistakes" could still be made, these tactics reifying the logic of risk-transfer that grounds them and further obscures the decision to engage in the first place: as Chamayou argues, "one can always claim afterwards that capture ... was 'infeasible' – failing to acknowledge that this technological incapacity was deliberately organized" (Chamayou 2015: 170). The resulting conversation becomes one about information gathering, surveillance, or other rational mechanisms of knowledge production on and of the combat mission rather than one about tenets and tactics. Applying Shaw's work to drone warfare, we see how– borrowing Jeremy Scahill's phrasing—the "assassination complex" unveils as an unquestioned, optimal *means* of engagement where previously there were myriad of different combat solutions (including *non-engagement*) (Scahill and The Staff of the Intercept 2016). As Chamayou argues:

> Once people's minds are implanted with the false proof that the drone is in principle a more precise weapon and, on that account, supposedly more in conformity with the principle of distinction, the necroethics of the drone abandons any discussion of fundamental issues and steers critics toward a debate on numbers in which, by reversing the onus of proof, those critics now have to establish empirically that this weapon, which they have just conceded in theory to be a priori more ethical, has in practice produced quite the opposite results – a fact that, once one has swallowed the original postulate, remains totally inexplicable other than by contingent circum-

> stances such as human misuse and errors in deployment. The instrument, in other respects, remains good in itself. (Chamayou 2015: 147)

The logic of risk transfer culminates in the technology of drone warfare and the tactics of "assassination-by-drone" for American militarism which, once established as the *means* of securing the United States and its allies, disavow critique through a slippage between technological limitations and tactical imperatives. The instrument of the drone becomes the site of ameliorating critiques of tactics through discourses of "more precision" to address critiques of "risk-transfer" and its tactics become a safe haven for the limitations and blowbacks of drone missile strikes, each belayed by claims of the mission being cheaper, less risky, and precise/safer for the non-combatants (Byman 2013). When considered in the context of the aegis of pre-emption, the drone becomes the perfect *means* to securitize American interests, perpetually, through transferring life-risks to the global periphery—all the while doing so in a cost-effective, risk-free (for the US military) way that minimizes traditional avenues of critique.

Imperial Arbitrage and Redistributive Precarity and Human Rights

> *The mode of risk that is flourishing across the horizons of contemporary economy and security operates according to a possibilistic logic. It does not deploy statistical probabilistic calculation in order to avert future risks but rather flourishes in conditions of declared constant emergency because decisions are taken on the basis of future possibilities, however improbable or unlikely.*
> —Louise Amoore - *The Politics of Possibility*

When the technology of the drone and "risk transfer" meets the strategy of preemptive "self-defense" against any imagined potential impediment to U.S. interests, we arrive at what this paper refers to as a form of "imperial arbitrage": in this case, the system formed at the nexus between the *justificatory logic* of predictive securitization and the *technological means* of "risk-free" (to the rights and lives of US citizens) interventions via assassination-by-drone in its actualization. Arbitrage is a financial term used to designate a risk-free means of profit by simultaneously buying an asset in one market and selling it in another for a profit; however, this paper radicalizes the term, following Carolyn Hardin's work in *Capturing Finance: Arbitrage and Social Domination*, as "arbitrage is a process of creating a novel comparison that leads to monopolistic appropriation, that is, capture" (Hardin 2021: 15). For Hardin, arbitrage is an apparatus of capture, one that

> does not take advantage of existing differences, but rather that it is a process that produces the conditions for comparison where none existed before in order to exploit them .... Capture is therefore a creative process, one that generates differential value measurements to allow for comparison and profit, but appears merely to find and exploit those differences. (Hardin 2021: 12)

Building from Hardin, this chapter argues that "imperial arbitrage" is a process by which an imperial center both re-entrenches and, to borrow Gayatri Spivak's usage "worlds" the global periphery while also policing and exploiting these differentiations in via "risk-free" interventions—empire maintained without risk. In the case of the US Drone program, we see an actualization of "imperial arbitrage" in both the worlding surveillance "from above"[7] and the "risk-free" (for the US) procedure of drone warfare to securitize by assassination-via-drone. If arbitrage is an apparatus of capture, the "imperial arbitrage" of the US drone program is a system which differentiates and exploits the global periphery's human rights, rendering all imminently killable, to (supposedly) securitize the imperial center. The result of these efforts to perpetually maintain US imperial hegemony globally in the name of national security is a dramatic, global redistribution of precarity[8] whereupon the rights of security for US citizens

[7] I am particularly invoking the panoptic presence of drone warfare here following the work of Caren Kaplan in *Aerial Aftermaths: Wartime from Above*. For more on the importance of the panoptic and aerial, please see both: Kaplan, Caren. *Aerial Aftermaths: Wartime from Above*. Durham: Duke University Press, 2018 and Spanos, William V. "Who Killed Alden Pyle?: The Oversight of Oversight in Graham Greene's *The Quiet American*". *American Exceptionalism in the Age of Globalization: The Specter of Vietnam*. Albany: State University of New York Press, 2008. 337–56.

[8] While not explicit to the argument of this paper, an understanding of precarity – the distribution of precariousness – is important. The relational rights, this paper is arguing, are inherently violated by national security and exploited in imperial arbitrage. In *Frames of War: When is Life Grievable?*, Judith Butler establishes a shared "precariousness" as a shared condition of life – or, that all life is vulnerable. For Butler, "precariousness has to be grasped not simply as a feature of *this* or *that* life, but as a generalized condition whose very generality can be denied only by denying precariousness itself"; yet, for Butler, the condition of precariousness leads to varying degrees of recognizability *of* precariousness. Butler asserts that precarity, as a politics of the recognizability of precariousness, results in differentiating grievability:

in any imagined future are privileged over the rights of those at the global periphery *in the actual present*. US drones kill today to potentially protect *tomorrow's* freedoms.

When considering the particularities of the form "imperial arbitrage" seen in the US Drone programs' preemptive securitization, the result is an autopoetic system that demands continual amplification and expansion. While the unceasing ability for the American imaginary to conjure up an enemy have been traced by other scholars,[9] Anne McClintock's "Paranoid Empire" speaks to the simultaneous nature of global power when projecting an imagined, unseen danger:

> the shared condition of precariousness leads not to reciprocal recognition, but to a specific exploitation of targeted populations, of lives that are not quite lives, cast as "destructible" and "ungrievable." Such populations are "lose-able," or can be forfeited, precisely because they are framed as being already lost or forfeited; they are cast as threats to human life as we know it rather than as living populations in need of protection from illegitimate state violence, famine, or pandemics. Consequently, when such lives are lost they are not grievable, since, in the twisted logic that rationalizes their death, the loss of such populations is deemed necessary to protect the lives of "the living. (Butler 2009: 31)

For Butler, the framing of precarity is the system which distinguishes lives as "living" – and grievable if killed – from those "ungrievable" others that are forfeitable. Building on Butler's work, Isabell Lorey in *State of Insecurity* notes on the striation of precarity:

> precarity can therefore be understood as a functional effect arising from the political and legal regulations that are specifically supposed to protect against general, existential precariousness. From this perspective, domination means the attempt to safeguard some people from existential precariousness, while at the same time this privilege of protection is based on a differential distribution of the precarity of all those who are perceived as other and considered less worthy of protection. (Lorey 2015: 22)

Viewing the work on precariousness from the perspective on human rights – particularly the right to life – reorients discussions on policies of *national* security as always already precaritizing, a phrasing implying redistributing who has the right to life (the national) and which are ungrievable (non-nationals). While implied in "risk-transfer" and the work of Shaw and the strategy sacrificing non-combatant lives as "collateral damage" for those of the nation, the strategies scale when mapped onto the nexus of imperial paranoia, drone warfare, and the risk management techniques of finance applied to relation security.

[9] For more information here, please see the work of William V. Spanos in *American Exceptionalism in the Age of Globalization: The Specter of Vietnam* (2018) and Richard Drinnon in *Facing West: The Metaphysics of Indian-Hating & Empire-Building* (1980).

> I conceive of paranoia as *an inherent contradiction with respect to power*: a double-sided phantasm that oscillates precariously between deliriums of grandeur and nightmares of perpetual threat, a deep and dangerous doubleness with respect to power that is held in unstable tension, but which, if suddenly destabilized (as after 9/11), can produce pyrotechnic displays of violence. (McClintock 2009: 53)

Building on McClintock, we can see how the *force* of "imperial paranoia" is what motivates the "imperial arbitrage" of pre-emptive drone securitization. When Masco notes that "the ability to shape public fears – to give image and form to threat – is one of the key powers of the counterterror state today," it speaks to a troubling dynamic when considering a paranoid empire (Masco 2014: 21). Operating as the sole entity able to make these distinctions, the counterterror state functions as the threshold of intelligibility of any and all risks—both in measuring who/what *is* and to what *extent* something constitutes a security risk but, even before such probabilities, determining the basis of what *constitutes* a "risk" or "threat" initially. Masco's claim that "precisely because [the logic of preemption] transforms the unknown into a space of terror requiring immediate action" when considering imperial paranoia becomes even more chilling: the future becomes the surface of unknowability that the paranoid US counterterror state reflects its worst fears back upon itself (Masco 2014: 17). Furthermore, the counterterror state's ability to unquestionably *measure*, *mark*, and *name* any uncertainty as a threat presents an unceasing imaginary supply of targets.

In this regard, the US drone program's "find, fix, and finish" [drone operator slang for articulating, locating, and killing a "enemy combatant"] tactics for eliminating threats become perpetual *and* expansionary. With interventions being "no risk"/"low-cost" to the US, traditional counterweights fail while the *force* of paranoia reads the future as an inexhaustible source of threats (Scahill and The Staff of the Intercept 2016: 40–54). This "perverse logic" causes a system where "threat (as pure potential) is used to enable a radically active and ever emerging counterterror state, allowing action to be favored over restraint, possibilities over capabilities, hypotheticals over knowledge" (Masco 2014: 17). The drone program becomes a complex system of perpetual intervention against any possible hindrance to the US vision of future of secure, national advantage; yet, rather than focusing on the probable, the imperial paranoia makes mere possibility actionable—preempting low-possibility and high impact scenarios that increasingly unlikely materialize.

It is here that the horror of what I am calling the "hellfire hedge" should become clear. When Amoore claims that "the methods and techniques of accounting and statistical business calculation were strictly brought to be *on* war," we can recode into financial terms to follow the logic that undergirds the US drone program: drones are a "risk-free" instrument engaged in forcibly "offloading" or "offshoring" the risks of empire—each hellfire strike becomes a hedge trade to reduce any potential fluctuation in the position of US dominance (Amoore 2013: 23). In finance, hedging gives its contract owner the ability to either "put" or "call" on a contract "option," allowing the investor to sell or buy at a previously agreed upon price rather than the current market value. It foundationally uses the ability to project and structure the limits of the future, which the contract guarantees, to "tame" uncertainty. Through the process of the justificatory discourse of preemption and the technological means of the drone, the United States can take options on human life at a *global scale* to ensure its own security. When we translate this logic to the Hellfire strike, the ability to "put" or "call" becomes the US ability to intervene and destroy such a life to hedge against its possibilities—any variable to US security and supremacy is killable to guarantee an "acceptable" range of future events. The system becomes a global war against possibility whose traumas are only felt at the local level of the global periphery—as each strike from the perspective of the US national security is always already justified ("to protect *our* freedoms"), precise ("surgical" and, thusly, "humane").

It is precisely this escalating and autopoietic trajectory, whereupon paranoia leads to securitization-by-death which begets increased funding *and more death*, that is seen in two quotes from insiders to the US Drone program. In an interview by *The Intercept* with Daniel Hale[10] about the construction of "baseball cards"[11] by the intelligence community, Hale recalled:

[10] At the time of the interview, Daniel Hale was listed an anonymous source who leaked the "Drone Papers" by the staff of the *The Intercept* to protect Hale as a source. However, as of Hale's arrest in 2019 I am retroactively attributing the source information.

[11] Making "baseball cards" is the term used to describe military's method for visualizing information regarding a prospective addition to the kill list that includes display data, relationship maps, in an effort to identify a "so-called life pattern" (Scahill and The Staff of the

> They make rushed decisions and are often wrong in their assessments. They jump to conclusions, and there is no going back to correct mistakes. Because there is an ever increasing demand for more targets to be added to the kill list, the mentality is "Just keep feeding the beast." (Scahill and The Staff of the Intercept 2016: 104)

Mirroring Hale's comments, albeit bigoted and vicious in its rhetoric, were made by (now "disgraced") former Lt. General Michael Flynn (Williams 2017). Flynn, who is credited as the Defense Intelligence Agency and JSOC's architect for the "find, fix, finish" doctrine, stated of the drone program:

> We've tended to say, 'Drop another bomb via a drone and put out a headline that we killed Abu Bag of Donuts,' and it makes us all feel good for twenty-four hours... and you know what? It doesn't matter. It just made them a martyr. It just created a new reason to fight us even harder. (Scahill and The Staff of the Intercept 2016: 47–48)

Both insiders reaffirming the drive of the program toward growth, regardless of reliability of information, correct risk assessments, collateral damage, or effectiveness at the goal of securitization. The death of *any* possible future threat was sufficient to order a strike—for 24 hours.

Conclusion: "Not A Bugsplat" the Impossibility of Human Rights in Drone Warfare

> *My grandma was teaching me how you can tell if the okra is ready to be picked. All of a sudden there was a big noise. Like a fire had happened... I had seen my grandmother right before it had happened but I couldn't see her after. It was really dark but I could hear [a] scream when it hit her... I really liked my grandma.*
>
> —Nabeela ur Rehman through a translator recalling the day her grandmother was killed. (Devereaux 2013)
>
> *I know Americans think drones are the answer, but I wish they could understand how I and other children in my community see drones.*
>
> —Zubair ur Rehman through a translator (Johnson 2013)

Intercept 2016). This is what is shown to the President prior to the approval of a targeted kill window.

Across the continuum of its technology, deployment, and operational rhetoric, drone warfare seems to resist social recognition between operator and victim. The drone operators sit a hemisphere away from the target in a "safe zone" (usually in the American southwest) and transmits signals across the fiber optic cable across the Atlantic to the Ramstein Air Base in Germany to a satellite uplink with the coverage of both Ramstein and the operation zone (to limit lag); the technology of the drone *forces* the operator and (those directing them) to only view the space from a distant, panoptic oversight—going so far as to call a gap in surveillance between drone feeds a "blink"; and rhetorically reinforces the already dehumanized targets by referring to targets in official documents as "heat signatures" (potential targets), a "jackpot" (a target hit), a "touchdown" (a target hit at night), or "bug-splats" (the post-Hellfire remains of the dead) (Scahill and The Staff of the Intercept 2016). Yet, speaking back through this dehumanizing continuum is the face of an unknown, child victim through the #NotABugSplat installation (#NotABugSplat 2023).

The #NotABugSplat installation, a "reaction to the dehumanizing nature of drone warfare" per one artist, is "a giant poster" of the "face of a little girl … her eyes searching for the whirring machines that destroyed her family" (Saifi 2014). The installation itself is "designed to be captured by satellites" and be seen by drone operators not as "an anonymous dot on the landscape, but an innocent child victim's face" (#notabugsplat.com). With the purpose of shaming drone operators, per one artist, the poster of the child is installed in a field outside of Peshawar, in the Kyber Pukhtoonkhwa region of Pakistan—a region heavily victimized by drone attacks (#notabugsplat.com). The #NotABugSplat installation, as such, *hijacks* the technology to undo the intended affordance of security and comfort of the operator, forcing them to *see* and *avow* what the technology of the drone, the logic of preemption, and the ideology of American exceptionalism want to keep illegible: the grievability of their still, yet uncounted, victims.

When the logics of financial capitalism are deployed in security, the result is that human rights—or even to be recognized as human—become commodified and exploitable. Security becomes a perpetual system of violent interventions, exploiting the rights of those on the global periphery, to preempt the possibility of a future where other rights are infringed; rights become "profits" for successfully absorbing uncertainty and reaping the rights of the present to insure those of the future for an elect few. In the dystopian logic of Philip K. Dick's "The Minority Report," assassinations-by-drone—a “risk-free” instrument of imperial arbitrage—are deployed to both execute others of “precrime,” killed by confidential tribunal for actions they may possibly commit in the paranoid future imagined by the US counterterror state (Dick 2002). The lives of those killed as “collateral damage” are treated as “acceptable losses” in the financial risk management plan and the technology used to implement it. In 2013, the Rehman family were called to Congress to describe what it is like to suffer through and partially survive a drone strike. In the testimony, where both epigraphs are pulled from, Zubair ur Rehman said: “I no longer love blue skies. In fact, I now prefer grey skies. The drones do not fly when the skies are grey” (as qtd in Abad-Santos 2013). We cannot claim that an inclusive *human* rights exist in an age of drone securitization; because, for some, the right to life is predicated upon if the sky is blue or gray.

References

#NotABugSplat. 2023. *NotABugSplat.com*. N.D. Online. notabugsplat.com. Accessed 30 September 2023.

Abad-Santos, Alexander. 2013. This 13-Year-Old Is Scared When the Sky Is Blue Because of Our Drones. *The Atlantic*, 29 Oct 2013. Online. https://www.theatlantic.com/politics/archive/2013/10/saddest-words-congresss-briefing-drone-strikes/354548/. Accessed 30 September 2023.

Amoore, Louise. 2013. *The Politics of Possibility: Risk and Security Beyond Probability*. Durham: Duke University Press.

Beckert, Jens. 2016. *Imagined Futures: Fictional Expectations and Capitalist Dynamics*. Cambridge: Harvard University Press.

Broder, John M. 2003. A NATION AT WAR; U.S. Military Has No Count of Iraqi Dead In Fighting. *The New York Times*, 2 April 2003. Online. https://www.nytimes.com/2003/04/02/world/nation-war-casualties-us-military-has-no-count-iraqi-dead-fighting.html. Accessed 13 September 2023.

Butler, Judith. 2009. *Frames of War: When is Life Grievable?* New York: Verso.

Byman, Daniel L. 2013. Why Drones Work: The Case for Washington's Weapon of Choice. *Brookings*, 17 June 2013. Online. https://www.brookings.edu/articles/why-drones-work-the-case-for-washingtons-weapon-of-choice/. Accessed 13 September 2023.

Chamayou, Gregoire. 2015. *A Theory of the Drone*. Translated by Janet Lloyd. New York: The New Press.

Devereaux, Ryan. 2013. Interview: Family of Grandmother Killed in US Drone Strike Arrive for Congress Visit. *The Guardian*, 27 October 2013. Online. https://www.theguardian.com/world/2013/oct/27/drones-attack-pakistan-family-rehman-congress. Accessed 30 September 2023.

Dick, Philip K. 2002. Minority Report. In *Selected Stories of Philip K. Dick*. New York: Random House, Inc.

Ezard, John. 2003. Rumsfelds Unknown Unknown Takes Prize. *The Guardian*, 1 December 2003. Online. https://www.theguardian.com/world/2003/dec/02/usa.johnezard. Accessed 10 October 2020.

Hardin, Carolyn. 2021. *Capturing Finance: Arbitrage and Social Domination*. Durham: Duke University Press.

Johnson, Carrie. 2013. Families of Drone Strike Victims Tell Their Stories. *NPR.org*, 30 October 2013. Online. https://www.npr.org/2013/10/30/241782633/families-of-drone-strike-victims-tell-their-stories. Accessed 30 September 2023.

Kaplan, Caren. 2018. *Aerial Aftermaths: Wartime from Above*. Durham: Duke University Press.

Knight, Frank H. 2014. *Risk, Uncertainty, and Profit*. 1921. Mansfield Centre: Martino Publishing.

Lewis, Michael W. 2013. Drones: Actually the Most Humane Form of Warfare Ever. *The Atlantic*, 21 August 2013. Accessed 23 August 2018.

Lorey, Isabell. 2015. *State of Insecurity: Government of the Precarious*. New York: Verso.

Luhman, Niklas. 2008. *Risk: A Sociological Theory*. 1993. New Brunswick: Transaction Publishing.

Martin, Randy. 2007. *An Empire of Indifference: American War and the Financial Logic of Risk Management*. Durham: Duke University Press.

Masco, Joseph. 2014. *Theater of Operations: National Security Affect from the Cold War to the War on Terror*. Durham: Duke University Press.

McClintock, Anne. 2009. Paranoid Empire: Specters from Guantanamo and Abu Ghraib. *Small Axe* 13:50–74.

Morris, Errol. 2014. The Certainty of Donald Rumsfeld. *The New York Times*, 25 March 2014. Online. https://opinionator.blogs.nytimes.com/2014/03/25/the-certainty-of-donald-rumsfeld-part-1/. Accessed 10 October 2020.

Rumsfeld, Donald. 2002. DoD News Briefing—Secretary Rumsfeld and Gen. Myers. 12 February 2002. http://archive.defense.gov/Transcripts/Transcript.aspx?TranscriptID=2636. Accessed 1 July 2017.

Saifi, Sophia. 2014. Not a 'Bug Splat:' Artists Give Drone Victims a Face in Pakistan. *CNN*, 9 April 2014. Online. Accessed 30 September 2023.

Savage, Charlie, and Scott Shane. 2016. U.S Reveals Death Toll from Airstrikes Outside War Zones. *The New York Times*, 1 July 2016. Online. https://www.nytimes.com/2016/07/02/world/us-reveals-death-toll-from-airstrikes-outside-of-war-zones.html. Accessed 10 October 2020.

Scahill, Jeremy, and The Staff of the Intercept. 2016. *The Assassination Complex*. New York: Simon and Schuster.

Shaw, Martin. 2005. *The New Western Way of War: Risk-Transfer War and its Crisis in Iraq*. Malden: Polity Press.

Steyn, Mark. 2013. Rummy Speaks the Truth, Not Gobbledgood. *The Telegraph*, 9 December 2013. Online. http://www.telegraph.co.uk/comment/personal-view/3599959/Rummy-speaks-the-truth-not-gobbledygook.html. Accessed 10 October 2020.

Williams, Jennifer. 2017. Disgraced Trump Adviser Mike Flynn Admits He Worked as a "Foreign Agent" for the Turkish government. *Vox*, 9 March 2017. Online. https://www.vox.com/world/2017/3/9/14868680/trump-adviser-michael-flynn-foreign-agent-turkey-lobby. Accessed 30 September 2023.

PART II

Drone Aesthetics: Resistance and Counter-Archive

CHAPTER 5

Look to the Skies: Drone Art in the Age of Telepresence

Jenna Ann Altomonte

"I wasn't scared of drones before, but now when they fly overhead I wonder, will I be next?" (Friedersdorf 2013). Stated by Nabila Rehman during her testimony to Amnesty International in 2013, she emphasizes the anxiety produced by the constant aerial presence of drones in her village. The title of the report, aptly named "'Will I Be Next': US Drone Stikes in Pakistan," is a "qualitative assessment based on detailed field research into nine of the 45 reported strikes that occurred in Pakistan's North Waziristan tribal agency between January 2012 and August 2013" (Amnesty International 2013). Rehman's statement echoes the sentiments of her community members and others residing in a region under constant aerial surveillance. A year prior, her grandmother, Mamana Bibi, died from a drone strike in their village of Ghundi Kala in North Waziristan, Pakistan. While gathering vegetables from a field when a missile from a drone hit the village, injuring several other relatives (Amnesty International 2013). Accompanied by her family, Nabila became one of the first survivors to testify about the effects and after-effects of drone strikes in Pakistan. Her

J. A. Altomonte (✉)
Mississippi State University, Starkville, MS, USA
e-mail: jaltomonte@caad.msstate.edu

M. W. Azeem (ed.), *Human Rights in the Age of Drones*, Palgrave Studies in Literature, Culture and Human Rights,
https://doi.org/10.1007/978-3-032-08191-9_5

testimony commented on the numerous casualties within her community and the catastrophic collateral damage caused by debris, shrapnel, and contamination from the missile strike.

Drones, also known as remotely piloted aircrafts (RPAs) or unmanned aerial vehicles (UAVs), provide military and intelligence communities with the ability to survey and neutralize potential and confirmed threats from long-range distances using remote or telepresent technology.[1] The original intention of these drones was to reduce casualties, limit the presence of ground troops, and provide surveillance support. Refined in the wake of 9/11, the *weaponized drone*, or unmanned combat aerial vehicle (UCAVs), enables the United States military to operate pilotless aircrafts with missile capabilities. However, critics cite concerns about the use, function, and deployment of weaponized drones, specifically in undeclared warzones. Populations classified as noncombatants or "civilians who do not take a direct part in hostilities" remain at significant risk due to the proximity of targeted terrorist cells in places such as North Pakistan (International Committee of the Red Cross 2019).

Concerning the modern use of weaponized drones, the crux of this chapter centers on *how* and *why* artists respond to aerial interventions in regions classified as undeclared warzones. Citing criticisms by Grégoire Chamayou and Roger Stahl, I interrogate a selection of artworks that magnify ethical and legal violations caused by drone strikes on noncombatants living in regions where formal declarations of war remain vague or undefined. The selection of artworks focuses specifically on the effects of said strikes on North Pakistan, a region once touted as the most drone-prone place on earth (Amnesty International 2013). In places such as Nabila Rehman's village, civilian deaths remain unreported or falsified. Thus, the artworks selected for this chapter seek to expose, subvert, and criticize the application of weaponized drones.

In the first piece by Pakistani artist Saks Afridi, titled *#NotABugSplat*, the artist worked in collaboration with French artist-activist JR to humanize victims of drone strikes. The site-specific work features a large portrait of drone victims and covers the length of a large field in North Pakistan. The second piece by artist James Bridle, titled *Dronestagram*, critiques the culture of secrecy surrounding drone strikes in both declared and undeclared war zones. The piece uses Instagram as a platform to announce the location of the strikes, complemented by aerial surveillance images. In

[1] The term *drone* will be used for consistency in reference to UAVs and RPAs.

the third drone-inspired series, artist Mahwish Chishty appropriates the body of the drone to recontextualize the function and purpose of an object coded as violent and intrusive. Two pieces, *The Reaper* and *The Predator*, merge imagery associated with traditional Pakistani truck art onto the body of the drone. Although playful in appearance, Chishty's colorful drone bodies assume a more subversive presence. Afridi, Bridle, and Chishty's works use a variety of digital and print-based media to expose the consequential after-effects of drone strikes on noncombatants living in North Pakistan. Each art piece serves as a *didactic* tool, a vehicle to educate viewers about the effects of drone strikes.

Defining the Drone: To Survey and Destroy

The *drone* is a militerm for unmanned aerial vehicles or an aircraft flown using remote support. Originally developed for surveillance and information gathering during World War I, the drone evolved from an observatory device to a weaponized tool capable of remote destruction over long distances.[2] In *War and Cinema: The Logics of Perception*, Paul Virilio cites World War I as the first modern event where short range, close-distance warfare was "superseded by long-range butchery" (Virilio 2009: 69–70). With the advent of airplane and aerial surveillance devices, reliance on remote reconnaissance gradually replaced the need for ground troops in conflict zones. According to Virilio, the rules of engagement shifted from reliance on the *visible made invisible* to the *invisible made visible* (Virilio 2009: 71). By World War II, the development of the modern drone arose with the combination of screenic hardware, cameras, and radio-operated

[2] In *Domesticating Drones: The Technology, Law, and Economics of Unmanned Aircrafts*, Henry H. Perritt, Jr and Eliot O. Sprague categorize drones into two categories: microdrones and macrodrones. Microdrones consist of lightweight, aerial devices weighing under 55 pounds. Microdrones can be operated using handheld devices or remote controls. AeroVironment's WASP III, a small, three-pound drone, requires only a hand-launch for short-range surveillance operations. The more substantial macrodrones weigh over 55 pounds and provide operators with long-range capabilities. Equipped with precision surveillance technology and/or weapons, macrodrones service the military and intelligence communities for information gathering missions and/or armed support. Macrodrones can travel over 8000 miles and at an altitude of nearly 60,000 feet. Popular macrodrones include the Global Hawk manufactured by Northrop-Grumman, the General Atomics MQ-1 Predators and MQ-9 Reapers (both combat capable). See Henry H. Perritt, Jr. and Eliot O. Sprague, *Domesticating Drones: The Technology, Law, and Economics of Unmanned Aircrafts* (New York: Routledge, 2017), 30–32.

aircrafts controlled by ground troops. Pilotless, these aircrafts required close operation and surveillance by manned aerial devices to assist with flight control (Chandler 2017: 89–90). The nascent technology provided operators the ability to control a plane after piloted take-off, crashing the armed devices into designated targets without endangering the operations crew (Gusterson 2016: 11). In the aftermath of the Iran–Iraq War of the 1980s and the Persian Gulf War of the 1990s, drone technology changed from surveillance-capable to weaponized. Macrodrones, such as the Predator and Reaper models, assumed weaponized status shortly after 9/11 ("Pentagon Plans for Cuts to Drone Budgets" 2014).[3]

In *A Theory of the Drone*, Grégoire Chamayou traces the genealogy of remote weaponry by focusing on the *implications* and after-effects of tele-present warfare on vulnerable bodies (Chamayou 2013: 11–12). Chamayou positions the 2001 launch of the Predator-based Hellfire AGM-114C missile as *the* moment when drones shifted from objects of surveillance and information gathering to a weaponized extension of the state (Chamayou 2013: 28–29). The drone operates as the eye and muscle of the state, surveilling and neutralizing risks or threats at an assured clear distance. However, what about regions where the United States has limited or no formal declarations of war? How do drone operations function outside ethical and legal frameworks as defined by international law?

In Pakistan, a country at the center of complex drone operations, artists and activists seek justice for victims injured or killed by American-initiated air strikes. In 2004, the United States began drone operations in North Waziristan, a region situated in the Khyber Pakhtunkhwa province (previously known as the Federally Administered Tribal Area or FATA) of Pakistan (Cavallaro et al. 2012). Known for a diverse tribal presence and vast mountainous landscape, the region is punctuated by several major cities, such as Peshawar. Until 2018, FATA remained under British protectorate via the colonial-era Frontier Crimes Regulations, a framework that governed Northwest Pakistan. Only in 2018, when FATA merged with

[3] In a study published in April 2003 by the Federation for American Scientists, 163 drones were in use by the United States military. By 2014, the US military counted 10,500 unmanned aerial devices in action, signifying the rise in remotely piloted aircrafts. In a study sponsored by the Brookings Institute in 2013, the number of drone pilots increased from 3.3% of total United States Air Force pilots in 2001 to 8.5%. See Jeremiah Gertler, "U.S. Unmanned Aerial Systems" (Congressional Research Service, Washington D.C., 2012), 7.

the Khyber Pakhtunkhwa province, did the FCR regulations dissolve (Akins 2017: 8–9).

Dereck Gregory (2017) defines this region as an Agambenesque *state of exception*, a "paradoxical space where divisions and interaction remain routine coperformances" (Gregory 2017: 29–30). To extrapolate on Gregory's position, the United States uses a defensive strategy to justify drone strikes in the Khyber Pakhtunkhwa province, citing self-defense and the need to neutralize threats to American security and sovereignty (Gregory 2017: 42–43). Originally, this pertained to operations after 9/11 in Afghanistan; however, the United States uses the borderlands on/between Pakistan as an extension of the warzone to search, survey, and neutralize possible terrorist activities. This defensive overreach produces major consequences for civilians living in regions where Al-Qaeda or Tehrik-i-Taliban Pakistan maintains presence (Nizami et al. 2018).

A 2018 study on the rise of terrorism in Pakistan argues that the increase in drone warfare correlates with a rise in radicalization, resulting in a "breeding ground of terrorism" (Nizami et al. 2018):

> Unmanned army drone strikes killed and maimed thousands of innocent civilians in poor and difficult-to-access regions of Pakistan. This infuriated people, leading them to take up arms against the perceived aggressors. This triggering of the relatives of the deceased to engage in such activity is the culture of revenge in Pakistan, which unfortunately can last for generations. (Nizami et al. 2018)

This led to an increase in anti-Western sentiment in North Waziristan, namely, in opposition to American drone intervention. In *Through the Crosshairs: War, Visual Culture, and the Weaponized Gaze*, Roger Stahl positions remote technology as *the* instrument of Western warfare (Stahl 2018: 3). He defines the *weaponized gaze* as the byproduct of Western defensive hegemony:

> The view through high-tech weapons has come to dominate the Western presentation of war. To a significant degree, the civic eye has migrated from the third-party witness to the first-person constituent of the weapon's gaze. Not only does the citizen increasingly apprehend war through this aperture, but this gaze has become a powerful means through which the military-industrial-media-complex apprehends civic consciousness-suspending it, as it [was] in a projected beam of light. This realignment, [which] I will refer

to as the 'weaponized gaze,' is anchored in the imagery of the targeting cameras. (Stahl 2018: 3)

Through this field of vision, the gaze is mediated by a multinational network of analysts, sensor operators, and pilots who control the militarized apparatus. The weaponized gaze not only surveys but also serves as an armed extension of the state defense system. Thus, the gaze mediates the civic responses/interactions via the drone apparatus.

What about those that operate and control the apparatus *behind* the weaponized gaze? Critics view drone pilots and operators as desensitized extensions of the state. In "Psychological Dimensions of Drone Warfare," Alaa Hijazi et al. investigate internal and external influences on drone operators and pilots.[4] Though data on the subject is elusive, the study critically evaluates the impact of various stressors, like screen time, temporal detachment, anonymity, apathy, and anxiety (Hijazi et al. 2017). The assumption that drone pilots and operators do not experience the direct act of killing, but rather neutralize combatants and noncombatants through the screen, presumes that they do not experience the traumatic after-effects.

Recent studies by the US Air Force document an increase in post-traumatic stress and acute stress disorders by operators, pilots, and analysts. In an interview with a former drone sensor operator, some of those studies explained the various stressors involved in working from a remote location and neutralizing potential threats from thousands of miles away:

> Ever step on ants and never give it another thought? That's what you are made to think of the targets – as just black blobs on a screen. You start to do these psychological gymnastics to make it easier to do what you have to do – they deserved it, they chose their side. You had to kill part of your con-

[4] The Hijazi et al. study explicitly states, "Although an ethical debate on drone use may be worthy, it was not the stated purpose of the task force to comment on the ethics or politics of drone warfare. Rather the purpose of this paper is to synthesize the available data regarding the psychological dimensions of drones and to identify gaps in the literature in need of new empirical information. Task force members were specifically recruited to reflect a range of opinions regarding the ethics of drones and came from a variety of backgrounds, clinical and experimental, some with military expertise, most without." (Hijazi et al. 2017). The study also recognizes the difficulty of obtaining drone operator data on individuals with Acute Stress Disorders (ASD), Post Traumatic Disorders (PTSD), and Disorders of Extreme Stress (DESNOS).

science to keep doing your job every day – and ignore those voices telling you this wasn't right. (Pilkington 2015)

Interviews with thousands of drone pilots and operators report symptoms ranging from fatigue to delusions and depression to suicidal thoughts and self-harm. Many cite the voyeuristic positioning of the drone camera as a catalyst. In *Drone: Remote Control Warfare,* Hugh Gusterson writes about the effects of "remote narrativization" that involves making "interpretive leaps, filling in informational gaps, and provide[s] framing moral judgements as they integrate shards of visual information and turn pixelated figures into personalities" (Gusterson 2016: 66–67).[5] From this position, operators admit to either humanizing or dehumanizing the "pixelated" figures on the screen.

Since the United States does not release consistent data on drone strike victims, investigative journalists, and nongovernmental organizations, such as the Bureau of Investigative Journalism (TBIJ is this correct acronym?) and Reprieve, report information on noncombatant injuries and deaths. On March 6, 2019, the former Trump administration published a decree limiting information on noncombatant casualties caused by drone strikes:

> [The report] revokes the requirement that the administration release an unclassified summary of 'the number of strikes undertaken by the United States Government against terrorist targets outside areas of active hostilities, as well as assessments of combatant and noncombatant deaths resulting from those strikes.' (Talev 2019)

According to this decree, information on noncombatant casualties, namely, in undeclared warzones, remains censored and/or highly redacted. To complicate this issue, International Humanitarian Law (IHL) under the auspices of the International Committee of the Red Cross (ICRC) provides a paradoxical framework concerning drone strikes on noncombatants. In *International Law and Drone Strikes in Pakistan: The Legal and*

[5] To alleviate this issue, engineers are working to humanize the drone interface to be more "user-friendly." Mike Patzek, an engineer at the Air Force Research Laboratory, reveals the proto-type for a "Siri-like" interface coded into future drones. Included in the new designs, Patzek references the introduction to tactile feedback, similar to gaming remotes that vibrate or shake. These new additions serve to make the human-mechanical connection more cohesive, increasing ease of access.

Sociopolitical Aspect, Sikander Ahmed Shah analyzes the language associated with drone use in accordance with IHL:

> Under IHL, there is a blanket prohibition on weapons that cause superfluous injury or unnecessary suffering, the main rationale behind these prohibitions is that they cause some form of 'permanent disability' or 'render death inevitable… the decision to deploy a UAV in a particular area almost always results in fatalities and there is little chance or opportunity of escape for those targeted. While the weapons used on drones might not be illegal *per se*-i.e., not causing superfluous injury- it is their use through the drones' platform, and the inescapability of the strikes themselves, which can result in unnecessary suffering and excessive injury. (Shah 2014: 169–170)

Thus, noncombatants injured or killed by drones often have limited legal recourse. Concerning this lack of transparency, artists such as Afridi, Bridle, and Chishty use drone strikes to confront the blurred legal status of American intervention in Pakistan.

Visibility and Victimhood: #*NotABugSplat*

To memorialize casualties caused by drone strikes in North Pakistan, artist Saks Afridi developed a large-scale, site-specific portrait project in 2014. Afridi, originally from Peshawar, Pakistan, created the piece in collaboration with French artist JR's *Inside Out* project. Starting in 2011, *Inside Out* serves as a global arts campaign encouraging collaboration and social equality. The project involves the use of giant portraiture, a signature in many of JR's projects in places such as the Separation Wall in Palestine and on the United States-Mexico border in San Diego/Tijuana. According to JR, the project

> gives everyone the opportunity to share their portrait and make a statement for what they stand for… and for people to share their untold stories and transform messages of personal identity into works of public art. (Afridi and JR 2014)

In regions where vulnerable populations face the direct effects of war, government intervention, and/or land-grabbing, *Inside Out* provides the opportunity to *make visible* the victims of these incursions. For example, an impactful project from 2011 focused on the portraits of Lakota tribal members in New York City. The three-word artist statement, "we still exist," criticizes the practice of erasure and land grabbing imparted on indigenous populations by the United States government. The projects vary according to the creator's theme or agenda; however, many iterations serve to bridge the communicative divide between disparate cultures and populations.

In *#NotABugSplat*, Afridi invites viewers to empathize with the victims of drone strikes. The term bugsplat serves as another militerm used by analysts and operators. Bugsplat first entered public usage in 2003 in a United States Department of Defense memo. In *Bugsplat: The Politics of Collateral Damage in Western Armed Conflicts*, Bruce Cronin (2018) outlines the term in relation to software programming. According to Cronin, *bugsplat* is

> software [that] examines a potential target by analyzing the surrounding terrain, the direction and angle of the proposed attack, and the particular characteristics of the munition selected for the strike, and then generates a bloblike image of an irregular-shaped 'probable-damage field' that 'looks like insects hitting a car windshield at high speed.' (Cronin 2018: 2)[6]

The field alerts analysts to the location of potential targets as a means of reducing civilian casualty rates. One official made the following observation after witnessing a strike:

> You say something like 'Show me the Bugsplat.' That's what we call the probability of a kill estimate when we are doing this final math before the 'Go go go' decision. You would actually get a picture of a compound, and there will be something on it that looks like a bugsplat actually with red, yellow, and green. (Pugliese 2017)

Although iteration is rarely used, *bugsplat* references the corporeal debris left behind in the wake of a drone strike. Both uses dehumanize the victim by reducing them to a slang term that correlates with dead insects smashed against the ground or windshield.

In his piece, Afridi uses the visage of child-victim orphaned by a US-initiated predator drone strike. The victim originates from Dande

[6]The software is now referred to as FAST-CD or Fast Assessment Strike Tool-Collateral Damage.

Darpakhel in North Waziristan (Saifi 2014).[7] The village, once touted as the most dangerous and highly droned location in Pakistan, cites hundreds of strikes since the late 2000s (Stanford Center for International Security and Cooperation, Stanford University 2018).[8] Noor Behram, a Pakistani photojournalist who spent the last decade documenting and photographing the after-effects of drone strikes in North Waziristan, captured the image of the young girl and her siblings. In an interview from 2009, Behram describes the sordid details of the strike that killed the girl's parents:

> These kids had no idea where their parents were. They [did not] know their parents were killed…there's no government here, no social network or security…people have to look after each other. (Ackerman 2011)[9]

Due to concerns about traveling to Dande Darpakhel, Afridi opted to display the piece in another village in Khyber Pakhtunkhwa. Derived from Behram's original photo, the composition centers on the young girl clutching a piece of debris (Behram 2010). Of the three surviving siblings, she gazes directly at the camera Cropped at the waist, the focus of the image centers on her face. Large dots cover the background of the piece, framing her body and providing contrast against the open field (Afridi and JR 2014). Printed in black and white, her portrait runs the entire length and width of the pasture. Afridi and his collaborators opted to print her portrait on durable material resistant to tearing and reusable by the local villagers (*#NotABugSplat*).

Returning to Stahl's definition of the weaponized gaze, I interpret Afridi's piece as presenting the victim in direct confrontation with the militarized apparatus of the drone. The piece counters the weaponized gaze by positioning the *victimized gaze* against the drones' operators. The victimized gaze supposes a defensive position, confronting the weaponized apparatus. Her portrait lies flat and unencumbered by debris and

[7] Information obtained from Shahzad Akbar, a human rights attorney and Reprieve affiliate. See Spencer Ackerman, "Rare Photographs show round Zero of the Drone War," *Wired*, December 12, 2011, accessed 20 August 2019, https://www.wired.com/2011/12/photos-pakistan-drone-war/.

[8] The region once housed members of the Haqqani Network, an insurgency group aligned with Al-Qaeda and known for their violent, guerrilla-style attacks.

[9] Ackerman, "Rare Photographs," https://www.wired.com/2011/12/photos-pakistan-drone-war/. Note: The children also lost two of their siblings in the blast.

foliage, providing viewers from above an unobstructed look at the girl's visage. The piece humanizes the victim, rather than reducing her and her family to a "bugsplat." What is most thought-provoking about Afridi's piece is the intention. Imagine if every victim of a drone strike in North Pakistan was provided a large-scale portrait as a form of memorialization. The sheer magnitude of such a project would require hundreds of squares to commemorate civilian victims, carpeting miles of land.[10]

Following Drone Strikes Online: Dronestagram

Afridi's piece used both the physical location of the portrait and online resources to memorialize the victims of drone strikes. Using site-specific locations in Pakistan, artist James Bridle engages the concept of *absence as presence* to inform digital users about the influx of drone strikes in undeclared warzones. In 2012, he started *Dronestagram,* a three-year, user-to-user project centered on mapping the locations of recent drone strikes in undeclared warzones in Pakistan and Yemen and declared warzones in Afghanistan (Dronestagram 2012). Using social media platforms and aerial footage gathered from Google Maps, Bridle published information about state-sponsored drone strikes. Bridle cites the Bureau of Investigative Journalism as a resource for uncovering and exposing drone strike zones, a source also cited by Afridi. Bridle also relied on independent investigative resources due to government censorship and the redaction of drone strike data.

To access and interact with *Dronestagram*, users first log in to his Instagram page at https://www.instagram.com/dronestagram/ (Dronestagram 2012).[11] An icon of a General Atomic MQ-9 Reaper drone serves as the profile picture, set atop an aerial image of a former strike zone (Bridle 2014). Clicking on an image from the third row, the following information provides data about the location, number of casualties, and date of the designed strike:

[10] Due to the ephemeral nature of the material and the location in rural Khyber Pakhtunkhwa, #NotABugSplat's physical presence lasted for only a short duration. Currently, the piece is available to view online via websites like, https://notabugsplat.com/, JR's Inside/Out project webpage at https://www.insideoutproject.net/en, and Saks Afridi's personal site at http://www.saksafridi.com/about-saks-art.

[11] Users could also access the page via Twitter and Tumblr.

> Dronestagram: December 20 2014: A US drone strike killed at least four militants, according to security officials. The strike reportedly killed militants who fought under local Pakistani taliban leader Hafiz Gul Bahadur. According to several sources, two missiles were fired at a compound. None of the dead have been identified, but there are reports that a high value target was killed in the strike. The Express Tribune, citing tribal sources, reported the dead "included one Arab and three Uzbek fighters – two of them members of the banned Tehreek-e Taliban Pakistan (TTP)." A senior security official told AFP: "A US drone fired two missiles at a compound in Mada Khail neighborhood of Datta Khail area in North Waziristan killing six persons. The death toll is expected to rise." #drone #drones #pakistan. (Dronestagram)

The village, Datta Khail, lies less than 60 kilometers from Dande Darpakhel, the location of the Afridi's child subject *#NotABugSplat*. Another post reads:

> Dronestagram "November 11 2014: between 4 and 7 killed by a CIA drone strike on the Dawa Toi valley, a heavily wooded area near the Afghan border, near to Datta Khel. The identities of those killed [are] unknown. #drone #drones #pakistan." (Dronestagram)

Bridle subverts the weaponized gaze by appropriating satellite images obtained via Google Maps. Rather than viewing the after-effects of drone strikes from the vantage of the victim or operator, this perspective derives from a civilian app accessible *en masse*. Stahl positions the drone eye as "anchored in the imagery of the targeting camera," mediated by operators, analysts, and pilots (Stahl 2018: 3). In the case of *Dronestagram,* the viewer-participant has control over the data captured by the targeting camera. Through Instagram, users can share and comment on the images, recontextualizing and reframing the content; an alternative vantage point mediated by the civilian viewer.

In *Dronestagram*, the viewer only sees satellite images curated by Bridle in the aftermath of the strike, decontextualized from footage viewed by the drone operator. Each image lacks visible bodies, only the built environments and rural terrain are visible. In many of his posts, the information is delayed 24–72 hours after the initial strike, obfuscating the exact location and timeframe of where and when the bombings occurred.[12] The

[12] Atmospheric interference from storms and debris obscures many of the images.

viewer assumes loss of life within the frame and is only informed of casualties by Bridle via the text box attached to each Instagram post. However, unlike Afridi, no giant portraits are visible from satellite view, only the assumed aftermath of a violent strike mediated online via social media platforms.

Reflections of Drone Warfare

Afridi and Bridle maintain social media presence, using tags and the digital platform to promote their drone-inspired projects. Mahwish Chishty in her work critiques the cultural implications of the drone program. Originating from Pakistan, Chishty uses the apparatus of the drone to educate viewers about Pakistani traditions directly affected by drone intervention. In a project started in 2018, she merges features of the drone with symbols of Pakistani culture. Part of the *Basant Portraits* series, her work focuses on children living at/near contentious border zones in the United States/Mexico and Afghanistan/Pakistan regions (Chishty 2018). Basant references the yearly kite festival held in Pakistan and India each spring (Desai 2010: 32–33). Communities gather to celebrate the season by flying brightly colored kites. However, with the advent of the drone program in Pakistan, communities refrain from flying kites for fear of drone strikes. In an iteration of the piece from 2018, Chishty includes colorful, hand-drawn kites suspended above silver emergency blankets:

> Children fly kites to mark the occasion of Basant by holding competitions, but common local kites are made of thin paper and wooden sticks that can easily tear or [become] weak in misty weather; hence, the sport cannot normally be enjoyed on cloudy days when drones don't operate. As part of this project, the artist works with Pakistani and American children to create and exchange durable kites that can be flown even on cloudy days. (Chishty 2019)

Juxtaposed to the kites, the piece includes two portraits painted atop a mirrored surface and embedded on silver emergency blankets. Referencing Afridi's portrait of the young girl from Dande Darpakhel in North Waziristan, Chishty also uses pixelated dots to create the visages of two children. Using Black 2.0, a pigment created by Stuart Semple and touted as the "most pigmented, flattest, mattest, black acrylic paint in the world," the pixelated dots serve as voids against the shimmering surface of the emergency blankets (Semple n.d.).[13] The blankets, synonymous with refugee and displaced populations, emphasize the children's portraits. The use of Black 2.0 pigment represents the type of paint used on stealth devices, a means of masking and concealing an object. In the installation, the portraits are made *more* visible by the pigment, subverting the original use of the stealth paint. Like Afridi's piece, the viewer is drawn to the pixelated visage of the portraits. The brightly painted kites are reflected against the backdrop of the portraits, a reference to the disrupted tradition impacted by drone strikes.

In another poignant representation of the *experience* of living under droned skies, Chishty adds a sonic element to her series. Two pieces titled *The Reaper* and *The Predator* depict drones rendered in Pakistani truck art designs. Like the Basant series, she draws on another Pakistani tradition of truck art, a practice originating from the 1920s (Stewart 2018). The tradition began with truckers embellishing corporate logos on their vehicles, eventually using the surface of trucks to compete with other companies and drivers. Artists adorn each truck with various motifs, such as stars, flowers, and hearts, and include portraits, landscapes, religious symbols, and text (Kienberger 2016: 84–87). In "On wings of diesel," Jamal J. Elias unpacks the rich history of truck (and greater vehicle) art in Pakistan, focusing specifically on the urban center in Karachi, the Rawalpindi-Islamabad corridor, and the Karakorum Highway (Elias 2003: 189). In his study, Elias noted five distinctive regional styles with unique symbols, motifs, and icons:

1. Punjabi style: most common…elaborate with metal cowling [and] rely heavily on hammered metal work and plastic applique in their decoration. [Trucks] are decorated with patterns made out of colored reflective tape.
2. Swati style: distinctive for their carved wooden doors…limited use of plastic and hammered metal work.
3. Peshawar style: …fall somewhere in between Punjabi and Swati.
4. Baluchi style: …larger trucks [that] use more geometric patterns on the side panels.

[13] Semple has strict rules on who can access Black 2.0 (just anyone besides artist Anish Kapoor).

5. Karachi style: has wooden panel above the windshield carved in relief with vegetative and floral motifs and colored iridescent paints. (Elias 2003: 189–192).[14]

In Chishty's *The Reaper*, the video runs for thirty-seven seconds. The drone was created using Premiere Pro and consists of painted segments and paper fragments cut and arranged to appear in motion and in the distinctive Punjabi style. In the video, the body of the drone stays within the frame; however, the painted eyes on the engine's body open and close while the loaded missiles glisten and shimmer. Throughout the video, humming noise plays at various frequencies. Chishty states,

> My inspiration for the Reaper sound comes from the 'singing comet' 67P/Churyumov-Gerasimenko (sounds recorded on the comet just last year), along with the drone sound (a steady hum). (Chishty n.d.)

For those living in North Waziristan, the sound of the drone serves as a trigger, inducing panic and anxiety. Referenced by survivors and witnesses to drone operations in Pakistan, the sight and sound of drones results in permanent psychological damage, including posttraumatic stress and acute stress disorders. In an Amnesty International report on drone strikes in Pakistan, one interviewee stated:

> Everyone is scared, and they can't get out of their house without any tension and from the fear of drone attacks. People are mentally disturbed as a result of the drone flights…We can't sleep because of the planes' loud sound. Even if they don't attack, we still have the fear of attack in our mind. (Amnesty International 2013)

The humming sound of the drone and the visualization of a gray body flying at low altitude trigger panic, anxiety, and other stress-related responses. Chishty subverts the body of the drone by remaking it in the Pakistani artistic traditions (Chishty 2016). The drone's hum is deadened,

[14] Elias also identifies six popular categories/motifs evident in Pakistani truck art: "1. Explicit religious symbols and icons; 2. Talismanic and fetish objects; 3. Talismanically or religiously loaded symbols; 4. Idealized elements of life; 5. Elements from modern life; and 6. The non-religious calligraphic program of the truck" (see Elias 2003: 192–194). Chishty's work employs a variety of motifs in *the Reaper* and *the Predator* videos, in particular vegetal motifs and iterations of the *nazar* or "bad/evil eye."

played in opposition to the "singing" noise emanating from the comet. This cacophony juxtaposes the naturally occurring phenomenon of the comet's sound with the artificial hum of the machine-driven drone.

In *The Predator*, the video runs for five minutes and twenty-seven seconds. Like *The Reaper*, the video includes the body of a drone painted in the truck art tradition. Situated at the front of the body, a pair of eyes blink complemented by a colorful spinning wheel on the multispectral targeting system camera. Traffic lights flash from green to yellow to red below the spinning wheel. In this video, the noise assaults the viewer with a variation of pitches and frequencies, ranging from near silence to sounds mimicking muffled screams. To create the noise, Chishty used sound recordings of the Aztec death whistle (Chishty). Used in ritual ceremonies celebrating death, the whistle consists of materials such as bone, clay, animal skin, and natural fibers (Watson 2008). According to studies by Roberto Velazquez (2008), an engineer and expert in pre-Columbian sounds/noise production, the death whistle evokes a noise similar to a scream or cry. The instrument would be played to assist the deceased in the afterlife (cited in NPR 2008). The video challenges viewers to speculate when the next cacophony begins. The various modulations mimic the unpredictability of drone strikes in Pakistan, forcing the listener to experience periods of calm punctuated by sounds of discord and tension.

Conclusion

Afridi, Bridle, and Chishty criticize the use, application, and deployment of drones by employing a variety of creative interventions. In particular, their work provides a space to critique drone programs deployed in regions where noncombatants suffer significant casualties. Just like these artists, a number of other artists, activists, filmmakers, and writers continue to expose the violent aftermath of drone strikes: Pratap Cahtterjee and Khalil's graphic novel, *Verax: The True History of Whistleblowers, Drone Warfare, and Mass Surveillance* (2017), illustrates the legacy of state-sponsored surveillance; Joseph DeLappe's drone-inspired series, including *Killbox* (2015–ongoing) and *Drone Strike Visualization*(2014–2015), critiques the aerial intervention programs in Pakistan; and *The Other Side* (2012), a film by Muhammad Danish Qasim, documents a child's radicalization after his home is hit by an American-led drone strike in Pakistan. Each of these artists uses their work as a didactic platform, a venue for educating the public about casualties associated with remote warfare. As the use of drones and remote technology increases in active and inactive warzones, artists and activists must continue to promote creative projects that challenge the after-effects of drone strikes. Returning to Nabila Rehman's testimony, no human should have to ponder "will I be next?"

References

Ackerman, Spencer. 2011. Rare Photographs Show Round Zero of the Drone War. *Wired*. December 12. https://www.wired.com/2011/12/photos-pakistan-drone-war/. Accessed 20 August 2019.

Afridi, Saks, and JR. 2014. #NotABugSplat. https://notabugsplat.com/. Accessed 20 August 2019.

Akins, Harrison. 2017. FATA and the Frontier Crimes Regulation in Pakistan: The Enduring Legacy of British Colonialism. *Policy Brief* 5:17, Howard H. Baker Jr. Center for Public Policy, University of Tennessee. http://bakercenter.utk.edu/wp-content/uploads/2017/11/PolicyBrief5-2017.pdf.

Behram, Noor. 2010. dande-darpa-khel-august-21-2009-2. https://www.wired.com/2011/12/photos-pakistan-drone-war/. Accessed 20 August 2019.

Bridle, James. 2014. Dronestagram. https://www.instagram.com/dronestagram/?hl=en. Accessed 20 August 2019.

Cavallaro, James, Sarah Knuckey, and Stephan Sonnenberg. 2012. *Living under Drones: Death, Injury, and Trauma to Civilians from US Drone Practices in Pakistan*. Stanford and New York: International Human Rights and Conflict Resolution Clinic, Stanford Law School; NYU School of Law, Global Justice Clinic. https://www-cdn.law.stanford.edu/wp-content/uploads/2015/07/Stanford-NYU-Living-Under-Drones.pdf.

Chamayou, Grégoire. 2013. *A Theory of the Drone*. Paris: The New Press.

Chandler, Katherine. 2017. American Kamikaze: Television-Guided Assault Drones in World War II. In *Life in the Age of Drone Warfare*, ed. Lisa Parks and Caren Kaplan, 89–111. Durham and London: Duke University Press.

Chishty, Mahwish. 2016. Covert War and Cultures Colliding. Imperial War Museum London. 20 December. https://imperialwarmuseum.wordpress.com/2016/12/20/iwm-talk-covert-war-and-colliding-cultures-by-mahwish-chishty/.

Chishty, Mahwish. 2018. Basant Portraits. https://www.mahachishty.com/work/#/basant-portraits/. Accessed 12 September 2019.

Chishty, Mahwish. 2019. Basant Portraits, Wall Text. Stamps Gallery. *Border Control: Traversing Horizons in Media Practice*. University of Michigan, Ann Arbor, MI.

Chishty, Mahwish. n.d. The Reaper. *Mahwish Chishty*. http://www.mahachishty.com/the-reaper/. Accessed 12 September 2019.

Cronin, Bruce. 2018. *Bugsplat: The Politics of Collateral Damage in Western Armed Conflicts*. New York: Oxford University Press.
Desai, Nikita. 2010. *A Different Freedom: Kite Flying in Western India; Culture and Tradition*. Newcastle upon Tyne: Cambridge Scholars Publishing.
Dronestagram. 2012. *Dronestagram*. https://dronestagram.tumblr.com/post/34245971902/ob298-october-24-2012-3-5-reported-killed-1. Accessed 25 August 2019.
Elias, Jamal J. 2003. On Wings of Diesel: Spiritual Space and Religious Imagination in Pakistani Truck Decoration. *Res: Anthropology and Aesthetics* 43:187–202.
Friedersdorf, Conor. 2013. 8-Year-Old Girl on Drones: 'When They Fly Overhead I Wonder, Will I Be Next?' *The Atlantic*, October 22. https://www.theatlantic.com/politics/archive/2013/10/8-year-old-girl-on-drones-when-they-fly-overhead-i-wonder-will-i-be-next/280753/. Accessed 16 June 2023.
Gertler, Jeremiah. 2012. *U.S. Unmanned Aerial Systems*. Washington, DC: Congressional Research Service.
Gregory, Dereck. 2017. Dirty Dancing: Drones and Death in the Borderlands. In *Life in the Age of Drone Warfare*, ed. Lisa Parks and Caren Kaplan, 25–58. Durham and London: Duke University Press.
Gusterson, Hugh. 2016. *Drone: Remote Control Warfare*. Cambridge: Massachusetts Institute of Technology Press.
Haqqani Network. 2018. Stanford Center for International Security and Cooperation, Stanford University. https://cisac.fsi.stanford.edu/mappingmilitants/profiles/haqqani-network#highlight_text_9408.
Hijazi, Alaa, Christopher J. Ferguson, Harold Hall, F. Mark Hovee, Richard Ferraro, and Sherrie Wilcox. 2017. Psychological Dimensions of Drone Warfare. *Current Psychology*. https://doi.org/10.1007/s12144-017-9684-7.
Inside Out: The People's Art Project. n.d. *Inside Out Project*. https://www.insideoutproject.net/en. Accessed 10 August 2019.
International Committee of the Red Cross. 2019. Rule 1. The Principle of Distinction Between Civilians and Combatants. *International Humanitarian Law Database*. https://ihl-databases.icrc.org/customary-ihl/eng/docs/v1_rul_rule1.
Kienberger, Richard. 2016. The Beauty Pageant. *Truck & Driver*, December, 84–87.
Nizami, Tamizuddin Asad, Tariq Mahmood Hassan, Sadia Yasir, Mowaddat Hussain Rana, and Fareed Aslam Minhas. 2018. Terrorism in Pakistan: The Psychosocial Context and Why It Matters. *British Journal of Psychiatry* 15 (1): 20–22. https://www.ncbi.nlm.nih.gov/pmc/articles/PMC6020923/. Accessed 06 August 2019.
Pentagon Plans for Cuts to Drone Budgets. 2014. *Military*. https://www.military.com/dodbuzz/2014/01/02/pentagon-plans-for-cuts-to-drone-budgets. Accessed 03 August 2019.

Perritt, Jr, H. Henry, and Eliot O. Sprague. 2017. *Domesticating Drones: The Technology, Law, and Economics of Unmanned Aircrafts.* New York: Routledge.

Pilkington, ed. 2015. Life as a Drone Operator: 'Ever Step on Ants and Never Give It Another Thought?' *The Guardian*, November 19. https://www.theguardian.com/world/2015/nov/18/life-as-a-drone-pilot-creech-air-force-base-nevada. Accessed 07 August 2019.

Pugliese, Joseph. 2017. Bugsplats and Jackpots: US Military Drone Operators Enjoy Games' Delight. *Newsweek*, September 18. https://www.newsweek.com/bugsplats-and-jackpots-us-military-drone-operators-enjoy-gamers-delight-667050. Accessed 03 August 2019.

Recreating the Sound of Aztec Death Whistles. 2008. *NPR*, July 1. https://www.npr.org/templates/story/story.php?storyId=92059649. Accessed 15 August 2019.

Roughton, Randy. 2011. Rise of the Drones—UAVs After 9–11. *Armed with Science*, October 3. http://science.dodlive.mil/2011/10/03/rise-of-the-drones-uavs-after-911/. Accessed 15 June 2023.

Saifi, Sophia. 2014. Not a 'Bug Splat:' Artists Give Drone Victims a Face in Pakistan. *CNN*, April 9. https://www.cnn.com/2014/04/09/world/asia/pakistan-drones-not-a-bug-splat/index.html. Accessed 15 August 2019.

Semple, Stuart. n.d. BLACK 2.0—The World's Mattest, Flattest, Black Art Material by Stuart Semple. *Stuart Semple.* http://stuartsemple.com/project/black-v1-0-beta-worlds-mattest-flattest-black-art-material/.

Shah, Sikander Ahmed. 2014. *International Law and Drone Strikes in Pakistan: The Legal and Socio-political Aspect.* London: Routledge.

Stahl, Roger. 2018. *Through the Crosshairs: War, Visual Culture, and the Weaponized Gaze.* New Brunswick: Rutgers University Press.

Stewart, Jessica. 2018. Colorful 'Jingle Trucks' Rule the Road in Pakistan. *My Modern Met*, April 10. https://mymodernmet.com/pakistan-truck-art/. Accessed 28 August 2019.

Talev, Margaret. 2019. President Trump Cancels Rule Requiring U.S. to Report Civilians Killed in Drone Strikes. *Time*, March 6. https://time.com/5546366/trump-cancels-drone-strike-rule/.

Virilio, Paul. 2009. *War and Cinema.* London: Verso.

Watson, Julie. 2008. Whistle Blows on Theory of Death. *The Courier Mail*, June 28.

'Will I Be Next?' US Drone Strikes in Pakistan. 2013. Amnesty International Report, London. https://www.amnestyusa.org/files/asa330132013en.pdf. Accessed 02 June 2023.

CHAPTER 6

Dispatches from Beneath the Flightpath: A Counter-Archive of Drone Warfare in Atef Abu Saif's *The Drone Eats with Me: A Gaza Diary*

Rachel Ann Walsh

"Life is what we have in between these wars."
—Atef Abu Saif, The Drone Eats with Me: A Gaza Diary

"Beyond the continual electric buzz of the drones, I can just make out the sound of the waves. If I die, it will be my only witness, I think."
—Atef Abu Saif, Don't Look Left: A Diary of Genocide

Introduction: Archiving Patterns of Disallowed Life in Gaza

During Israel's 2014 "Protective Edge" siege against Gaza, novelist Atef Abu Saif wrote a series of articles that originally appeared in the *Guardian*, *Slate*, and the *New York Times*, and were later elaborated as the memoir,

R. A. Walsh (✉)
English Department, Bowling Green State University, Bowling Green, OH, USA
e-mail: walshr@bgsu.edu

M. W. Azeem (ed.), *Human Rights in the Age of Drones*, Palgrave Studies in Literature, Culture and Human Rights,
https://doi.org/10.1007/978-3-032-08191-9_6

The Drone Eats with Me: A Gaza Diary. Written in English and organized as diary entries that chronicle the 51 days of the Israeli attacks, *Drone*'s serialized form poses the question of what it means to document Palestinian life from a place that has been zoned for annihilation and implies the related inquiry of what it means to address an Anglo-American readership that is implicated in that very eradication. Notably, its U.K. Beacon Press edition was published in 2015, the same year the U.N.'s Conference on Trade and Development issued its widely cited report warning that due to Israel's suffocating blockade and the "de-development" that resulted from its consecutive military operations ("Cast Lead" in 2008–2009, "Pillar of Cloud" in 2012, then and "Protective Edge" in 2014) Gaza would become "unlivable by 2020."[1] The report's survey of Gaza's imminent collapse and its use of the antiseptic euphemism of "de-development" established, Jasbir K. Puar trenchantly remarks, "a perverse apocalyptic timeline" similar to those predicting the "demise of the planet due to climate change."[2] These doomsday clocks run on a "prehensive" logic that produces a narrative in which the authors of the unfolding disaster (i.e. "the tragedy in Gaza") are disappeared in an egregiously passive formulation that she paraphrases as "this thing is happening to us, when, indeed, we made it happen."[3]

2025 has been a particularly perverse anniversary of the U.N.'s report. As of this writing, it feels as if the most powerful nations in the global North are watching that clock run out as we witness what has been widely characterized by activists, journalists, and artists as a live-streamed genocide. As of this writing, Israel's and the United States' disproportionate response to Hamas's October 7 attacks may result in the complete destruction of Gaza. In response to this horrifying possibility, Atef Abu Saif published *Don't Look Left: A Diary of Genocide* in late 2023. The text reads as a sequel to his 2014 account of the Protective Edge campaign and chronicles Palestinians' attempts to survive in Northern Gaza as they are herded into refugee camps in Rafah where, in the months after Saif's last entry, they were targets of a bombardment of airstrikes. In an early and tragically prescient entry dated October 11, Saif and his son, Yasser, listen

[1] United Nations Conference and Trade and Development, *Report on UNCTAD assistance to the Palestinian people: Developments in the economy of the Occupied Palestinian Territory* (Geneva: UNCTAD, 2015), 11.

[2] Jasbir K. Puar, *The Right to Maim: Debility, Capacity, Disability*, (Durham: Duke University Press, 2017), 148.

[3] Puar, 148.

to the BBC and in response to his son's question "What does 'genocide' mean?" Saif explains, "'Everything that's happening around us.'"[4] Just as in 2014, when the IDF violated the Geneva Conventions by subjecting Gaza to "collective punishment," the direct deaths of Palestinian civilians have been numbered at over 67,000.[5] And as it did in 2015, the U.N. has once again employed the tropeology of the doomsday clock; in November 2023, it warned that time was running out to "prevent" a genocide that, as South Africa charged through the International Court of Justice has, in fact, been occurring.[6] Voicing this charge in the pages of the *Boston Review*, Ariella Azoulay observed in December 2023—the same month in which Saif's memoir ends—that the "25,000 tons of explosives—equivalent to two nuclear bombs" have resulted in the "destruction of [the] geophysical archive of the Nakba, and the second mass expulsion of those who effectively became its archivists—Palestinians who are familiar with every bit and piece of it."[7]

In light of how Saif's 2015 and 2023 memoirs function as archives that pay witness to what Saree Makdisi and Gil Z. Hochberg respectively insist is the ongoing continuation of the Nakba[8] and in light of the outsized role drone technology—now "enhanced" by A.I.[9]—plays in that continuation, we would do well to revisit *The Drone Eats With Me*. As Tobi Smethurst and Stef Craps have argued, Saif's 2015 memoir has become a canonical text within the expanding corpus of drone-inspired art and literature. Its reportage fulfills what Sunny Moraine identifies as one of the early impera-

[4] Atef Abu Saif, *Don't Look Left: A Diary of Genocide*, (Great Britain: Comma Press, 2023), 20.

[5] See Rashid Khalidi, "Collective Punishment in Gaza," *The New Yorker*, July 29, 2014, https://www.newyorker.com/news/news-desk/collective-punishment-gaza and Mallory Moench, "Nearly 70% of Gaza war dead are women and children, UN says," November 8, 2024, https://www.bbc.com/news/articles/cn5well1pgdo

[6] "Gaza is 'running out of time' UN experts warn, demanding a ceasefire to prevent genocide," U.N., November 2, 2023, https://www.un.org/unispal/document/gaza-is-running-out-of-time-un-experts-warn-demanding-a-ceasefire-to-prevent-genocide/

[7] Ariella Azoulay, "Seeing Genocide," *Boston Review*, December 8, 2023, https://www.bostonreview.net/articles/seeing-genocide/

[8] Saree Makdisi, *Tolerance is a Wasteland: Palestine and the Culture of Denial*, (University of California Press, 2022), and Gil Z. Hochberg, *Becoming Palestine: Toward an Archival Imagination of the Future*, (Durham: Duke University Press, 2021).

[9] Harry Davies, Bethan McKernan, and Dan Sabbagh, "'The Gospel': how Israel uses AI to select bombing targets in Gaza," *The Guardian*, December 1, 2023, https://www.theguardian.com/world/2023/dec/01/the-gospel-how-israel-uses-ai-to-select-bombing-targets

tives of the genre: to recuperate the humanity of those who have been reduced to pixelated targets.[10] Indeed, *The Drone Eats with Me* uses the form of the memoir, a central genre within human rights literature, to confront readers with the ways in which Palestinians lives have been disallowed. In so doing, it intervenes in the archival operations of the drone. The drone, Grégoire Chamayou has shown, is fundamentally an archiving machine; its ability to map "a cartography of lives" serves as the "epistemic basis for armed surveillance."[11] The "*patterns of life*"[12] that it records—movements of a population always read as suspect—constitute a weaponized data collection or, a "file that, once it becomes thick enough, will become a death warrant."[13] What authorizes the execution of the death warrant, though, Hugh Gusterson observes, is the "remote narrativization" whereby "after a frame has been put in place, ambiguous information is interpreted within that frame, informational gaps are ignored, and moral judgments are rendered."[14] In Saif's depiction of Palestinians' attempts to survive these remotely realized and murderous fictions, he exercises what Nicholas Mirzoeff has theorized as the right to look in the face of the settler colonial state's standard operating procedure of producing state-authorized archives as it destroys the archives of those it subjugates.[15] The importance of Saif's counter-archival work cannot be overstated in light of the pronounced role that Israel's archival practices have played in the dispossession of Palestinians. Following Edward Said, Gil Z. Hochberg rehearses that alongside Israel's investment in "creating an elaborate archive of archaeological findings meant to prove the historical ties of Jews to the land," it "confiscated, looted, and absorbed into its various archives collections... rendering Palestinian archives invisible, 'missing,' or non-existent."[16] Saif's serial documentation of the 51 days of

[10] Tobi Smethurst and Stef Craps, "Toward an Understanding of Drone Fiction," *The Journal of War and Culture Studies* 12, no. 1, (2019): 99.

[11] Grégoire Chamayou, *A Theory of a Drone,* trans. Janet Lloyd, (New York: The New Press, 2015), 48.

[12] Chamayou, 49, emphasis mine.

[13] Chamayou, 49.

[14] Hugh Gusterson, *Drone: Remote Control Warfare*, (Cambridge, MA: MIT Press, 2017), 69.

[15] Nicholas Mirzoeff, *The Right to Look: A Counterhistory of Visuality* (Durham: Duke University Press, 2011).

[16] Gil Z. Hochberg, *Becoming Palestine: Toward an Archival Imagination of the Future* (Durham University Press, 2021), 25–26.

the siege and his location of the siege within the longer history of the Nakba operates as a defiant corrective to these erasures.

Saif's assembled archive, however, expresses an ambivalence about the framework of "humanization" that Moraine identifies as the raison d'être of drone literature and the limited conditions under which Palestinians appear *as human* to readers in the Global North. Straddling the overlapping genres of the eye-witness account and human rights literature, Saif's memoir inhabits a post-Second Intifada visual field in which, Hochberg writes, Palestinians are all too frequently "granted two positions from which they may speak and appear: that of victimization, which manifests in images of wounded, unarmed bodies, and that of defiance, which manifests in images of armed freedom fighters."[17] As Hochberg acknowledges in her afterword to *Visual Occupations*, (a text that went to press during the 2014 siege), the pervasiveness of drone technology has complicated this field by realizing a "new *mode of visualization*: one that eliminates the possibility of witnessing, while rendering those who are subjected to live *under the drones* completely invisible despite their hypervisibility."[18] Hochberg's observations may, at this point, be familiar but I leverage them to argue that Saif's *Drone* invites us to re-approach the memoir as a post-9/11 cultural practice of counter-archiving that contests both how drone warfare eliminates the "possibility of witnessing" and the ways in which Palestine and Palestinians have been precariously positioned within the framework of international human rights law. Reviewing Palestine's paradoxical status as being excluded from the guarantees of international human rights laws and yet "defined by astute attention to law and legal controversy," Noura Erakat reminds us that international human rights law is derived from a colonial order and shaped by power relations, as well as, to recall Judith Butler, the norm of the human.[19] Erakat also emphasizes that these power relations are not fixed and human rights law can be repurposed for more liberatory ends. Saif's account of the siege operates, I contend, within this spirit and with these ends in view. It documents the human rights violations experienced by Palestinians in Gaza while elucidating the ways in which Palestinians have been excluded from and/or

[17] Hochberg, 124–25.

[18] Hochberg, 166.

[19] Noura Erakat, *Justice for Some: Law and the Question of Palestine*, (Stanford: Stanford University Press, 2019), 3–5. See also, Judith Butler, *Frames of War: When is Life Grievable?* (New York: Verso Books, 2009).

only selectively incorporated into the framework of human rights and the human.

Just as Saif's memoir critically engages with the framework of human rights, it also anticipates the greater attention that is now devoted to the role the U.S.-Israel alliance has played in shaping the post-9/11 "age of drones" that we inhabit. In the aftermath of the 9/11 attacks that coincided with the Second Intifada, Israel used the United States' pursuit of what Ronak Kapadia has termed its "forever wars," to legitimate its own use of preemptive strikes in the occupied territories. The U.S.'s and Israel's shared argument—that terrorism was an exceptional enemy that must be met with exceptional and extra-legal strategies—merely advanced one whose origins, Erakat observes, can be traced back to the Balfour Declaration of 1917. Since its founding, Israel has long claimed a "sui generis" status and constructed a latticework of lawfare to circumvent international laws governing warfare and human rights.[20] This latticework has been legitimated by the United States' financial support and its outsized role in the U.N. Security Council. As the United States' and Israel's counterterrorism practices became more tightly interwoven, particularly as the Obama administration increasingly relied on drone strikes, "Israel's violations steadily escaped the zone of brazen violations and moved into the scope of legitimacy."[21] This scope of legitimacy led to Gaza in being used as a "colonial laboratory for experimentation with weapons and tactics in the so-called Global War on Terror."[22] As the Global War on Terror came home to American neighborhoods, U.S. police forces underwent training in Israel, and adopted the same racial profiling software and crowd-control chemicals pioneered and produced by the Israeli security apparatus.[23] In my conclusion, I address how Saif's theorization of the experience of being viewed through a drone's viewfinder—rendered at once hypervisible as a target but disappeared as a human being with rights—speaks to the parallels that Black American and Palestinian activists drew between Gaza and Ferguson in the summer of 2014. The transnational and multiracial coalitions that emerged between Palestinian and BLM activists in 2014 predicted and laid the foundation for the current

[20] Erakat, 15.

[21] Erakat, 193.

[22] Erakat, 197.

[23] *Researching the American-Israeli Alliance* and *Jewish Voice for Peace*, "Deadly Exchange: The Dangerous Consequences of American Law Enforcement Trainings in Israel," (September 2018): 1–38.

protests against the genocide in Gaza and evidence an anti-colonial analytic for examining the human rights violations of Palestinians.

Mapping Gaza: Inhabiting the Landscapes of Israel and Palestine

In his afterword to the U.K. Comma Press edition of Saif's memoir, founding editor Ra Page shares that it emerged out of his earlier collaboration with Saif, *The Book of Gaza*. The latter was an anthology of short fiction designed to foreground the "domestic, ordinary" register of life in Gaza and serve as a corrective to the typical war-porn fare consisting of stock-images depicting "the angry funeral processions, the suited Hamas/Israeli spokesmen standing behind banks of microphones—images that are both extremely familiar and *utterly impossible to connect to*."[24] In contrast to these commonplace yet estranging photographs, Page shares that he hoped to foster an emotional familiarity with the topography of life in Gaza. He posits that the global outpouring of sympathy in the aftermath of the 9/11 attacks could be partially attributed to the fact that so many people had "mentally inhabited" New York City even if they had never traveled there, and admits that he had hoped a similar affective investment might be brokered for Gaza. The damage caused by the unrelenting drone strikes during the Protective Edge campaign, however, disabused him of such hopes. "There is no stability in Gaza," Page notes, "on which to build a reader-familiarity, let alone an iconography.... How can any literature get a purchase on this landscape in the writer's imagination, when the landscape itself doesn't have any long-term purchase on the Palestinian soil?"[25] While Page characterizes his aspiration to familiarize "Western readers" with Gaza as "naïve," I would counter that it harbors a set of instructive assumptions. The post-9/11 Manhattan he evokes is one of a victimized, still-shining city on the hill, imagined as a space of multicultural tolerance, and tasked with upholding an Enlightenment humanism in the face of a "barbarism" racialized as Muslim and Arab. The U.S. exceptionalism that generates this image of NYC is mirrored by and authorizes Israel's exceptionalism as "the lone democracy in the desert" menaced by the same dark and despotic forces. "Who can judge democratic Israel,"

[24] Ra Page, "Editor's Note to the UK Edition," *The Drone Eats with Me: A Gaza Diary*, (Boston: Beacon Press, 2015), 243, emphasis mine.

[25] Saif, 247.

Ta-Nehisi Coates trenchantly quips, "which must exist in 'that part of the world' where child brides, chemical weapons, and bin Laden reign?"[26]

Crucially, Saif's memoir refuses this exceptionalism and revises the failed analogy that his collaborator initially pursued by likening Gaza's destroyed infrastructure to Baghdad, Iraq. In his entry, "The Shuja'iyya Massacre, Sunday, 27th, July," Saif and a friend drive down Baghdad Street and he dwells on the irony of the street name by comparing the destruction they survey with "the scenes left behind by the American and British armies in Iraq after the 2003 invasion. Houses no longer have any shape or form, a balcony sits in the middle of the street like a broken chair."[27] Through Saif's labeling of the wreckage caused by the aerial bombardment as a "massacre,"—a term more typically employed to describe atrocities committed by armed forces with boots on the ground—Saif refuses the sanitizing euphemisms of drone warfare like "surgical strike" and recalls us to a broader truth that the "war torn" landscapes of Baghdad and Gaza evidence: the streets of these cities are unfamiliar to "Western readers" because they have been deliberately unmade. In his entry, "The War on Beauty, Monday, August 25th," Saif remarks, "They have targeted every modern building, every attractive piece of architecture.... They want nothing to be left but a gray, rubble-strewn slum."[28] His observation draws out the greater insight contained in his colleague's ambition for their earlier project; settler colonial-apartheid and neocolonial regimes design landscapes and recruit enfranchised audiences to imaginatively inhabit them. Through the destruction and renaming of villages, Makdisi rehearses, Israel has attempted to "rewrite the territory and landscape of Palestine, to eliminate the indigenous Palestinian presence."[29] This incomplete project, undermined by the tell-tale traces of the ruins of villages and the resistance of Palestinians themselves, has, he shows, partially been executed through the ecological remaking of the landscape---"making the desert bloom" by destroying the indigenous flora and planting forests to create the illusion of a simultaneously Biblical and vaguely European pastoral vista.[30] The "war on beauty" that Saif documents is the part and parcel of this aesthetic project; the decimated buildings and streets of Gaza

[26] Ta-Nehisi Coates, *The Message*, (New York: Penguin Random House, 2024), 176.
[27] Saif, 102.
[28] Saif, 228.
[29] Makdisi, 22.
[30] Makdisi, 32–33.

are the corollary of the pastoralism of Israeli landscapes. The contrast between debris and forests is indicative of what Hochberg has elsewhere characterized as the binaristic framing of Israel as being generative force of the democracy and life and Palestine as a space and people "of violence, self-destruction, victimization, and (a culture of) death."[31] Drone showcases the consequences of this framing by including GPS-style maps of Gaza as they would appear through the viewfinder of a drone. Each map has a pixelated quality and only features the names of camps, such as Jabalia—the camp where Saif was born[32] and to which he repeatedly returns with his family—and targeted landmarks along with notations about the occupation such as those informing the reader that Gaza's airport closed in 2002 and the Rafah border of southern Gaza was sealed off in 2014. These maps orient the reader through what they refuse to provide. The streets and landmarks are only accompanied by numbers rather than visual icons; the grayscale system of shading (some districts and refugee camps are depicted as slightly darker than others) is not explicated for the reader. The denial of visually engaging images is pointed. Through the viewfinder of the drone, informed by the discursive construction of Gaza as an exceptional, death-driven enemy territory, the streets, monuments, and refugee camps are all marked as potential targets.

This viewfinder framing of Palestinians and the lands that they inhabit as destroyed and destroying and therefore, unworthy of self-determination and ultimately, outside of the frame of the human, mirrors what Atanasoski and Vora refer to as "technoliberalism" that guides drone technologies and their operations. In *Surrogate Humanity*, they extend Lisa Lowe's insight that the liberal humanism of the Enlightenment applied only to those who defined themselves against racialized populations deemed incapable of realizing the vaunted ideals of freedom and self-governance. Drones and killer robots, which have been lauded, despite all evidence to the contrary, for their precision and lack of human prejudices and biases, are programmed by the same racial grammar of the Enlightenment. The drone, in particular, performs a pernicious sleight of hand: "The fantasy of remote control manifest in the drone takes the human colonist/interventioneer out of the frame of action.... [it] thus renders the fantasy of remote control as a reconceptualization of empire that, by being human-free, can

[31] Hochberg, 10.
[32] Saif, *Don't Look Left*, 39.

disassociate its power from earlier modes of colonial conquest."[33] Saif's memoir refuses the historical amnesia facilitated by drone technology; in numerous entries, the surveilling movements of the drone activate earlier memories of the occupation. When an UNRWA worker requests that Palestinians not to carry belongings with them to the refugee camps because such objects might be read by the circling drones as "'weaponry or rocket fuel,'"[34] Saif recalls his experience of the first Intifada. At the age of fifteen, he is shot twice by IDF soldiers for throwing stones and imprisoned for seven months in a camp in the Negev desert. Saif's interweaving of these memories refuses any "dissociation," to borrow Atanasoski and Vora's phrasing, of drone strikes—conceptualized as a "post-occupation" technology—from earlier periods of settler-colonial violence.

The dissociation of drone warfare from earlier forms of settle-colonialism has been integral to Israel's legitimation of their usage. Surveying the history of Israeli "state lawfare" developed to circumvent international human rights law, Lisa Hajjar recounts that its targeted assassination program was authorized, in part, by Israel's argument that the West Bank and Gaza are not, in fact, occupied "because they had not been sovereign to the states displaced in the [1967] war (i.e. Jordan and Egypt)."[35] This argument gained greater traction with the withdrawal of IDF troops from Gaza in 2005. When the occupation took to the skies and the IDF intensified its control over Gaza's land, sea, and air spaces, Eyal Weizman reviews, Israel characterized its continuing sovereignty as an "'invisible occupation'... and/or 'an occupation in disappearance'"[36] and described the relocation of its locus of power as a shift from "'*occupation to technology*.'"[37] Saif's memoir exposes the lie of this nomenclatural shift. Observing a drone hovering above a car on Day 29 of the siege when a truce has been declared, he reflects, "It seems Israel will never leave Gaza. It always here, even if its soldiers are not visible... The occupation is now truly twenty-first century---the best drone technology in the world is being deployed

[33] Neda Atanasoski and Kalindi Vora, *Surrogate Humanity: Race, Robots, and the Politics of Technological Futures*, (Durham: Duke University Press, 2019), 149.

[34] Saif, 58.

[35] Lisa Hajjar, "Lawfare and Armed Conflicts: A Comparative Analysis of Israeli and U.S. Targeted Killing Polices and Legal Challenges against Them," in *Life in the Age of Drone Warfare*, ed. Lisa Parks and Caren Kaplan (Durham: Duke University Press, 2017), 61.

[36] Eyal Weizman, *Hollow Land: Israel's Architecture of Occupation*, (New York: Verso Books, 2007), 436.

[37] Weizman, 459, emphasis mine.

up there, just to keep us occupied."[38] Israel's "disappearance" and denial of its occupation, Saif, Hajjar, Weizman, and Erakat have respectively argued, is the "essential element to legitimize them [Palestinian territories] as sites of warfare" and therefore evade the Fourth Geneva Convention's prohibition against waging war against an occupied territory.[39] By an obscene paradox, the drone is one of the crucial means by which the IDF denies its occupation and the violence of its warfare, instead claiming that drones are a more humane form of technology. Indeed, "humanitarian," Weizman notes, is the privileged descriptor applied to the technological apparatus of the "invisible" occupation.[40] "The 'humanitarian' rhetoric of the current phase of the occupation," he warns, "is part of a general attempt to normalize it. The urgent and important criticism that peace organizations often level at the IDF---that it is dehumanizing its enemies—masks another more dangerous process by which the military incorporates into its operations the logic of, and even seeks to cooperate directly with, the very humanitarian and human rights organizations that oppose it."[41] Uncovering further evidence of this masking, the *Intercept* reported that in the summer of 2014, the IDF claimed, through its public relations unit, "that the live feed videos provided by drones enabled its air force to avoid killing Palestinian civilians."[42] Saif's war reportage sharply refutes the IDF's claims and critiques the humanitarian framework employed by both the IDF and the international news media by examining how Palestinians have been excluded or only selectively incorporated into the category of the human.

Doing the Numbers: Human Data in the Sensorium of Drone Warfare

At its heart, *The Drone Eats with Me* is a teaching text that places the "Protective Edge" campaign in a longer history of the devaluation of Palestinian lives and guides readers through a daily accounting of the

[38] Saif, 149.

[39] Hajjar, "Lawfare," 63.

[40] Weizman, 297.

[41] Weizman, 297–98.

[42] See Smethurst and Craps, "Toward an Understanding of Drone Fiction," 92. Robert Mackey, "Secret Israeli Report Reveals Armed Drone Killed Four Boys Playing on Gaza Beach in 2014," *Intercept*, August 11, 2018, https://theintercept.com/2018/08/11/israel-palestine-drone-strike-operation-protective-edge/

ongoing violation of their human rights. In his second entry, Saif recalls that when the "Cast Lead" invasion of 2008 began he was giving a lecture on human rights and democracy in a building near one of the first targets of the siege.[43] His catalogue of such macabre ironies strategically draws on the braided history of international human rights and world literature. World literature, Joseph Slaughter argues, "cooperate[s] with human rights to naturalize their common sense---to give law the Gramscian force of culture."[44] The "naturalization" of the commonsensical suppositions of human rights is achieved, Slaughter diagrams, through the "transitive grammar" that structures international human rights law and the eighteenth-century *Bildungsroman*. They rely on an "as if" temporality that engenders a "narrative aspirationalism" and projects the reader into a future when the human person *will have become* recognized as a human person with inalienable and universal rights.[45] To be sure, *The Drone Eats with Me* is a memoir rather than a novel that chronicles the education of a protagonist who develops into an enfranchised citizen, yet even accounting for these differences of genre, there is pointedly no such "as if" temporality at work in *Drone*. Rather than being driven by plot, Saif's memoir documents the denial of any sense of futurity and calls into question the potential efficacy of his testimony. In an entry entitled, "Who Will Convince Them?," Saif poses a series of questions that challenge the visuality of the drone as well as the international community's refusal to hold Israel accountable for its crimes.

> Who will convince this generation of Israelis that what they've done this summer is a crime?... Who will convince the drone operator that the people of Gaza are not characters in a video game?... [T]hat the buildings he sees on his screen are not graphics, but homes... Who will convince the international community that it has a responsibility to be objective when things like this happen?[46]

Like the memoir as a whole, these questions issue an imperative to future readers but the entry concludes with the angry and despondent reflection that Palestinians can only depend on themselves. This

[43] Saif, 8.

[44] Joseph Slaughter, *Human Rights, Inc.: World Literature, Narrative Form, and International Law*, (New York: Fordham University Press, 2007), 25.

[45] Slaughter, 26.

[46] Saif, 66.

despondency permeates the text as a whole. As Saif moves from the beginning of the siege to its conclusion, his entries are marked by stasis and uncertainty rather than a sense of propulsion toward a hoped-for end. People endeavor to make it through another day by adapting to the "dumb logic of... mission goals"[47] largely unknown to them and in a space where wartime precarity blurs into the quotidian violence of the occupation.

Saif highlights the blurred temporalities between the siege and the occupation when, in his first entry, dated July 7, he and his friends and family exchanges theories on when and whether the siege will begin. Their speculations are scored to "SMS news updates [that] interrupt the evening's conversation, with innocent little pings"[48] and they soon learn that it has already started with a strike.

> At around 9 p.m. this evening, a drone attacked a group of people near Beit Hanoun, two miles north of Jabaliya Camp.... Half an hour later another drone fired on three people on the street in the western side of Gaza City. At the time, these were reported as one-offs, the way bad traffic accidents would be.... Two drone strikes don't make a war. This is what the radio calls an 'escalation in tension.'[49]

Saif's deadpan summation, "two drone strikes don't make a war" and the initial reporting of the strikes as comparable to traffic accidents that briefly impede and disrupt the movement of people underscore the degree to which drone strikes trouble the fragile distinction between occupation and war.

Recurrently throughout *Drone*, Saif vacillates between depicting the overwhelming sensorium of the siege as simultaneously surreal and overly familiar. On the twenty-eighth day of the war, Saif observes that "the sound of explosions... the blinding light given off just before a drone attack... the Israeli army's recorded message on your mobile saying that you stay where you are at your own risk" have all become "utterly normal."[50] Transcribing an overheard conversation between two men during the truce, he later recounts one man telling the other of his recent return to his decimated home in Beit Hanoun. "I didn't recognize the street I'd lived on for forty-five years.... I spent that day running between

[47] Saif, 66.
[48] Saif, 2.
[49] Saif, 3.
[50] Saif, 140.

shells like I was playing a video game. Like I was a character in the game, someone else was playing me."[51] The man's de-realized experience of himself as an avatar whose movements are determined by an unseen player or designer echoes Saif's claim that Palestinians are "objects that the war machine plays with."[52] The fragment of this overheard conversation is but one instance of Saif's repeated and, by now, well-worn analogy of drone warfare to video games. The man's characterization of himself as a character played by someone else, though, complicates the comparison; in first-person shooter games, Smethurst and Craps note, users face off against an armed rather than entirely vulnerable opponent and, in sharp contrast to the man's experience, they are the shooter, determining the movement of their avatar.[53] Unlike these war games, Palestinians in Gaza cannot reliably employ any strategy as the rules and territory of the "game" are constantly shifting. Bitterly referring to the siege as an "endless game. Nothing but a game" Saif reports, "Last night Israel announced the termination of its operations in Gaza. But tonight four people from one family have been killed and others injured."[54] One of his neighbors later quips that he wants to believe news of a truce, but "that drone up there doesn't."[55] Each entry conveys the experience of inhabiting a terrain in which the international laws have limited application.

Many of Saif's entries in *The Drone Eats with Me* enunciate these limitations by likening the viewfinder of the predator drone to the humanitarian gaze of the international community. As targeted data points that might warrant a strike, Palestinians are hyper-visible; as global citizens, though, they have disappeared and frequently only come into view of the Western news media in the aftermath of their deaths or as the specter of death hovers above them. Within this vein, Saif sardonically relates a conversation in which he is positioned as a representative of a soon-to-be-destroyed land by a French woman whose phone call reaches him despite the power outages. The caller expresses her support for Saif and his family by first asking him to verify his imperiled location: "Is this Gaza?... Are you Palestinian?"[56] This surreal exchange between the French woman, calling from the liberal, Global North and Saif, who politely receives the recognition this

[51] Saif, 146.
[52] Saif, 151.
[53] Smethurst and Craps, "Toward an Understanding of Drone Fiction," 97.
[54] Saif, 139.
[55] Saif, 145.
[56] Saif, 26–27.

other world has bestowed in the form of "solidarity expressed in passionate words,"[57] is immediately followed by a passage in which he describes how the siege has remapped Gaza by reducing the number of the areas that offer only tenuous guarantees of safety. He curtly runs through the lengthening roster of prohibited spaces, "We shouldn't be near the border to the east, or the north. We shouldn't be near the beach. We shouldn't be near any government headquarters either"[58] before informing the reader:

> People look to anything that makes them feel safer, anything that props up their world a bit longer before the inevitable collapse. Our fates are all in the hands of a drone operator in a military base somewhere just over the Israeli border.... He might decide to terminate a life of someone walking along the pavement... The operator practices his aim at his own discretion, energized by the trust and power that has been put in his hands by his superiors.[59]

His imagining of the drone operator refutes the bogus-yet-still-rehearsed alibis for drone warfare as well as the discursive construction of the IDF as the "most moral" army.[60] The "discretion" that the drone operator (imagined as an immature and petty sovereign in many of Saif's descriptions) exercises through a decisive click is at once arbitrary and highly orchestrated. Saif's portrait of the high-tech production of Gaza as an exceptional space with aerial checkpoints that menace the movements of Palestinians resonates with Chamayou's theorization of the drone as an innovation of the "hunter-state" which remade the spatial and temporal dimensions of warfare in the aftermath of 9/11.[61] Under the watch of the hunter-state, "armed violence is no longer defined within the boundaries of a demarcated zone but simply by the presence of an enemy-prey who, so to speak, carries with it its own little mobile zone of hostility."[62] Chamayou's conception of the "hunter state" is mirrored in Saif's use of the organizing motif of the drone as a predatory and consuming force that looms over them as they observe Ramadan. Implicitly capitalizing on the term "predator drone," he emphasizes that raids more frequently occur

[57] Saif, 27.
[58] Saif, 30.
[59] Saif, 31.
[60] See Hochberg, *Visual Occupations*, 31.
[61] Chamayou, 53.
[62] Chamayou, 52.

during they break their fast for iftar.[63] As he and his wife Hanna prepare suhoor, "Fear and anxiety eat with us. The unknown eats with us. The F16 eats with us. The drone, and its operator somewhere out in Israel, eats with us."[64] Moving from the ambient negative affects that permeate their home to the foreshortened horizon of their future ("The unknown eats with us"), Saif concludes with a stark condemnation of the consuming drone and the hunter-state that deploys it. Here, as throughout his memoir, he reverses the vertical axis of the settler-colonial power that Israel employs to monitor and police the Palestinian territories, and provides a counter-portrait of its surveilled and asphyxiated life.[65]

Saif's production of a counter-portrait, moreover, indicts the hunter-state that consumes Gaza and the international news media for which Palestinians exist only in their deaths. In his chapter, "I Do Not Want to Be a Number," he describes the news media as being another predatory force that feasts on Gaza and reduces its people to numbers to be tallied up in the final death toll of the siege.

> Imagine it. Imagine what it must be like to be converted into a number. That you are not 'Atef Abu Saif.' You are 'Victim Number 568.' You are merely a digit in a much larger number, one that just keeps on growing.... In a crowd of other numbers, the importance of every number disappears, because what is important is the Big Number.... Journalists like catastrophes. They like numbers, statistics, data. They like the sight of tears and emotions in front of the camera. Destruction is a rich meal for the camera.[66]

As with so many passages in his memoir, this one stages a confrontation with its presumed audience in the Global North that has little to no connection with the Palestinian diaspora and critiques what Hochberg has diagnosed as perverse forms of "hypervisibility" experienced by Palestinians. Palestinians frequently only come into view of news media and human rights organizations, Hochberg argues, in the moment of their

[63] Saif, 11.

[64] Saif, 32.

[65] In Puar's *The Right to Maim: Debility, Capacity, Disability*, she augments Omar Jabary Salamanca's characterization of Israel's control over Gaza as "asphixatory control" by writing "The capacity to asphyxiate is not a metaphor: while the West Bank is controlled largely through checkpoints, the Gaza Strip is suffocated through choke points. The intensification of policing and control thus happens through, and not despite, 'disengagement' and disinvestment, not through checkpoints but through choke points" (135).

[66] Saif, 76–77.

annihilation and are all too often positioned as "an instrument meant to facilitate the ethical response of others."[67] Saif's entry resists this instrumentalization and instead issues a demand for empathy while refusing any appropriation of the anguish that the text requires the reader to imagine. Saif's inclusion of his name is an assertion of his specific, individual experience which will ultimately be denied by the conversion of his person into one number that adds up to the eventual "Big Number." His acerbic criticisms of the international news media "they like numbers, statistics, data" implicate the news media in the same economy of knowledge production that guides the operation of the drone and which the drone strikes themselves generate. Imperial warfare, Kapadia elucidates, relies upon a "calculus... a particular method or system of reasoning used by the state in its often senseless enumeration of wartime violence."[68] In turn, this calculus generates "body counts, combat time, military budgets, and the price of oil."[69] Saif implicates the international news media in the same calculus that it purports to condemn. Like drone surveillance, the news media produces Gaza as a series of numerical data points: the number of potential militants, the number of civilian casualties, the number of buildings providing shelter for potential terrorist activities, the number of homes destroyed.

These tallies, in turn, Puar notes, determine the ways in which Israel wages war. Writing on the heels of the "Protective Edge" campaign and after she had conducted fieldwork in the West Bank and occupied East Jerusalem, she argues that Israel's "tactical calculations of settler colonial rule" have been cynically guided by the policy of shooting to maim rather than shooting to kill. Following Tanya Reinhart who reports that, during and after the second intifada, the IDF sought to ensure that "Palestinian casualties [remained] low to deflect attention, sympathy, and solidarity from the Palestinian struggle,"[70] Puar elaborates that these "tactical calculations" occlude a biopolitics of maiming which "functions as slow but simultaneously intensive death-making, as targeting to maim is an accelerated assault on both bodily and infrastructural forms... Maiming functions as 'will not let die' and, its supposed humanitarian complement, 'will not make die.' Maiming masquerades as 'let live' when in fact it acts as 'will

[67] Hochberg, *Visual Occupations*, 119.
[68] Kapadia, 24.
[69] Kapadia, 22.
[70] Puar, 131.

not let die.'"[71] Saif's statement of refusal "I do not want to be a number" articulates a protest against having his life subsumed by an index of suffering that obfuscates the depth and scale of debilitated life.

Living through the growing tally of deaths that will be ratified as the "Big Number," Saif entreats the reader to understand these numbers as stories of communal loss and anticipates the rallying cry now uttered at protests occurring worldwide, "every life a universe":

> The Kawareh family---from Khan Younis, whom the drone decided to prevent from enjoying a meal on the roof of their small building under the moonlight---they were not just 'SIX.' They were six infinitely rich, infinitely unknowable stories that came to a stop when a dumb missile fell from a drone and tore their bodies apart. Six novels that Mahfouz, Dickens, or Márquez could not have written satisfactorily.... Instead, they are tales that have cascaded into the news as numbers:... Every number is a world in itself.[72]

As he insists on the "infinite" and unquantifiable richness of the Kawareh family, Saif contrasts the intelligence of the lives of the Kawareh family members with the "dumb missile" that ended them. By citing Egyptian Nobel Laureate Naguib Mahfouz, Charles Dickens, and Colombian Laureate Gabriel García Marquez, Saif alludes to the novel as a vaunted medium of Enlightenment humanism but slightly revises its canon of world literature (Mahfouz takes pride of place over Charles Dickens). Saif's reference to the novel as the paradigmatic vehicle for portraying the life of the citizen that, in turn, is symptomatic of the vitality of the nation-state, performs a pointed reversal. Outside of the Westphalian nation-state system, in the exceptional zone of occupied Gaza, the promise of the members of the Kawareh family being recognized as "right-and-duty-bearing citizens"[73] has been voided from the start. The counterfactual gesture of imagining their endlessly unspooling narratives and the complexities that they would have contained, is cruelly truncated and converted into the numbered detritus of the war.

Reiterating the refrain that he does not want to be included within the ever-expanding and obfuscating roster of lost lives and destroyed worlds, Saif insists, "I do not want to be a small number in a large one, a part of

[71] Puar 139.
[72] Saif, 77.
[73] Slaughter, 61.

the data. I don't want to be an image among thousands of images that the activists and sympathizers share and post on their Facebook walls, or Twitter accounts, rained down on with likes and comments."[74] Occluded in life, consumed in death as a digitized spectacle of suffering, Palestinians are registered as bits of information by the occupying drones and the international news media that is complicit in the operations of the IDF. Saif's acerbic description of the social media response to the stolen lives that are repurposed as consumable images whose circulation generates a form of social capital, "rained down on with likes and comments" aligns, in uncomfortable proximity, such acts of conscientious consumption with the bombs rained down by the predator drone. In a chapter titled, "This is Fame," he imagines the belated news media attention Palestinians receive in death. Inserting the reader once more into his own uncertain relationship with life and death, he writes, "In a split second, you can simultaneously cease to exist and become a news item. You swap your existence for TV airtime, radio coverage... A few minutes later, your name appears again—in full this time—in the news ticker along the bottom of the TV screen."[75] Here, it is only in death that Palestinians are fleetingly individuated within the larger number and achieve some visibility in the ethico-political horizon of the international news media as the tragic evidence of seemingly unpreventable war crimes. Saif's archive rejects this empty and self-absolving form of witnessing as well as the false promise that a particular threshold could be met that would, in turn, result in the U.S.'s withdrawal of its financial support for the occupation, and members of the U.N. Security Council holding Israel accountable for its war crimes. Through its serialized account, *Drone* demands that the reader examine the unlikely conditions under which Palestinians have survived in Gaza and the human rights protections they have been denied.

Conclusion: From the River to the Sea, or Toward an Anti-Colonial Analytic

As I noted in my introduction, Saif's most recent work, *Don't Look Left*, documents his survival of the initial unfolding of the genocide in Gaza before he and his son, Yasser, were able to flee to Egypt. After earlier observing how "hospitals have been 'legitimate targets,' turned into war

[74] Saif, 77–78.
[75] Saif, 172.

zones... and the international community just whistled to itself,"[76] he reveals that journalists and U.N. organizations have "abandoned" Gaza.

> Despite the Red Cross's mandate being to guarantee the protection of the civilians in times of war it left those civilians for war to just kill them. The UN did the same thing. Is anyone innocent, in these situations? Why... in other parts of the world, do they stay at their posts and keep working, or keep reporting? Why do those places get protection, while Gaza barely sees them for dust?[77]

Saif's anguished questions confront readers with the same insidious paradox that he earlier chronicled in *Drone*. Similar to the 51 days of the Protective Edge campaign, the genocide against Palestinians has been well-documented and spectacularized across news and social media platforms, yet the United States, which bears responsibility for the abandonment Saif documents, funds IDF bombs with one hand while attempting to launder its reputation by providing humanitarian aid with another. In so doing, Omar El Akkad compellingly argues, the U.S. has exposed its commitment to human rights as a "shell of modern liberalism and the capitalist thing it serves."[78]

The application of human rights law, though, as South Africa's ICJ case has demonstrated, and as Erakat holds, is malleable. Like Erakat, I want to maintain hope that it can recalibrated by "subaltern movements mobiliz[ing] various forms of coercive pressure, including crude violence, massive uprisings, civil disobedience, and boycott."[79] Since the summer of 2014, when Palestinian-American activists joined Black Lives Matter protesters in the Ferguson uprising and Black Lives Matter activists and writers visited Palestine to, as Marc Lamont Hill characterized his own journey, further develop an "anti-colonial praxis"[80]of solidarity, transnational and multiracial coalitions have emerged to challenge Israeli apartheid and the U.S.'s sponsorship of its crimes. In the United States, these multiracial coalitions, often led by those within or with ties to the Palestinian dias-

[76] Saif, 141.

[77] Saif, 240.

[78] Omar El Akkad, *One Day, Everyone Will Have Always Been Against This*, (New York: Alfred A. Knopf, 2025), 28.

[79] Erakat, 9.

[80] Marc Lamont Hill, "From Ferguson to Palestine: Reimagining Transnational Solidarity Through Difference," *Biography*, 41, no. 4 (Fall 2018): 942–957.

pora, have driven the city and campus protests, the renewed Boycott, Divestment, and Sanctions campaigns, and the widespread support for a ceasefire. That these movements have been met with such draconian attempts at suppression by liberal institutions is proof both of how Palestine constitutes the exception for liberal humanism within the U.S. and how such movements are actively imagining an anti-colonial humanism. Like Saif's two memoirs, these campaigns amplify the testimonies and archives produced by those within Gaza and the occupied territories. Collectively, they demand an end to the genocidal violence and a path forward for Palestinian self-determination.

References

Atanasoski, Neda, and Kalindi Vora. 2019. *Surrogate Humanity: Race, Robots, and the Politics of Technological Futures*. Durham: Duke University Press.

Azoulay, Ariella Aisha. 2023. Seeing Genocide. *The Boston Review*, 8 December 2023. https://www.bostonreview.net/articles/seeing-genocide/. Accessed 14 December 2023.

Butler, Judith. 2009. *Frames of War: When is Life Grievable?* New York: Verso.

Chamayou, Grégoire. 2015. *A Theory of the Drone*. Translated by Janet Lloyd. New York: The New Press.

Coates, Ta-Nehisi. 2024. *The Message*. New York: Penguin Random House Press.

Davies, Harry, Bethan McKernan, and Dan Sabbagh. 2023. 'The Gospel': How Israel Uses AI to Select Bombing Targets in Gaza. *The Guardian*, 1 December 2023. https://www.theguardian.com/world/2023/dec/01/the-gospel-how-israel-uses-ai-to-select-bombing-targets.

El Akkad, Omar. 2025. *One Day, Everyone Will Have Always Been Against This*. New York: Alfred A. Knopf.

Erakat, Noura. 2019. *Justice for Some: Law and the Question of Palestine*. Stanford: Stanford University Press.

Gusterson, Hugh. 2017. *Drone: Remote Control Warfare*. Cambridge: MIT Press.

Hajjar, Lisa. 2017. Lawfare and Armed Conflicts: A Comparative Analysis of Israeli and U.S. Targeted Killing Polices and Legal Challenges against Them. In *Life in the Age of Drone Warfare*, ed. Lisa Parks and Caren Kaplan, 59–88. Durham: Duke University Press.

Hill, Marc Lamont. 2018. From Ferguson to Palestine: Reimagining Transnational Solidarity Through Difference. *Biography* 41 (4): 942–957. https://doi.org/10.1353/bio.2018.0086.

Hochberg, Gil Z. 2015. *Visual Occupations: Violence and Visibility in a Conflict Zone*. Durham: Duke University Press.

Hochberg, Gil Z. 2021. *Becoming Palestine: Toward an Archival Imagination for the Future*. Durham: Duke University Press.
Kapadia, Ronak K. 2019. *Insurgent Aesthetics: Security and the Queer Life of the Forever War*. Durham: Duke University Press.
Khalidi, Rashid. 2014. Collective Punishment in Gaza. *The New Yorker*, 29 July 2014. https://www.newyorker.com/news/news-desk/collective-punishment-gaza.
Mackey, Robert. 2018. Secret Israeli Report Reveals Armed Drone Killed Four Boys Playing on Gaza Beach in 2014. *Intercept*, 11 August 2018. https://theintercept.com/2018/08/11/israel-palestine-drone-strike-operation-protective-edge/.
Makdisi, Saree. 2022. *Tolerance is a Wasteland: Palestine and the Culture of Denial*. Oakland: University of California Press.
Mirzoeff, Nicholas. 2011. *The Right to Look: A Counterhistory of Visuality*. Durham: Duke University Press.
Moench, Mallory. 2024. Nearly 70% of Gaza War Dead Are Women and Children, UN Says. *BBC News*, 8 November 2024. https://www.bbc.com/news/articles/cn5wel11pgdo.
Puar, Jasbir K. 2017. *The Right to Maim: Debility, Capacity, Disability*. Durham: Duke University Press.
Researching the American-Israeli Alliance and *Jewish Voice for Peace*. 2018. Deadly Exchange: The Dangerous Consequences of American Law Enforcement Trainings in Israel. September 2018, 1–38.
Saif, Atef Abu. 2016. *The Drone Eats with Me: A Gaza Diary*. Boston: Beacon Press.
Saif, Atef Abu. 2023. *Don't Look Left: A Diary of Genocide*. Great Britain: Comma Press.
Slaughter, Joseph. 2007. *Human Rights Inc.: World Literature, Narrative Form, and International Law*. New York: Fordham University Press.
Smethurst, Tobi, and Stef Craps. 2019. Towards an Understanding of Drone Fiction. *Journal of War and Culture Studies* 12 (1): 85–102. https://doi.org/10.1080/17526272.2018.1514759.
United Nations Conference on Trade and Development. 2015. *Report on UNCTAD Assistance to the Palestinian People: Developments in the Economy of the Occupied Palestinian Territory*. Geneva: UNCTD.
Weizman, Eyal. 2007. *Hollow Land: Israel's Architecture of Occupation*. New York: Verso Books.

CHAPTER 7

How to Share Space with a Drone: James Bridle's Drone Shadow at the Imperial War Museum

S. F. Maxwell

In his work on the Israeli occupation of Palestinian territories, Eyal Weizman describes how the airspace above Gaza and the West Bank is used as a site of surveillance and control (Weizman 2002). He writes:

> The West Bank must currently be the most intensively observed and photographed terrain in the world. In a 'vacuum-cleaner' approach to intelligence gathering, sensors aboard unmanned air vehicles (UAVs), aerial reconnaissance jets, early warning Hawkeye planes, and even an Earth-Observation Image Satellite, snatch most signals out of the air. Every floor in every house, every car, every telephone call or radio transmission, even the smallest event that occurs on the terrain, can thus be monitored, policed or destroyed from the air. (Weizman 2002: Part 11)

Weizman's description of intelligence gathering in the West Bank communicates the enormous control that drones can exert over populations

S. F. Maxwell (✉)
Independent Scholar, Sheffield, UK

M. W. Azeem (ed.), *Human Rights in the Age of Drones*, Palgrave Studies in Literature, Culture and Human Rights,
https://doi.org/10.1007/978-3-032-08191-9_7

via surveillance. Though they are touted to be precision weapons, their information-gathering operation functions via undiscerning generality. The data extracted by the drone is used to analyse and interpret specific kinds of behaviours, and to reveal links between individuals. This process disintegrates the objects of their surveillance into data points, split apart into nodes for the extraction of information. In this framework, human beings are stripped of their subjecthood. It is an act of rupture that lies beneath the drone's surveillance network and beyond the very real physical threats they pose to life and to wellbeing.

In the West Bank, drone operations treat an entire geographical area and its population as a target. Where the drones are deployed, their 'kill box' strategy dissects the area into three-dimensional conflict arenas that allow operators to categorise the space within. Derek Gregory has termed this 'battlespace' a 'grey zone' in which the legality of drone use is murky (Gregory 2011: 242). When a target is located, a drone within the same 'box' is able to surveil or destroy at will without further supervision from higher up the 'kill chain' (Currier 2023). Once a 'target' of either data extraction or destruction, an individual is separated from their other social, political, and in this instance geographical, contexts (Weber 2009: 4). What I describe is an ontological rupture that takes place as a result of the act of targeting by military drones, the operative strategy of which depends upon the geographical packaging of space into militarised sections, creating the preconditions for what Andrea Miller describes as a form of contemporary war in which 'the boundaries between human and nonhuman organisms, things, and their ambient environments are rendered indistinct' (Miller 2017: 115). Miller goes on to refer to how the operation of military drones and their network of pilots, satellites and coordinators instigates a 'series of spatiotemporal splits' (Miller 2017: 116). This is emphasised in *The Drone Eats with Me: Diaries from a City Under Fire* by Atef Abu Saif, in which he recalls the Israeli bombardment of Gaza in 2014 (Abu Saif 2015). To describe the effects on his life of drone operations overhead, Abu Saif uses primarily aural language. He repeatedly describes the sounds of Israeli drones flying above Gaza as an 'inevitable whir… sounding so close it could be right beside us' (Abu Saif 2015: 4). His words describe the drones as psychological torturers: 'If you allow yourself to listen to them, you'll never sleep' (Abu Saif 2015: 189). Discourse surrounding drones thus demonstrates a duality whereby the drone is at once a vivid and destructive violator of human peace and freedoms, and a politically opaque state weapon whose true operational strategy is barely known by those living in nations whose state forces deploy them.

From the autumn of 2017 to the spring of 2018, the Imperial War Museum (IWM) in London held an exhibition about the complex politics of the drone, and other elements of contemporary warfare.[1] The exhibition featured a large number of conflict-inspired works, linked by the themes '9/11', 'State Control', 'Weapons' and 'Home.' I visited the exhibition twice, recording my impressions with the intention of creating a form of ethnographic journal. Here I recount my interaction with just one installation; a piece by James Bridle entitled *Drone Shadow*, a painted outline of a Predator drone, to-scale, on the museum's floor (Bridle 2017).

Bridle, an artist and writer based in Athens, began the *Drone Shadow* series in 2012 with collaborator Einar Sneve Martinussen, after recognising their unfamiliarity with the physical reality of military drone technology. Bridle sought 'the ability to touch the cold metal of [a drone], to measure oneself against it' (Bridle 2012). *Drone Shadows*, 1:1 scale representations of different types of weaponized drone, are now repeated as commissions for galleries and public art events. On their blog, Bridle writes:

> We all live under the shadow of the drone, although most of us are lucky enough not to live under its direct fire. But the attitude they represent—of technology used for obscuration and violence; of the obfuscation of morality and culpability; of the illusion of omniscience and omnipotence; of the lesser value of other people's lives; of, frankly, endless war—should concern us all. (Bridle 2012).

The implication made by drones of endless war is also referred to by Weizman in connection with military discourse surrounding airpower and drone usage by Israeli forces:

> The quest to make war more 'humane' - which has been written into different conventions and laws of war since the nineteenth century - may under certain conditions similarly result in making it more imaginable, more frequent. By regulating violence... society may end up legitimising war, and even prolonging it (Weizman 2007: 251).

The geo-political model upon which the drone and its data networks function, and even the discourse via which it is explained to the civilian

[1] *Age of Terror: Art Since 9/11.*

population, creates the conditions necessary for a state of potentially endless war and violence. This symptom of the drone age coalesces with the state of what Hansen terms 'twenty-first-century media', the source of a novel renegotiation of subjectivity provoked by the digital age (Hansen 2015: 3–7). Sarah Lucie works with Hansen's terminology in her writing on how performance can function as resistance to symptoms of living alongside the 'datasphere': 'twenty-first-century media—where a human's qualities are translated into data that goes on to interact in algorithmic technology and machine-learning systems in particular—creates an expanded human object that is distributed in time and space' (Lucie 2021: 320). Certainly the boundaries between the corporeal body and its environment become blurred, then, in a world—this world—of unboundaried war and the data networks upon which it is hosted, and through which it is described and narrativised.

Recounting my experience viewing *Drone Shadow* in London in 2018 is an exploratory exercise. I consider the bodily rupture as a consequence of both wartime violence and, conceptually, a symptom of being recontextualised by the datasphere. These two forms of rupture are exemplified in the militarised drone, a tool of data-collection and destruction so comprehensive and inescapable that, as Weizman writes, even 'the smallest event that occurs on the terrain, can… be monitored, policed or destroyed from the air' (Weizman 2002). I consider specifically the meanings created in the time and place of my encounter, by both the space and the art, and by my presence as the viewer in question. Particular to the exhibitionary complex, Bennett describes 'a technology of vision which served not to atomize and disperse the crowd but to regulate it, and to do so by rendering it visible to itself, by making the crowd itself the ultimate spectacle' (Bennett 1988: 81). Understanding the drone as an agent of rupture to both the body and the sense of self merited to the human by virtue of our subjecthood as human beings, I place myself in the museum for this analysis in order to harness its capacity to 'render' [the crowd] visible to 'itself', and therefore to assist in an act of self-affirmation that resists the rupturing of the drone, while at the same time interrogating its capacity to decontextualise and harm its targets.

The Museum

I arrive at the IWM on a warm Wednesday at 10:30. There are steps leading up to the wide doors, and already a steady flow of people are wandering about in the indeterminate way particular to the museum or gallery environment. The *Drone Shadow* on display, like the others in the series, is a 1:1 scale outline of a Predator drone, one thick white line painted onto the floor of the grand atrium (Bridle 2017). The hall is large, framed on two sides by the open balconies of each storey of the building, and on the far side by a staircase from which to access these floors. In the central space, designed to be viewed from all angles and elevations, are suspended two military aircraft and a flying bomb. They hang in a tight grouping, at angles suggesting the dynamics of a peculiarly crowded flight frozen in time.[2] I observe the crowd of visitors. Most of the visitors are school children being shepherded around in large, loud groups. They are talking and laughing, taking photographs of each other, and wandering to and from the bathrooms. As I look around, few people appear to notice or acknowledge the planes and rockets above and around them. The display is a vigorous attempt at drama, and I am amused that the rushed overexcitement of the visitors has drowned it out rather than the other way around. The museum's V2 rocket reaches up from ground level to the third floor, a towering obelisk from which I find myself recoiling. A group of visitors chat happily at its base.[3]

In *Visual Methodologies*, Gillian Rose describes the effects of museum architecture, recalling that entrance halls such as the IWM's 'were designed to be as inspiring and uplifting as the understanding of culture and science

[2] The display at the IWM atrium includes the following artefacts: *Fieseler FI-103 V1 Flying Bomb*, German V1 flying bomb, MUN 3854 <https://www.iwm.org.uk/collections/item/object/30020791> [accessed 3 January 2019]. *BAE Harrier GR.9*, British jet aircraft, 2010.30.8 <https://www.iwm.org.uk/collections/item/object/70000429> [accessed 3 January 2019]. *Supermarine Spitfire MK.IA*, British fighter aircraft, 2010.285.1 <https://www.iwm.org.uk/collections/item/object/70000222> [accessed 3 January 2019]. *V2 (Vergeltungs-Waffe 2) Rocket (Sectioned)*, German V2 rocket, MUN 3853.2 <https://www.iwm.org.uk/collections/item/object/30020790> [accessed 15 June 2018]. *Baghdad, March 5th 2007*, wreckage from a car bomb, Imperial War Museum, London. <https://www.iwm.org.uk/collections/item/object/70000413> [accessed 15 June 2018].

[3] James Bridle's website shows the layout of the Drone Shadow IWM among the other artefacts in the atrium, including *Baghdad, March 5th 2007*. In this image it is easy to see how, when full of visitors, the artwork is (literally) overlooked. https://jamesbridle.com/works/drone-shadow-iwm

articulated within' (Rose 2002: 172). In this model, artefacts become advertisements for the building that houses them, crowd-bringers whose presence relates more to the museum as a commodified space than as an educational one.[4] Here, the museum displays itself rather than its collection, resulting in a space which does not quietly corral or direct visitors, or otherwise regulate them in the manner of a dedicated exhibition space. We are free to gather in groups, to talk loudly, and to ignore the objects as we please. However, the nature of an open space, plus each floor's open gallery, '[affords] a superior vantage point from which the lay-out of the whole and the activities of other visitors [can] also be observed' (Bennett 1988: 81). Visitors to the IWM's atrium unwittingly become part of the museum's display. It is a celebration of spectacle and empire, and therefore its spectator-subjects are as necessary to its purpose as its displays.[5]

In his article 'But Who Actually Watched Mark Lewis's Films at the Louvre?' Raymond Bellour describes two visits to the Louvre he made in 2014 and 2015 (Bellour 2016). Bellour records his attempts to watch films by Canadian artist Mark Lewis, whose work explores cinematic optics and history. After introducing the artist, Bellour takes a step back from the discussion to consider whether the environment of the Louvre exhibition helped or hindered his viewing of the films on display. He reflects that 'it seemed the conditions of projection might have been too adverse to the sustained effort required from the viewer willing to watch them' (Bellour 2016: 238), due to the arrangement of the room and the quality of the light within, and the distracting sounds of gallery-visitors walking past or hovering at the entrance. At the IWM, the placement of the *Drone Shadow* blends the piece so smoothly into the environment that all the

[4] At London's Natural History Museum, 'Dippy' the fossilised diplodocus became the face of the site after being featured in the museum's vast Hintze Hall for thirty-eight years. In 2017 the display was replaced by 'Hope', a skeleton of a blue whale, which is mounted as if diving towards onlookers. The museum has announced a series of 'star specimens' which are to be displayed beneath the whale. The use of language as marketing, including the naming of the artefacts, emphasises the way these 'star' objects are used to create spectacle and define the commodity value of the museum. Star specimens of Hintze Hall revealed. 2017. Natural History Museum, 30 June 2017. http://www.nhm.ac.uk/discover/news/2017/june/star-specimens-of-hintze-hall-revealed.html Accessed 23 April 2018.

[5] Looking down at my notebook, I am conscious that in this environment of promoted self-surveillance, I am probably its most active participant. It is also not lost on me that in observing the museum's visitors, I am enacting my own form of data-gathering. In avoiding 'taking aim at' the visitors, figuratively speaking, I seek to communicate my impressions rather than act 'to occupy and to appropriate' (Weber 2009: 105).

surrounding distraction seems, from my position on the second-floor balcony, to be a part of the artwork, like a developing commentary on the political opacity of the drone program, or on the themes of 'everywhere war': the drone outline a suggestion of possible presence rather than a cemented one like the decommissioned objects around it. Bellour's gallery visit prompted him to wonder 'what happens to the visitor as soon as [s]he enters the museum, leaving [her] familiar identity behind to virtually become a viewer of paintings[?]' (Bellour 2016: 241). He conceives of a shedding that occurs, a leaving behind of oneself. I imagine the new skin one wears at the museum: the social identity of viewership, worn in the environment of the observed object.

Sarah Lucie explores our relation with objecthood via her gallery visit to see the installation of *Hansel and Gretel* by Jacques Herzog, Pierre de Meuron and Ai Weiwei, with Damian Woetzel, after her visit in 2017 (Lucie 2021). In the exhibit, 'participants', as Lucie terms the audience, 'are tracked by infrared cameras and overhead drones that are continuously capturing images, which are then projected onto the dark ground' (Lucie 2021: 328). She describes the playful interaction between the participants and the drones, describing the blurred role of object and subject taken on by visitors to the space: 'bodies' locations in time and space... activate the installation' (Lucie 2021: 329). Bridle's work endows its viewers with agency, then, in a reversal of the real drone's impact on personhood. While *Drone Shadow* is not directly playful or interactive like *Hansel and Gretel*, there is still the indication that art-viewing can be more than just viewing, and this challenges the immovable object/viewer relationship created by the museum's display objects.

Drone Shadow speaks to the simultaneity of the visible and the invisible at work in the operational politics of the drone. The presence of a *Drone Shadow* on this site, a place laden with 'imperial' history, engenders a feeling of responsibility specific to this iteration of the project. The IWM *Drone Shadow* questions the motivations and meanings represented by the museum in which it is housed. A revealing statement from the museum website makes this claim: 'founded while the First World War was still raging, it [the IWM] gives voice to the extraordinary experiences of ordinary people forced to live their lives in a world torn apart by conflict'.[6] The IWM's description of itself fails to locate the museum within a temporal or geopolitical framework; the 'ordinary people' it mentions are nameless

[6] Discover IWM London.

and placeless, just as the ambiguous 'world torn apart' they inhabit denotes a global interest. The vagueness belies the very title of the building and its 'imperial' interests. A small comment in *Punch* magazine contemporaneous to the IWM's first few years gives a different impression of the original purpose of the building:

> One of the most striking of the collection of exhibits... [at the Imperial War Museum] is the Air Force map for carrying out the British plan for bombing Berlin. Specimens of the bombs... are also included in this museum of war souvenirs with the object of demonstrating the resources of the Empire and giving a stimulus to its trade.[7]

Punch includes this extract from the *South African Paper* with the caption, 'if at first you don't succeed, try, try, trinitrotoluene [TNT]'. This caption drily conveys the fact that Britain's imperial interests, the spoils of which form the museum's exhibits, were predicated upon economic and military control. The attitude to the IWM represented in *Punch* in 1920 suggests something more in keeping with the political agenda suggested by the museum's name: a 'demonstration' of the British Empire's power. Gaynor Kavanagh claims that 'it was first imagined that the exhibits [at the IWM] would be largely captured trophies', speaking to the imperialist politics at the centre of its early development (Kavanagh 1988: 84). From this vantage, Bridle's *Drone Shadow* is an explicit representation of British military resources, and its lack of physical form an indication that this weapon is currently elsewhere, 'on loan' to our present conflicts.

The Shadow

I wind my way up the stairs to view the atrium from a higher vantage point. The *Drone Shadow* fits easily into the melange of weaponry and military vehicles displayed in the museum's entrance hall. It is egregious, though, too, as the only part of the display specifically created as a work of art. The surrounding war machines are objects removed from a historical military context and repurposed to suit the museum's desired projection of itself. Their meanings are shaped by this recontextualisation, and by the visitors' expectations of museum artefacts. They are static, silent, and

[7] This paper was published three months after the opening of IWM London at the Crystal Palace in June 1920 (Advertisement 1920).

explicitly strung up and mounted as if to avoid any semblance of movement or of presence. They remain in the past, somewhere beyond the possibility of our physical interaction, beyond the signs instructing us to look but not touch. They are dead objects. Bridle's work takes on a specific meaning in this context: the outline of the drone suggests that something has been removed, like a patch without dust in a display case, or tape on a theatre stage denoting where a prop ought to stand: rather than an artwork, the white lines indicate something that is missing, and remind us that the drone, unlike the V2 and the doodlebug above it, is a contemporary tool of war. This thought brings me to the temporality of the installation: like the real-world drone, the shadow representation has a murky relation to time and space. From my position above *Drone Shadow*, the artwork clearly sits alongside the other artefacts close by. Contextualised in this way, it appears to have not yet taken its place in the atrium; the drawn outline an indicator of something yet to arrive.

In their writings about *Drone Shadows*, James Bridle states that it is the continued and increasing threat posed by drones that inspired the creation of the series. They attempt to render the drone visible because, in their words, 'in operation, their very point is invisibility' (Bridle 2012). It is not the object's shadow, then, but the implied shadows cast by government secrecy, extreme and imprecise violence, international conflict, and ever-smarter technologies of war, which makes Bridle's piece so unsettling. During my visit to the IWM, I linger in the entrance hall, observing how groups of visitors use the space as a meeting point, perhaps waiting for others, or using the cafe or cloakrooms nearby. The people standing here by *Drone Shadow* have either just arrived or are preparing to leave the museum, and in either case appear distracted; overwhelmed by the cacophony of exhibits with which they have immediately been met, or fatigued from hours of focused looking-at-things. People mill about the area, standing on the drone, noticing it absently, poking it with the toes of their shoes. Some read the adjacent plaque. Some step awkwardly off the white lines, unused to walking directly onto an art exhibit, or unaware of its significance unless they notice its nearby museum label. Most are oblivious to the crowds of people lining the staircase trying to photograph an unobstructed view of the hall. I observe visitors spending time viewing the innards of the V2, as though trying to make sense of these undone objects, imagining their past lives. In between them, the drone is paid less attention. The dynamic between viewer and object is much clearer and more linear with the artefacts; they are offered up by the museum to be admired and gazed upon, whereas *Drone Shadow*, not being 'a thing' in the same way, demands a different form of audience interaction. The missing 'fill' created by the empty outline means that when walking over it, the viewer takes up the role of shadow-caster in reference to the shadow beneath them. It is in this sense an interactive piece of art that prompts through its lack—the lack of a tangible form—a continuing dialogue with its audience. The dialogue is dynamic, and like the 'everywhere war', seems inevitable, a result of the designed absence the artwork incorporates (Gregory 2011).

Moving to stand on top of the *Drone Shadow*, I observe how my position in the space affects the way I view the artwork. Its placement on the floor removes the sense of reverent respect with which museum visitors are trained to view exhibits. Occasionally in a museum we are invited to touch an object, cautiously, for some specific sensory purpose. Here, the shadow can be easily missed by those walking directly upon it. Close by, its label describes the piece and advertises the accompanying exhibition for which *Drone Shadow* is a signpost: *Age of Terror: Art Since 9/11*. Seeing the sign before realising that one is standing upon the artwork creates a momentary lag before the *Drone Shadow* is understood as an art piece. This delay in recognition is part of how the piece creates meaning, in that it sneaks up on the visitors, who share their space with the piece in extreme proximity. The drone, via its outline, is not visible at first but then is *right there* beneath you. By rejecting the conventional uses of space in a museum, Bridle's work explores the chaotic temporality of the military drone: its technologies of vision endow it with an omniscience that precludes the dimension of time from having relevance with regard to evasion. It is not possible to flee, one is always watched; it is not possible to hide, the drone waits. Once in place as a technology and as a military tool, it cannot be unmade. When established over a location, the drone is a constant from which it is impossible to hide (Weizman 2002). This oppressive omnipresence and its consequent enduring sense of threat not only have potential to inflict physical destruction but also physically damage those in the target zones, and most ominously, these factors are organised by the legally uncertain boundaries of the 'battlespace', which present possible outcomes summarised by Human Rights Watch as 'contrary to international law' (Gregory 2011: 242). Bridle's work acknowledges this through mimetic gesture, since by removing the drone's body and instead implying it, the drone becomes contradictorily both present and absent, conceptual rather than physical, in all time and all the time.

The renegotiation of space and time is central to *Drone Shadow*, just as it is central to the networked applications of the real world drone. If the piece surprises people with a sudden visibility, it also renders the space that it takes up chaotic and difficult to define. The floor remains the floor of a museum, part of a functional and necessary infrastructure. Once the piece has been placed upon it, the floor becomes art (even the space that isn't painted upon becomes a potential canvas), which toys with the conventional segregations of space between visitor and exhibit in the museum. The form of the piece is significant: it is an outline, so despite the reference to shadows, Bridle chose not to use a filled-in shape for the *Drone Shadows* series. As the viewer may stand within the boundaries of the shape, as though impossibly inside the drone itself, the shape provides another dimension to the piece. Rather than a two-dimensional shape, upon which the viewer walks, the drone becomes three-dimensional once we stand within its edges in a merging of human and drone. The shape of the artwork gestures upwards, into the air above it, where the physical body of the viewer takes on the role of the imagined physical body of the drone. The strange blending that results does not mimic the drone's physical form but the network of information, communication, and targeting upon which it operates, and through which we conduct our lives in the 'datasphere' (Lucie 2021).

Let us think about shadows. *Drone Shadow* relates to the object that casts the shadow, which is not present but implied. By referring to these images as shadows, Bridle emphasises the absence of the drone. Its absence is a political as well as physical lack of visibility or coherence: the drone's body is necessarily not there, as it is enmeshed so deeply within a military system of secrecy and obfuscation. Writing about forms of post-atomic seeing, Akira Mizuta Lippit writes, 'invisibility functions not as the negation of visibility but as a form of visibility given to be seen, but unseen. Visual but invisible' (Lippit 2005: 84). Bridle's *Drone Shadows*, like Trevor Paglen's *Drones* photographs, depend upon the visuality of the drone—its visual existence—even if the drones themselves are not visible (Paglen 2010–2015). In Paglen's artwork, the viewer searches for the drone in the image, thus creating a process of watching or surveillance between viewer and artwork (Maxwell 2022). In Bridle's work, the implication of the drone does not encourage the viewer to spend more time with the artwork, instead creating a feeling in the viewer that lingers beyond the moment of seeing. Bridle reminds us that drones are flying without providing a captured example of one to display to us; the drone remains an unseen ephemeral threat, its terrifying potential undiminished. It is as though the drone has already flown past, evading our gaze, leaving only an indication that it was there above us moments ago, like a snapshot of a passing aircraft. Lippit describes a relationship between invisibility and power, noting that 'power is most often expressed as the ability to cause swift and undetected destruction' (Lippit 2005: 92). Military drones are an archetype of power under this definition, but they are only one part of a long history of airborne death machines.

Lippit examines the atomic bombings of Hiroshima and Nagasaki, events that have a strong link to the concept of the shadow in relation to the photographic effects of the blasts' blinding light. 'Seared organic and nonorganic matter left dark stains, opaque artefacts of once vital bodies, on the pavements and other surfaces of this grotesque theatre' (Lippit 2005: 94). The connection between death, photography and the shadow apparent in the *Drone Shadow* series recalls this ultimate destruction. Visually, even if they are not true shadows, Bridle's outline design is entirely shadowy in light of Paul Virilio's words on photography, quoted by Lippit: 'what appears in the heart of darkrooms is no longer a luminous outline but a shadow, one which sometimes, as in Hiroshima, is carried to the depths of cellars and vaults' (Lippit 2005: 94). In bringing together both the 'luminous outline' and the 'shadow,' Bridle's work echoes Virilio's link between atomic bombing and photography. The *Drone Shadow* is almost a photograph, but perhaps also an exposure cast onto the ground from above, illuminating both the outline of the machine and the shadow of death that follows in its wake.

The conceptual link between the *Drone Shadow* and atomic shadows indicates a shared narrative concerning military technologies and their aftermaths. Bridle's artwork is not a modern retelling of an atomic past, however, nor does the work seek to memorialise or explicitly acknowledge victims of atomic warfare. I have drawn a connection between the two in order to consider the implication of the shadow as a visual event in the study of war machines. If atomic shadows inform our understanding of Bridle's work, it is because of their shared absent subjects. The lack of the human body in an atomic shadow and of the drone in *Drone Shadow* establishes both shadows in time as well as space. The 'opaque artefacts of once vital bodies' are uncanny remnants of living people, killed by the radiant heat of an atomic bombing (Lippit 2005: 94). These shadows tell us both of the prior existence and the ultimate absence of the individual whose mark is left behind. We know that not only was a person previously in this space, but that a catastrophic event occurred which caused their permanent lack. The shadow retains this meaning, impossibly preserving the mark of the body it signifies. It is impossible because a shadow should not be able to exist without the thing that casts it, yet here the violence of the bomb ripped into the temporality of the event of the shadow-casting, separating the individual from their shadow, and leaving the trace of its violence as a permanent image.

Hans Christian Andersen's fairy tale 'The Shadow' tells of the separation of the shadow from its body in a less violent form.[8] Andersen's story addresses how injustice and greed (represented by the shadow) can overwhelm good and morality (the learned man). Mapping this fable onto Bridle's *Drone Shadow* indicates that the shadow without its caster is a representation of lack. A lack of form (or as in the story, a lack of a moral soul) that, by way of having been represented visually, has been given a form that only mimics reality rather than being itself real. The sense of lack in *Drone Shadow* is not only an absence of form but also a seeking of form, just as in the story the man's shadow desires to cast a shadow of its own in order to become a real man. The drone's shadow has the quality of being incomplete without its caster, the real drone. It is for this reason that standing on the *Drone Shadow*, I am aware of the irrational urge to look above me, as if in seeing a real drone flying, the artwork would be relieved of its sense of lack, and something about it would be satisfied. As there is no real drone, the artwork continues to discomfit me, to suggest something incomplete, and due to this, it has the impression of seeking something. In this gesture of seeking, a sense of dynamism or changeableness is inscribed in the work.

Drone Shadow is a shadow without its associated object. The object, the drone, is not like that of the atomic shadow traces, because it has not previously existed in the space denoted by the outline. Instead, Bridle's *Drone Shadow* indicates the possibility of a drone. As we have seen, the design of the artwork makes it possible to overlook, or to have it sneak up on the viewer. It is also indicative of the absent machine in deployment. In the context of Lippit's work, it seems to acknowledge a prior violence. Thus,

[8] In the story a learned man loses his shadow. When they are reunited many years later, the man finds his shadow has become a man itself, using its formlessness to discover people's secrets to grow rich. Meanwhile the learned man becomes thin and poor because his writings on goodness and morality are unsuccessful. The pair slowly exchange roles until the shadow has its 'former master' executed (Andersen 1997).

looking neither forward nor backward in time, but every way at once, the *Drone Shadow* is paranoid art.

> The unidirectionally future-oriented vigilance of paranoia generates, paradoxically, a complex relation to temporality that burrows both backward and forward: because there must be no bad surprises, and because learning of the possibility of a bad surprise would itself constitute a bad surprise, paranoia requires that bad news be always already known. (Kosofsky Sedgwick 2003: 130)

Eve Kosofsky Sedgwick describes a contradictory methodology that turns both to the past and to the future, despite being 'unidirectionally future-oriented.' This paradoxical relation to temporality is apparent in *Drone Shadow*: the artwork is a symbolic warning of something that may occur in the future, yet because of its title as a shadow, it is at the same time an indicator of something that *has been* present. This temporal complexity recalls Jacques Derrida's article 'Spectres of Marx,' in which he claims that 'one can never distinguish between the future-to-come and the coming-back of a spectre' (Derrida 1994: 35). (Here I make a conceptual link between the notions of shadow and spectre, both being forms of simulacra or the implications of more tangible things.) The spectre's existence in time is uncertain, 'already promised but only promised' (Derrida 1994: 35). We cannot know if it has been, or is yet to be, or indeed if it exists in both states at once. This uncertainty is how Bridle's work grabs at its viewer, since it is not simply an object around which one can manoeuvre, imaginatively or physically, but also an idea, a 'promise,' offering something deeply sinister and yet visibly, materially sparse. The space between the lines creates the emptiness implied by the notion of the spectral.

There is a bluntness in how the outline is drawn, relating to the particular thickness of the lines and the bright white paint and the curve of the drone's nose. It reminds me that these machines are bizarre looking, beluga-like, their function-over-form aesthetic somehow jarring with the nostalgic tone often used when one hears of the beauty of the Spitfire or even the terrifying symmetry of the V2 rocket. I struggle to assimilate this gawky shape into my mental timeline of historical aircraft and weapons, and this lack of fitting in or of making sense only makes the drone harder to comprehend. I notice, too, that the outline design is reminiscent of the chalk outline at a crime scene, as if someone had drawn around a dead body. Whether a trope of crime fiction or a real investigative practice, the chalk outline is the implication of something gruesome that leaves space for a viewer's imagination, the foundation of dark jokes on television and in film. What is not seen, what is censored, draws the attention of the viewer even more than the captivating horror of a corpse. The visual association between the chalk outline and *Drone Shadow* implies in the latter the aftermath of a crime. Perhaps whatever object those white lines denote is too unpleasant to be displayed in the full weight of its reality. Thus, the outline is suggestive of an event that has already come to pass; the drone's destructive powers indicated in retrospect.

An outline that replaces the un-viewable corpse is a representative substitute, one that might indicate both *what* and *where*. In this sense, the outline is a map, an X that marks the spot. In *Warped Space*, Anthony Vidler describes the imprecision of the 'X' when used to map space. 'Objects can be presented in the courtroom,' he writes, 'but spaces have always to be imagined, and represented; and representation has, from the early nineteenth century at least, been an art, controlled by psychological projection and careful artifice, more than a science' (Vidler 2000: 123). If Bridle's X-as-drone is a form of mapping, by which to indicate the place occupied by the drone, it is susceptible to the same crises of representation described by Vidler in his criminological example of spatial understanding. Bridle's X does not mark a true spot, as we see that the drone is not present, nor would it cast such a shadow were it to be on display.[9] The *Drone Shadow* represents possible and plausible space, in the same way that the scene of a crime might be described and imagined in a courtroom as a representative fiction.

Entering the Space of the Drone

Drone Shadow has complex conceptual resonances, relating to temporal and spatial uncertainties and the critical absence of the drone's body. When we come to meet the artwork itself, the outline becomes important because it changes the way the viewer interacts with the work. The design invites interaction because Bridle places it beneath our feet, in a space occupied by our bodies. In the case of the IWM *Drone Shadow*, though not outdoors in a truly public space, visitors cross its path due to the location of the lines of the floor. If we briefly imagine that this image of the

[9] While Vidler does not expound on the significance of the X shape, it seems fitting that the drone's angular geometry resembles an X.

drone is filled in to form a solid shape, we would find that to walk across it means to stand *on* the drone. As an outline, I stand *in* the shape and therefore, although the image and I exist in different dimensions of space, it is as though I am within the drone's body. This is not a possible place to inhabit, however. Jordan Crandall describes how the unmanned aerial vehicle changes its meaning when viewed as a weapon or tool, rather than as an alternative form of aeroplane. 'To get *in* the robotic vehicle… is not to enter into an enclosure. There is no entering it as one would a cabin, for its nature is operational, not spatial. […] By way of the pilotless, we access the cabinless' (Crandall 2017: 326). We ought therefore not to think of the unmanned aerial vehicle as a vehicle, since this title conjures the idea of a vacant space within, of an empty chair surrounded by knobs and dials. But the drone is not a tool to transport the human body. 'In an operational and ontological sense, it is not that there is no pilot inside, but that there is no inside' (Crandall 2017: 329). If I cannot enter an object that has 'no inside,' no interior space literally or conceptually, it becomes very difficult to imagine myself inside the drone without some kind of unification taking place.[10]

Now that my gaze is focused on the floor beneath me, I am reminded that it is this terrestrial surface upon which the drone's operation begins and ends. The drone's operator has no relation with flight at all: a different team are responsible for the drone's take-off and landing, in between which they handover to the group responsible for the surveillance and ordnance operations. The operator who watches what the drone's camera broadcasts has no sense of the sky, as instead their gaze is trained on the ground seeking out its targets, preparing its weaponry, interpreting the topography of the world from above. Their focus is on the visceral, tangible lifeforms beneath them, but their gesture of looking—reliant as it is on their own corporeal forms—is entirely detached from anything organic, dependent instead upon the mediation provided by drone, camera, satellite and screen. The decision to strike leads to impact, where the worlds of machine and human fuse at ground zero, the site of impact, always upon the earth's surface, the place where shadows are cast. The ground plays its

[10] I recall here the fate of Gottfried in Thomas Pynchon's *Gravity's Rainbow*, for whom a specialised V2 rocket became a tomb. It had to be adapted to admit him, 'not a Procrustean bed, but modified to take him. The two, boy and Rocket, concurrently designed.' He was not forced in, it was designed, and this sense of forethought haunts *Drone Shadow* too, as though the drone had been waiting for you to step inside (Pynchon 2013: 891).

role in this operation. To make art that is drawn directly onto the ground is to take the artwork to the place at the end of the drone's strategic journey: the final stop. A site either destroyed by the drone's missile or captured in its all-seeing gaze: this is where *Drone Shadow* operates.

Drone Shadows are designed not to be exclusive images, but reproducible ones. While James Bridle remains the author of the artwork as an idea and an image, they encourage their audience to make their own shadows using schematics they provide in their *Drone Shadow Handbook.*[11] The handbook gives details of how to paint the drones to a 1:1 scale, which Bridle explains is necessary because 'they are intended to convey the reality of the size and shape of actual drones' (Bridle 2013). They provide schematics not only for the Predator but also the Global Hawk, Reaper and Hermes drones. The information is available for free but also to purchase, as though giving the user the chance to donate towards the project. The existence of the handbook and its easy availability change the nature of the *Drone Shadows* from traditional artworks into graffiti-like images, street art with anonymous creators that might pop up at any time, anywhere. This is critical to a piece of art about political machines, since this too is the nature of the shadows' real counterparts. The idea that a shadow like this might emerge anywhere in the viewer's domestic space at any time is a central part of the discomfort these images create. While street art more generally plays a decorative role in urban spaces, these drones are deliberately unadorned and functional with regard to their aesthetic properties. Bridle writes in the handbook that although colours can be used, 'white is the strongest colour for drawing...on dark surfaces, and stands out the best during the day and night' (Bridle 2013). It is apparent that visibility is the primary desired effect, rejecting real world drones' trope of invisibility. The schematics are not playful, but clinical, their tone instructive. These artworks are, in Bridle's words from the handbook, 'diagram[s] of a political system' (Bridle 2013). It follows that the final work is also part of this diagram, an image rendered in its most basic form, showing a system defined by oppressive force.

Outside and exposed, rendered in chalk or paint, a *Drone Shadow* will quickly pass out of visibility. It will be in existence a few days or perhaps

[11] Bridle's *Handbook* for recreating his work is available at his website. The site claims that 'the *Handbook* has enabled the creation of many *Drone Shadows* in many locations, without the involvement of the artist.' Like a pilot from the drone, Bridle has distanced himself from the work, allowing it to travel and spread without its author.

weeks, briefly enough that it does not risk passing into the banal or commonplace. It does not blend into its surroundings. It can be viewed close up, and from nearby buildings, but it can also be viewed from high above, from a Google satellite, for instance, or from a drone. Its viewership is not therefore limited to museum visitors or members of the public. Bridle's *Drone Shadow Handbook*, besides allowing the *Shadows* to exist beyond exhibition spaces, provides blueprints that mimic the unknown schematics that exist for the real drones. The *Drone Shadows* themselves look a little like blueprints, clinical and directive, as though pre-existing the real drone. At first glance, Bridle's art causes its viewer to look to the present moment, to search for or at least consider the entity that is casting the shadow on which we are standing. Seeing its absence, we feel that we are looking at the shadow of something that *has been*. However, if we see the design as like a blueprint, the aesthetic qualities of the artwork suggest a machine that is yet to come, and therefore it functions to indicate the drone-filled world of which we are only at the beginning.

Drone Shadow exhibits both temporary and spatial complexity. Its manipulation of the horizontal and vertical planes inhabited by viewer and artwork are cause for a renegotiated form of interactive art-watching. This invites questions of accountability—the positioning of *Drone Shadow* on the ground means that the involvement of the watcher, or walker, is a central part of how they create meaning. They exist in our spaces, and subsequently we inhabit theirs. I posit that understanding how this merging correlates to the real world is a necessary element of ontological analysis of the droned world, since while there is certainly scope for new perspectives and new subjectivities in drone technologies—as Sarah Lucie experienced viewing *Hansel and Gretel*—there is also a risk of finding ourselves aligned with technology that threatens our autonomy and creates spaces of death all around us.

> The performance suggests the body-object as it exists in the contemporary culture of surveillance must be understood also as a cyborgian body-object, where the body extends in time and space to include its data-body representation as an agentic object itself. (Lucie 2021: 332–3)

Lucie's reflections on her own exhibition experience bring together the 'cyborgian' contexts present in the 'droned' body that emerges after interacting with *Drone Shadow*. In disrupting the role of the art-viewer through the strange rupture of the subject and object at work in *Drone Shadow*,

Bridle echoes the many forms of ontological rupture that occur as a result of drone warfare. The painted drones are simultaneously in development, in use, imagined and real, invisible and ubiquitous. In creating the shadow without a body, Bridle positions the drone in a specific but undiscoverable place, somewhere, but nowhere. Without a body, they can be everywhere, and if they are everywhere they can be there at any and all times. Here lies drone paranoia, creating in the viewer a shadow-like version of the feeling of dread that drones are designed to inspire, enhanced by the way they involve the physical body of their viewer to complete their own form. They move from being placeless (and thus anywhere or everywhere) to being part of us, and in the moment that viewer and drone fuse together, the artwork becomes part of our past, present and future. In the IWM, the stasis and sense of permanence in the usual exhibits is disturbed by the drone-object and its disorienting absorption of the visiting bodies. Where Miller referred to 'spatiotemporal splits' occurring in the wake of drone warfare, Bridle's work enacts a spatiotemporal renegotiation of subject-hood, that simultaneously forewarns and mimics the phenomenological rupturing provoked by the age of drones.

After several hours of work in the museum, I leave the exhibition and walk out through the atrium, over the *Drone Shadow* and out into the cool bright day where I look up to the sky.

References

Abu Saif, Atef. 2015. *The Drone Eats with Me: Diaries from a City under Fire*. Manchester: Comma Press.

Advertisement. 1920. Company's Water is on to the House and Cowshed. *Punch*. https://link.gale.com/apps/doc/ES700056429/PNCH?u=su_uk&sid=PNCH&xid=0da957a9. Accessed 23 February 2021.

Age of Terror: Art since 9/11. 2017–2018. Imperial War Museum London.

Andersen, Hans Christian. 1997. *The Complete Fairy Tales of Hans Christian Andersen*, 383–395. Ware: Wordsworth Editions Limited.

Bellour, Raymond. 2016. But Who Actually Watched Mark Lewis's Films at the Louvre? In *Screens: From Materiality to Spectatorship—A Historical and Theoretical Reassessment*, ed. Dominique Chateau and José Moure. Amsterdam: Amsterdam University Press.

Bennett, Tony. 1988. The Exhibitionary Complex. *New Formations* 4: 73–102. https://banmarchive.org.uk/new-formations/number-4-spring-1988/the-exhibitionary-complex. Accessed 30 September 2023.

Bridle, James. 2012. Under the Shadow of the Drone. *Booktwo*, 11 October 2012. http://booktwo.org/notebook/drone-shadows/. Accessed 30 September 2023.

Bridle, James. 2013. *Drone Shadow Handbook*. STML. Flickr.com. https://www.flickr.com/photos/stml/sets/72157638510036333/. Accessed 30 September 2023.

Bridle, James. 2017. *Drone Shadow*. London: Imperial War Museum. Mixed Media.

Crandall, Jordan. 2017. Materialities of the Robotic. In *Life in the Age of Drone Warfare*, ed. Lisa Parks and Caren Kaplan, 324–342. Durham: Duke University Press.

Currier, Cora. 2023. The Kill Chain. *The Intercept*. https://theintercept.com/drone-papers/the-kill-chain/. Accessed 30 September 2023.

Derrida, Jacques. 1994. Spectres of Marx. *New Left Review* 205.

Discover IWM London. Visit IWM London—Plan Your Visit | Imperial War Museums. IWM.co.uk. www.iwm.org.uk/visits/iwm-london. Accessed 23 February 2021.

Gregory, Derek. 2011. The Everywhere War. *The Geographic Journal* 177:238–250. https://doi.org/10.1111/j.1475-4959.2011.00426.x. Accessed 30 September 2023.

Hansen, Mark B. N. 2015. *Feed-Forward: On the Future of Twenty-First-Century Media*. Chicago: Chicago University Press.

Kavanagh, Gaynor. 1988. Museum as Memorial: The Origins of the Imperial War Museum. *Journal of Contemporary History* 23 (1): 77–97. https://doi.org/10.1177/002200948802300105. Accessed 9 June 2021.

Kosofsky Sedgwick, Eve. 2003. *Touching Feeling: Affect, Pedagogy, Performativity*. Durham: Durham University Press.

Lippit, Akira Mizuta. 2005. *Atomic Light (Shadow Optics)*. Minneapolis: University of Minnesota Press.

Lucie, Sarah. 2021. Human Objecthood in the Datasphere: The Body as Resistant Material in Twenty-First-Century Media. *Theatre Journal* 73:319–337. https://doi.org/10.1353/tj.2021.0070.

Maxwell, S. F. 2022. An Investigation into Trevor Paglen's Drones Photographs, Military Targeting, and Looking Slowly. *Journal of War and Culture Studies* 15 (4): 476–493. https://doi.org/10.1080/17526272.2022.2116186.

Miller, Andrea. 2017. (Im)material Terror: Incitement to Violence Discourse as Racializing Technology in the War on Terror. In *Life in the Age of Drone Warfare*, ed. Lisa Parks and Caren Kaplan. Durham: Duke University Press.

Paglen, Trevor. 2010–2015. *Drones*. Photographs. https://paglen.studio/2020/01/21/untitled-drones/. Accessed 30 September 2023.

Pynchon, Thomas. 2013. *Gravity's Rainbow*. London: Vintage Books.

Rose, Gillian. 2002. *Visual Methodologies*. London: SAGE Publications Ltd.

Vidler, Anthony. 2000. *Warped Space: Art, Architecture and Anxiety in Modern Culture*. Cambridge: The MIT Press.

Weber, Samuel. 2009. *Targets of Opportunity: On the Militarization of Thinking*. New York City: Fordham University Press.

Weizman, Eyal. 2002. The Politics of Verticality. *openDemocracy*. https://www.opendemocracy.net/en/article_810jsp/. Accessed 30 September 2023.

Weizman, Eyal. 2007. *Hollow Land: Israel's Architecture of Occupation*. London: Verso.

CHAPTER 8

'None of the Guilty Will Be Spared': Atmospheric Terror in George Brant's *Grounded*

Daniel O'Gorman

George Brant's *Grounded*, first performed in 2013, dramatises the impact of US-led drone deployment on both the experience and the perception of so-called counterterrorist warfare in the twenty-first century. The play takes the form of a one-actress monologue in which a female fighter pilot tells the story of her forced reskilling as a drone operator, a process that leads to her developing a crisis of conscience that reaches a head when she refuses orders to strike a target because she can see a small child running across her screen. Drawing on theories of spatial violence and justice, this chapter argues that *Grounded* makes tangible to its audience an *atmospheric* circumscription of liveable space that is most immediately obvious in the experience of those under the drones' watch, but that is also more surreptitiously present in Western societies, enacted and tolerated in the name of securitisation.

D. O'Gorman (✉)
School of English, University of Leeds, Leeds, UK
e-mail: d.ogorman@leeds.ac.uk

M. W. Azeem (ed.), *Human Rights in the Age of Drones*, Palgrave Studies in Literature, Culture and Human Rights,
https://doi.org/10.1007/978-3-032-08191-9_8

As the European Center for Constitutional and Human Rights (ECCHR) reported in 2017, 'civilian populations in regions such as Afghanistan/Pakistan, Yemen, Somalia, Libya or Syria/Iraq, are living under a growing number of drone attacks' (ECCHR 2017: 11). What is more,

> With the ongoing threat and the uncertainty of when and where the next strike will happen, their experience can only be described as living under a constant threat of terror – no established battlefields which locals could avoid entering, no predictability as to when and where airstrikes will happen and what will constitute a target. (11)

Similarly, an influential Stanford and NYU report, *Living Under Drones* (2011), states its findings on US drone surveillance clearly: 'Their presence terrorizes men, women, and children, giving rise to anxiety and psychological trauma among civilian communities. Those living under drones have to face the constant worry that a deadly strike may be fired at any moment, and the knowledge that they are powerless to protect themselves' (vii).

'It's not fair / Not really', Brant's Pilot says at midway through the play, already beginning to lose faith in the morality of her work: 'We should make an announcement / Attention People of the Grey Desert / Everything is Witnessed / The Moment You Step Outside You are Under Suspicion / That would be fair' (2013: 45–6). The stark asymmetry of power that she describes is in line with the atmosphere of terror that drones create in communities under their gaze. Like **judgement** meted out by a vengeful god, an entire neighbourhood can be flattened with barely a moment's warning. Brant's Pilot is aware of this, and repeatedly speaks in godlike terms, repeating the phrase 'None of the Guilty Will Be Spared' (71). The play's challenge to the US drone program is not based on a critique of the technology as such, but rather on the way it foregrounds the imperial logic that military drones as we know them are shaped by and sustain: a logic that is made plain in their brazenly necropolitical names: 'Predator drone', 'Reaper drone', 'Hellfire missile'. Although *Grounded* is ostensibly a personal morality narrative, it also holds up for examination the language of morality itself: categories like 'innocent' and 'guilty' become increasingly blurred. Through this examination, it encourages wider structural critique of a neoliberal security state that, through its 'fear of fundamentalism', all too often allows drone strikes to 'drop off the radar as a human rights concern' (ECCHR 2017: 20).

The chapter will begin with a brief note in support of existing theorisations of drone warfare as *atmospheric* in nature. It will then divide its analysis of Brant's play across two further sections. The first will focus on the play's dramatisation of a *circumscription* of everyday space through technologies of surveillance. The second will show how the play renders perceptible a politically expedient *invisibilisation* of this surveillance, and the violence it enables, in public life.

Atmosphere

Both the policing of space and invisibilising of violence that drones enable render *atmosphere* a particularly useful term to describe Brant's engagement with them in *Grounded*, because 'atmosphere' describes our sense of the space around ourselves or our communities. It is an *affective* experience: one that can sometimes be hard to pin down or put into words, but that still influences our behaviour and the way we go about our lives.

There are several ways in which theorists have begun to define this creeping encroachment of space that drone technology has enabled in the twenty-first century. Brian Massumi, for instance, calls it 'ontopower': that is, an 'environmental power' that 'alters the life environment's conditions of emergence' (2015: 40). He distinguishes it from Foucauldian biopower by shifting his focus from a political control over life as such, to political control over the spatial conditions—or environment—within which life is enabled. Similarly, both Ian Shaw and Andreas Philippopoulos-Mihalopoulos have invoked Peter Sloterdijk's theorisation of 'atmospheric warfare' in their analyses of drones. Shaw ties the concept to a Marxist critique of the way drones enhance capitalism's 'atmospheric enclosure' of geographical space (2015: 3–4), while Philippopoulos-Mihalopoulos uses it to describe how drones enable a creeping—and deeply disturbing—'invisibilisation' of state violence enacted under the guise of counterterrorism:

> Drone atmospherics is … [a] case of all-inclusive *atmosphere* in which law becomes fully materialised and thus invisibilised. Drones act from an already partitioned air according to the specific needs of the atmosphere in whose service they are. (2015: 133)

By 'already partitioned air', Philippopoulos-Mihalopoulos means a separation of global space into that which is perceived as relatively 'secure' and that which is perceived as 'insecure'. It is not drones themselves that do this dividing: this perception is already in place before the drones are deployed. What they do, rather, is contribute to an enforcement of counterterrorist policy in the insecure zones through violence that is harder for publics in more secure spaces to fully perceive. This is because one of the purposes of drones is to carry out a kind of *perpetual policing*. As Mark Neocleous argues in *War Power, Police Power*, drones are an example of 'air power technology designed for war but being used in civilian spaces for police purposes, and so it is yet another step in the "militarisation of policing" and "policization of the military"' (2014: 156). And as Neocleous points out elsewhere, despite the apparent technological novelty, their use in the perpetual surveillance of formerly colonised nations puts them on a *continuum* with the colonial wars of the 1920s, when violent policing was justified in a struggle against so-called insurgents.

The effects of continual drone surveillance on communities, even when no missiles are fired, are both material and severe. They create an atmosphere of perpetual terror, in which entire communities are forced to live in relentless anxiety about the violence that might explode around them at any moment. In *Terror from the Air*, Peter Sloterdijk describes the use of gas and napalm in twentieth-century warfare as a form of 'environmental terror', turning the very space in which one exists into a weapon of war (2009: 17). However, the distance from which a drone can identify and fire at its target take this concept to a new psychological extreme.

As Achille Mbembe has argued, 'in our contemporary world, weapons are deployed in the interest of maximally destroying persons and creating *death-worlds*, that is, new and unique forms of social existence in which vast populations are subjected to living conditions that confer upon them the status of the *living dead*' (2019, 92). Brant's play shows how drones intensify such 'death-worlds'. While not the *only* weapon used to engender such spaces, they are amongst the most severe in their effects, the extreme atmospheric violence they inflict on communities alone giving the lie to justifications of their use based on claims about precision targeting and the minimisation of civilian casualties. Although this chapter focuses on US drone warfare during the Obama presidency (in which the Bush administration's 'war on terror' was quietly continued, mostly away from the headlines), it is worth noting that the critique levelled by *Grounded* also holds relevance for the deployment of drone warfare in other, more recent contexts: for instance, in the way that smaller, more nimble quadcopters have been put to lethal use on civilian populations in Ukraine and in Gaza.

Circumscription

The Pilot's story takes place in Nevada, the location switching between her mundane daily shifts manning a Reaper drone at a local military base, and her increasingly tense marriage at home, as she and her husband bring up their young girl. The play script calls for a set design that 'contribute[s] to a growing sense of unease throughout', and that 'should be more abstract than literal, or perhaps transform the literal into the abstract' (2013: 19). In Christopher Haydon's 2013 production of the play at the Gate Theatre in London, Lucy Ellinson's Pilot recounts her story in the past tense, on an unadorned, dark square stage, with the audience surrounding her. As the play progresses, it becomes clear that she is in a military prison cell. She says this in the play's closing lines, but it is also literalised by a gradual changing of the light to highlight a netted cube that surrounds her on the stage. The audience can see her, but it is implied that she can't see them back. The gazer becomes the gazed at, witnessed on all sides by an audience who become a kind of jury, silently passing judgement upon her just as she has repeatedly passed judgement upon the blurry figures on her screen. It is only in the play's final moment—to which this chapter will later return—that she breaks the apparent fourth wall and directly addresses the audience, warning them to avoid taking their assumed privacy for granted: 'You who ... think you are safe / Know this / Know That You are Not Safe' (71).

Brant has explained in interviews that what intrigued him most about drone pilots was the fact that they are based in the United States and are able to go home to their families every night, something unprecedented in American military history (2016: n. pg.). Nonetheless, statistics show that on average they still tend to experience similar levels of PTSD to traditional fighter pilots (Dao 2013). In *Grounded*, the case is slightly different. The Pilot is deeply depressed to be relegated to what she calls the 'Chair Force' (24) following her return to work after the birth of her daughter. Far from being traumatised by her time in the US Air Force, she misses the thrill of it immensely and is emotionally torn by the demands of her newfound motherhood: 'I'll scream if I don't get up and out', she says early on in the play, 'I was born for this but I was born for that too I don't can't can't not be up there be up alone alone in my sky' (2013: 28). From the play's opening sequence, in which she harks back to her jet-fighting days, it is clear that the younger self that she inhabits has internalised the 'us vs. them' rhetoric of the war on terror and believes herself to be fighting the good fight:

> I'm in the blue for a reason
> I have missiles to launch
> I have Sidewinders
> I have Mavericks
> I rain them down on the minarets and concrete below me
> The structures that break up the sand
> I break them back down
> Return them to desert
> To particles
> Sand. (21)

The unambiguous joy—even *jouissance*—that she displays in the celebration of her jet plane's destructive power here is chilling. An association between terrorism and Islam is subtly established through the reference to minarets, and the Pilot's deep-seated Islamophobia signalled through her revelry at reducing the structures to dust.

The passage evidences what Sara Ahmed has described as a 'sliding between [the] signs' of Islam and terrorism, resulting in a '"sticking" [of] signs to bodies: the bodies who "could be terrorists" are the ones who "might look" Muslim' (2014 [2004], 76). As Ahmed goes on, 'it is this could-be-ness, this detachment, which also allows the restriction on the mobility of those bodies that are read *as associated with terrorism*: Islam, Arab, Asian, East, and so on. Fear sticks to these bodies (and to the bodies of "rogue states") that "could be" terrorist, where the "could be" extends to the power to detain' (79). Ahmed is primarily concerned here with the detention of individuals under heightened post-9/11 counterterrorism laws, but what *Grounded* sets up from the start is a demonstration of how drone warfare enables an extension of this logic to entire communities placed under surveillance in regions identified as 'terrorist' in Asia, Africa, and the Middle East.

A sliding between signs is evident in the Pilot's personal life, too: it is only when the Pilot is grounded by her pregnancy and redeployed at the drone operation base that her emotional and psychological wellbeing starts to fray, and that she in turn begins to develop a sense of unease at the racism at play in this worldview. In the lead-up to this realisation, however, she finds the domestic space of her suburban home increasingly bland and constricting. As a result, she experiences a disorienting blurring of the boundary between the military and the domestic: 'Home will be training too', she says, 'driving to war like it's shift work / Like I'm punching the clock' (36). Something is missing for the Pilot, and her increasing disconnectedness impacts their relationship, the intimate space of their bedroom becoming isolating and lonely. There is 'no sex for a while' (62), until, by accident, they discover her military suit to re-spark some passion (64), the domain of a faraway war enmeshing even more closely with that of their home.

It is, of course, nothing new for war to seep into everyday life: PTSD, for example, is one of many ways that it can maintain a profound presence in the lives of those who have experienced warfare, whether soldiers, aid workers or refugees, long after they have left the physical space of the conflict zone. Likewise, shifts in counterterrorism policy, news reportage, surveillance, and attitudes towards minority communities, especially Muslims, are all examples of ways in which the logic of warfare can extend into spaces far outside of the physical location of the war. However, there is a newfound, technologically enabled immediacy underpinning the war's presence in the Pilot's domestic life: something akin to what Doreen Massey has described as 'that throwntogetherness' of a shared space, 'the unavoidable challenge of negotiating a here-and-now … and a negotiation which must take place within and between both human and nonhuman' (2007: 140). The war no longer *extends* its reach into her home life temporally, but has become *interwoven* with it spatially (it is happening in synchronous real time, excruciatingly slow and mundane, alongside—and gradually encroaching upon—her everyday family life). This synchronicity is emphasised in the way the Pilot's narrative weaves the spaces together in its telling, with words and phrases reflecting one another as in a poem:

> [Eric] smiles
> We eat
> We stare at a screen and then go to sleep
>
> Drop Sam off
> Drive through the desert
> Stare at a screen at a road in the desert
> A road that's twelve hours ahead
> But only 1.2 seconds away. (43)

The resonances created in this short passage between the couple's home television screen and the screen of her drone transmission, as well as between two roads in two deserts in two different continents, help underscore the disorienting experience of global space that the Pilot is experiencing because of the technology she works with. The lines 'A road that's twelve hours ahead / but only 1.2 seconds away' make little logical sense as a sentence, but convey a sense of the technology's overwhelming power, defying geographical logic. As a result, it poses a profound challenge to the Pilot's worldview: that is, what has until now been her capacity for literally *viewing the world.*

What is more, through her surveillance of the Middle Eastern desert, the Pilot gradually becomes more sensitive to the surveillance under which her own life is ineluctably placed daily. On a trip to the shopping mall with her daughter, she fixates on a CCTV camera on the wall:

> I look up
> See the little black circle in the corner of the wall
> They're watching us
> Someone is watching us
> That's finc
> Fair enough
> But Attention People of the Boulevard Mall:
> My Daughter is Not the Guilty and her Stroller is Not a Jeep
> We are the Innocent
> You Let Us Pass
> …
> there's always a camera right
> JC Penney or Afghanistan
> Everything is Witnessed. (48)

Similarly, she becomes affected by the practice of 'sleeve shaking' that her husband is required to do at the end of every shift at the Las Vegas Pyramid casino where he works:

> Clap off the game. Blackjack. The end of my shift.
> *(He performs a blackjack dealer "nothing up my sleeves" move with his hands to the eye in the sky.)*
> *(Of the eye in the sky.)* To let it know I've got no chips up my sleeve. … I clap and I'm done. I leave the table and I'm done for the day. (51)

Both of these observations from everyday life are fleeting, but together point towards a connection between surveillance and capital: The Pilot's fixation on the CCTV cameras offers a forewarning of the creeping technological enclosure in her homeland: an atmosphere that has already long been felt far more sharply by Americans who most closely resemble the general profile of the 'could-be' Islamic terrorist (see, for example, the Bush Administration's PATRIOT Act in 2001, or the more recent 'Muslim Ban', instigated by Donald Trump in 2017). As Christine Evans has argued,

> Point of view and mode of mapping both enact and disguise power; controlling them is key to the pursuit (and laundered representation) of virtuous war. This point underlies one of *Grounded*'s most vital moves: connecting the surveillance technologies that enable drone warfare to globalized neoliberal conditions of work and commerce. (2015: 667)

The play shows that the security provided by drone surveillance is merely one facet of a broader neoliberal drive towards securitisation. As Frédéric Gros puts it, 'The exponential growth in social inequalities will, without doubt, demand ever more "securitarian" mechanisms .... Neoliberal regimes are doomed to become police states, as it will become ever more necessary to contain the explosions of misery' (186). Terrorist attacks in the West are, of course, the most literal manifestations of such 'explosions of misery', and Brant's Pilot finds herself at the forefront of the state's mission to prevent them, fighting terror with another kind of terror: one enabled by the drone's ability to project a sense of omniscient, panoptical surveillance.

At the centre of this surveillance is, of course, the military base where the Pilot is stationed. The base has a claustrophobic atmosphere built up around it from the start: she describes it as 'an air-conditioned trailer that seals me off completely from all sky all blue' [38]. What is notable, however, is that she describes the screen that she is now required to stare at for hours on end, as 'not like a videogame / A videogame has color / I stare at grey' (38). The grey comes in stark contrast to what she repeatedly and longingly describes as 'the Blue' of the vast Middle Eastern skies in which she used to fly. What is more, the distinction that she makes between the drone screen and a video game is significant because it complicates the equivalence that is frequently made between the two in discourse on drone warfare. A video game, no matter how realistic or immersive, is always a kind of *fiction* (albeit an interactive one), whereas the task of drone operation, no matter how seemingly virtual or abstracted, is always a representation of *reality*.[1] As the Pilot keeps repeating, it is an extremely *boring* reality, which comes in contrast to the fast-paced action and excitement of most computer games. Indeed, one of the key points that the play aims to make clear about drones is that the danger they pose is *not* so much that they encourage their operators to mistake what is on their screen for a video-game-like simulation of reality. Rather, the screen—coupled with a kind of Kafkaesque bureaucracy and plain, monotonous boredom—contributes to an *exacerbation* of the divisive 'us vs them' fictions that *already* underpin discourse surrounding the so-called 'war on terror' (Jackson 2005; O'Gorman 2015).

As Achille Mbembe has argued in relation to the primacy of screens more generally in twenty-first century life: 'The screen is the new scene. The screen does not only seek to abolish the distance between fiction and reality. It has become reality-generating. It forms part of the conditions of the century' (2019, 181). In other words, it's not the virtuality, but rather the disorienting *reality-generation* of the desert on her screen—and a creeping *real*isation (quite literally) of the imperial project with which she is actively complicit—that prompts such deep-seated unease for the Pilot. This unease begins with a gradually increasing tendency to psychologically dissociate: 'The eye in the sky / That's me / That's me now / I fly a plane and stare at a screen that stares at the ground / I don't see anything / And that's good / Just grey putty / Nothing / Nothing / Nothing / Nothing' (39). The reality of the Middle Eastern desert represented in front of her eyes is hard for her to compute: she knows it is real, but there is something so deeply inhuman and mechanical about the way that it is mediated that it is difficult for her to *feel* it as real: the landscape just looks like grey putty, and the people on the ground are 'putty people' (41). The use of 'putty' as a metaphor is significant because it implies moldability and, as such, subjectivity: the people are subject to any reality that she and her team choose to inflict on them. This is, of course, the case physically (she can annihilate them at the touch of a button), but it is also the case emotionally: in her mind, the identities of these blurry figures are moulded into the

[1] For example, as Joseph Pugliese reports: 'Remarking on the crossover between gaming technologies and drone operations, Predator sensor operator, Staff Sgt. Nicolette Sebastian, explains that a drone 'operation is a lot like Play Station … "Oh, it's a gamer's delight."' Joseph Pugliese, 'How drones are gamifying war in America's casino capital', *LSE US Centre Blog* <https://blogs.lse.ac.uk/usappblog/2017/09/15/how-drones-are-gamifying-war-in-americas-casino-capital/>

shape of suspected terrorists and terrorist sympathisers, literalising Ahmed's point about 'sticky' signifiers.

The 'putty' metaphor helps to articulate the plasticity of the Orientalist othering in which she is participating. However, it also articulates the *ease* with which its structural *enclosing* of identities can lead to devastating physical violence. As the Pilot articulates elsewhere: 'A dot … zooms in to a man which pans to be several men by the side of the road two miles up from our boys' (41). In her allusion to her drone's Gorgon Stare capabilities here, what is presented to the audience is a clear depiction of the camera's capacity for atmospheric enclosure: it literalises an ideological map—or 'imaginative geography', to borrow Derek Gregory's take on Edward Said's phrase (1994: 204)—that distinguishes certain dots (suspicious 'military aged males' [2013: 41]) from others ('our boys' [41]). Although the Pilot is never able to fully articulate the 'imaginative' aspect of this ideological mapping, the camera's zooming works to both literalise and amplify this fictive dimension in a way that nonetheless causes her to become increasingly disturbed. As Elise Morrison has argued, 'The Pilot's tragic story destabilize[s] divisions between guilt and innocence, watcher and watched, familiar and foreign in which justifications for global surveillance programs and drone strikes are grounded' (2014: 168). The technologically enabled experience of watching blurry dots transform into perceived friends or foes makes it difficult for the Pilot to sustain the illusive binaries upon which her understanding of the world—as well as the justification for her actions—relies: 'good' and 'evil'; 'innocent' and 'guilty'; 'citizen' and 'terrorist'; 'us' and 'them'. It is not so much the case that the action on the monitor is reduced to a fiction, but rather that an already-existing fiction *inherent to her worldview* is brought to the fore.

The drone screen casts into doubt her most fundamental ideological assumptions. She becomes aware that she is simultaneously both involved in and detached from the lives depicted on her screen, and the resulting spatial dysphoria prompts a gradual dissolving of her sense of self. As Grégoire Chamayou puts it in *Drone Theory*:

> For classic soldiers, the transition from war to peace is a notoriously delicate phase. In this switch from one moral ground to another difficulties in adaption or reintegration may surface, for the return to civilian life requires periods of decompression. The fact is that even if they never leave their country, drone operators who "telecommute to the war-zone" have to manage the equivalent of such a switch twice a day, very fast and almost without

> transition. The problem lies in a ceaseless to-ing and fro-ing between two worlds that are opposed in every way. (2015 [2013]: 119)

What Chamayou is referring to is precisely the kind of schism between the spaces of war and peace, or military and civilian space, that Brant's Pilot is forced to straddle on a daily basis. The technology that she uses in her work brings into collision 'the two worlds opposed in every way' that Chamayou describes, and it becomes impossible for her to maintain a sense of distance between the Middle Eastern landscape on the screen and the American one in which she lives. The screen works as a nodal point that brings into contact a constellation of disparate realities. Part of the reason the screen gradually prompts an unravelling of the Pilot's sense of self is because she starts to see the ways in which the very fictionality of its digitalised, pixelated *mise-en-scène* reflects, like a mirror, the 'imaginary order' (Lacan 2006 [1949]: 75–81) of her own deeply-held ideological convictions about good and evil, innocence and guilt. In doing so, it prompts her to begin dissociating from a United States counterterrorism discourse that has over the years come to form a constitutive part of her self-understanding as both a soldier and a citizen.

Invisibilisation

The Pilot's increasing awareness not only of the imperialistic spatial circumscription to which she is contributing, but also of the ways this process is 'invisibilised' through the distancing effects of drone technology, are particularly apparent in the contrasting manner in which she describes the occasions on which she is given orders to fire a missile at a target. In the first, she is euphoric: she and her team both cheer at the successful elimination of a group of the 'putty people', and she 'high-five[s]' her nineteen-year-old colleague to celebrate (2013: 42). For the first time in her new role, she feels the white-knuckle thrill that she used to experience in the sky: 'My knuckles are white white' she says, 'Was I flying was that flying / they're white like they used to be / White' (42). Her euphoria, and the sense of unease with which we are encouraged to respond to it, is compounded moments later when she does the same again with another group of figures on the ground. She jubilates in the godlike power that she has been granted by the drone: 'You can't hide from the eye in the sky my children', she says, 'We look down from above we see all and we have / pronounced you guilty' (44).

The reference to the men as 'children' here is significant because of the way it contrasts with the play's motherhood motif: unlike her daughter Samantha, a vulnerable baby to be unconditionally cared for, the 'children' here have sinned and are punished by a wrathful god. On a more mundane level, they are reduced to naughty children who require disciplining. This idea returns with bitter irony at the play's conclusion, when the Pilot reflects on her own disciplining and punishment by the military system. She is 'Grounded' in her new 'court-martial home', and this reveals the play's ironic double-meaning: the title refers not only to her reskilling as part of the 'Chair Force', but also to her demotion from heroic soldier to powerless child, 'grounded' for her misbehaviour.

The absurdity of her situation comes across through the grotesque cognitive dissonance that she displays when, this time, she notices body parts on her screen: 'Those must be body parts' she says, 'Guilty body parts' (44). The audience has no way to gauge the accuracy of this ascription of 'guilt' on the targeted people, but this is precisely the point: no matter how ostensibly 'justifiable' their targeting may have been according to military rules or international law, the absurdity of the phrase 'Guilty body parts' belies the sheer scale of dissociation enabled by the technology. The victims have been othered to such a degree that even their body parts can be described as 'guilty'.

However, this absurd ascription of guilt to the body parts is also a necessary defensive reflex for the Pilot as it temporarily protects her from having to think of the victims as fully human, and in turn from having to question the morality of her actions. They de-invisibilise the violence in which she is implicated, making it impossible to ignore. The body parts counteract what Eyal Weizman has described as the culture of 'Glomarization' that has been deliberately fostered by successive US Governments in response to questions about drone strikes. The term stems from the 'Glomar Response', which was a strategy first used by the CIA in 1975, after its ship, the *Glomar Explorer*, sunk a Soviet nuclear submarine. Instead of denying the attack with a straightforward phrase like 'This is untrue' or 'this did not happen', which both would have required a plausible counternarrative, the US government employed 'a form of denial that aims to add no information whatsoever': they said '"[we can] *neither confirm nor deny* the existence or nonexistence" of such covert activity' (2017, 33). This strategy has been used frequently ever since, especially with regard to drone strikes, which tend to be treated with secrecy. As Weizman puts it:

> Glomarization is not only a rhetorical formulation ...; it is also based on a territorial blockade meant to make unavailable access to ground-level images and testimonies and on the fact that traces of the violence cannot be identified in the resolution of available satellite images. ... Drone strikes can thus be understood not as a direct, linear relation between a drone, via a missile, and a target, but rather as a set of operations enabled by the production of thresholds – territorial, juridical, and visual. Juridical thresholds extraterritorialize entire territories, physical thresholds filter the movement of people in and out of regions, and photographic thresholds filter objects in and out of visibility. (33)

By refusing to confirm nor deny the occurrence of a drone strike, the authorities prevent the strike from becoming concretised in people's minds: it remains distant and easy to forget about, like a half-remembered dream that slips from memory before one fully awakes. As James Bridle has put it in another discussion of this strategy, the phrase 'we can neither confirm nor deny' functions as 'a kind of magic spell, or political technology, transforming civil life into a conflict between government and the governed as assuredly as any military technology – and creating a new kind of truth in the process' (2018, 162).

The Pilot, therefore, is in a unique position in that she bypasses the Glomarisation process in some ways, but is still kept in the dark about *why* her targets *are* targets. She can affirm that a strike of some kind *has* taken place, but is not in a position to say *whom* it is that has been struck, beyond a vague faith in her superiors to accurately determine the 'guilty' from the 'innocent'. In other words, she is compelled to adhere to the narrative of 'good vs evil' that Glomarisation, as a kind of ideological 'filter' or 'blockade', is designed to uphold, at the same time as this narrative is directly challenged by the gruesome asymmetrical violence that she can see exploding right before her eyes.

Maintaining the 'good vs evil' narrative of the war on terror, then, requires for the Pilot a dissociation that invisibilises the humanity of the perceived enemy to the point that there is little to distinguish living bodies ('putty people') from exploded limbs, not just visually but also *affectively*: both are 'guilty' because the guilt that has been ascribed to them has little to do with any material actions that they may or may not have taken. It is a guilt that is predetermined by the fictional binaries of 'good' and 'evil', 'civilised' and 'uncivilised', or 'us' and 'them' that underpin the imperial logic of the so-called war on terror and reflect what Ronak K. Kapadia has described as 'The abstract sense of a temporal limitlessness of a planetary forever war' (8). As Kapadia puts it:

> Along with the lack of sustained public consciousness of US involvement in all-out global warfare, this borderless vision of twenty-first-century military empire links temporally and spatially dispersed bodies and geographies through differential forms of management and extermination, revealing the nation as a "forever war" machine: seemingly enduring, mutable, and eternal. (8)

The Pilot's guilt, stemming from her own growing 'consciousness' about the nature of US global warfare, is *projected onto*, rather than *created by*, the drone screen. The Pilot's euphoria in response to these initial killings stems from a belief in the *fiction* that she is on the side of good against evil: a fiction that was, perhaps surprisingly, *easier* to maintain in her previous role as a fighter pilot. As a fighter pilot, she was not required to stare at her targets for days on end, nor to pay too close attention to the gory aftermath of her strikes.

Given its interest in the invisibilisation of drone violence, one might raise some concerns here about whether *Grounded*'s intense focus on perpetrator trauma comes at the expense of an equally intense focus on the Pilot's victims, or on the vast disparities between them in terms of power and history. As Inderpal Grewal has convincingly argued, '[the play's] reliance on empathy as the powerful ethic to resist new wars remains limited by a refusal to address any difference between the history of empire and its historical targets' (2017: 354). Moreover, she makes following the crucial point:

> Human witnessing and human embodiment by Americans become the play's tools for resistance. The power and limit of this embodied witnessing emerges via the white body of Pilot .... Here, even the impact of neoliberal politics remains confined to an American subject, rather than to its broader, global effects. (354)

Grewal is right to critique the play's limitations on the grounds of its sole focus on the Pilot. Nonetheless, there is also something to be gained from considering these limitations from a different angle. On one, basic level (and to be fair to Brant), the play's monologue form automatically renders complex postcolonial historicisation difficult. On another level, however, its hyper-specific focus on the American Pilot is valuable because it highlights the unique position that drone pilots occupy in the context of the war on terror: they sit at the threshold between the homeland and the conflict zone, and as a result experience a sort of atmospheric disorientation whereby their sense of being-in-the-world is stretched and warped in extreme and unsustainable ways. As Alan Gibbs puts it in a discussion of drone operators in *Contemporary American Trauma Narratives*, 'if trauma is deliberately and exclusively associated with victimhood, then this dangerously excludes the possibility that if one suffers trauma one can be a perpetrator' (2014: 199). The play's focus on the Pilot gives an indication of how the American general public might be affected by drone strikes, were the injustice they inflict made more visible: the point is not only about producing empathy (which, of course, has its limits), but also, more simply, about acknowledging injustice.

Drone technology and the propaganda surrounding it have enabled an entrenchment of the widespread sense that 'precision' strikes are doing the 'good' work of killing distant terrorists on humanity's behalf. As John Kaag and Sarah Kreps point out:

> Poll data suggest that the American public is widely accepting – while at the same time somewhat ignorant – of US drone strikes abroad. A large majority (65 percent) of Americans claim that they have heard a lot about the US drone program, but when asked where most strikes are occurring, most Americans either cite the wrong country or do not know where those strikes are carried out. More broadly, an astounding majority of people (75 percent) report that they nevertheless *approve* of these targeting practices, even though their knowledge of the policy is dubious. Yet, *in the very same poll*, only a quarter of respondents aver that drone strikes are legal. (2014: 23)

Again, *Grounded* invites its audience to pay attention to the Pilot's psychological and emotional degeneration precisely because it occurs at the meeting point of the two worlds described here—the American public sphere, on the one hand, and the unknown countries in which strikes are happening, on the other. As a result, the astonishing cognitive dissonance that Kaag and Kreps describe becomes much harder for the Pilot, and, in turn for the audience, to sustain. The broad recognition amongst those polled that the strikes are illegal constitutes an inversion of Hannah Arendt's notion of the 'banality of evil' (2006 [1963]): in this instance, the normalisation of state violence is enabled not through a thoughtless belief in the inherent good of the bureaucratic process, but through a thoughtless belief in in the inherent good of the violence itself.

In a brief commentary on the play in his essay, 'Drone Geographies', Derek Gregory describes this dissonance as an inability to consistently maintain the kind of 'remote split' that Stanley Milgram famously described in his experiments on obedience to authority in the early 1960s. Milgram argued that compliance, even when being asked to inflict pain, is made more likely by a physical separation between the act and its consequences. He called this separation a 'remote split', and Gregory uses the idea to suggest that a similar practice has been at play in media and political discourse on drone strikes in the context the war on terror. He points out that, in the name of security, the Obama administration regularly performed a version of the Glomarisation tactic whereby 'the veil of official secrecy [was] deliberately let slip once, twice, three times [... working] to draw its audience's eye towards the American body politic and away from the Pakistani bodies on the ground' (9).

In contrast, Brant's Pilot finds susceptibility to the 'remote slip' decreasing:

> [She] describes the difficulty of maintaining the separation necessary for her to decompress, and gradually and ever more insistently one space keeps superimposing itself over the other; the fixed, precise sensor of the Gorgon Stare [the name of the powerful camera mounted on the drone] yields to a blurred vision in which she finds it virtually impossible to know where (or who) she is. (Gregory 2014: 9)

This digitalised folding of distant terrains, and the resultant dissolving of the Pilot's sense of self, reaches a head at the end of the play, when the Pilot describes her crisis of conscience upon being given orders to fire another missile on a later occasion, following many days of maddeningly uneventful boredom while trailing a vehicle containing another potential target, 'twelve hours a day' (57). The man, officially referred to as 'Number Two' (57), remains in his vehicle for days, rousing suspicion but also preventing a positive identification:

> He just drives around in my car
> I think he knows we're there
> We're miles above him but I think he knows
> So he doesn't get out

> If he got out we'd have target certainty and it would be
> over
> ...
> How does he piss?
> Into a cup or something?
> Number Two is the one who calls himself a prophet
> Perhaps prophets don't piss. (57)

By referring to his vehicle as 'my car', the Pilot's language reveals a continuation of the slippage between worlds that she has been experiencing elsewhere in her life, whether at home, at the military base, or in the shopping mall. Her fixation on the question of how the man 'pisses', meanwhile helps underscore the radical contemporaneity of their lives through the sheer mundaneness of the time she has spent with him, once again emphasising a newfound, technologically enabled temporal interweaving of disparate global spaces. The conceptual juxtaposition of 'prophet' and 'piss', likewise, evidences a fraying of her faith in the fictive binaries she has been encouraged to believe exist between them. Eventually, he is forced to emerge, when – having idled outside his home for some time – a young girl emerges from the house and 'Runs out toward the car / a little girl running / Her face a body of blurs' (67). The 'Prophet' jumps out of his car and 'leaps limping toward her waving his arms / He's waving her away from the car trying / to keep her safe' (67). The limp matches the profile of the Pilot's target, and she is given clearance to fire, but she hesitates:

> The girl
> Her face
> She stops running and I see it
> Her face
> I see it clearly
> I can see her
>
> It's Sam
> ...
> The team screams fire and all it would take is my thumb
> my thumb has orders to annihilate but it's her and I
> can't kill her I can't kill her I can't. (67–8)

The Pilot knows she will be immediately overridden, so she decides to crash her drone, an act that leads to her present incarceration. However, her drone has been secretly surveilled from above ('There was another Reaper above me I didn't know was / another god above me' [2013: 69]), and a missile is fired anyway:

> The team cheers as my daughter dies
> As her arms and legs fly off in separate directions
> As her pulp is mixed with the car and the Prophet and the sand
> As her pulp dissolves into the grey
> There is only the grey now
> Only the grey. (2013: 70)

The radical contemporaneity of 'life-world' and 'death-world' has here reached an apex, the gruesome emphasis on body parts once again underlining Mbembe's point about the screen's capacity for 'reality-generation', as it conveys the child's death to the Pilot in horrifically material terms. What we might term the 'ungrievable' invisibility of the girl's life in the eyes of the American military—the judgement that she is *surplus* to the greater good of American security—is precisely what renders her death all the more grievable to the Pilot (Butler 2009: 22). The 'us vs. them' identity binaries so common to discourse surrounding the war on terror have disintegrated, and everyday understandings of what terrorism constitutes have, for her, been turned on their head. As Elise Morrison argues, 'The Pilot's tragic story destabilize[s] divisions between guilt and innocence, watcher and watched, familiar and foreign in which justifications for global surveillance programs and drone strikes are grounded' (2014: 168). While terrorist attacks in Western nations, like the 2015 attacks on *Charlie Hebdo* and the Bataclan music venue in Paris, prompt outpourings of grief from around the world, more frequent acts of terror in Muslim nations often pass with much less remark in the West, and the mediated, sometimes 'collateral' killing of civilians in drone strikes barely even registers as an event, let alone an act of terror.

It is only after she has related this incident that it becomes apparent that, throughout the play, the Pilot has been speaking from inside a military prison cell. It has until now been unclear to whom she has been addressing her tale. At this point, however, there is a shift: '*She takes in her audience*' (70), before directly addressing them:

> You who watch me
> Who observe me watch my every move here and I know
> you watch me I know there is a camera somewhere for
> Everything is Witnessed. (70)

When the Pilot addresses her audience, and the space of the stage encloses on itself as its resemblance to a cell becomes more apparent, the audience members are placed briefly into the role of the godlike watcher, gazing down upon the 'guilty'. Jacqueline Viskup describes the play's engagement of the audience in this way as evidence of its innovation within the genre of the 'surveillance tragedy', prompting them 'to harness their autonomy and agency and judiciously resist a decline into a fully militant society' (2017: 304). There is a dissonance here between the direct address, in which she actively stares her audience in the face, and the *content* of what she is saying, which reveals that she can't see the 'camera' that she knows is watching her. Indeed, as Harrop has pointed out in reference to London's Gate Theatre production:

> It's an irony of contemporary theatrical artifice that Ellinson can't see us at this moment, since she is brightly lit and we are in darkness. But as she glares out of her prison, it certainly feels as though she can … The watchers may become the watched. "There" may one day become "here" (181).

This dissonance disrupts the panoptical effect that the set design has so far maintained. In this moment, audience members are prompted to feel a similar sense of creeping paranoia about all of the ways that they are being technologically surveilled themselves, both in the moment (via the theatre's CCTV cameras) and in their lives more generally (via their smartphones and other electronic devices). As Inga Meier has put it, we as spectators 'are not separate from the representations we choose to engage. When we leave the theatre, we will turn on our cell phones. Our journey home will be captured by cameras following our movements as we navigate the city streets' (2018: 74). The act of theatrical spectatorship is metaphorised, becoming one with the act of surveillance, as the audience gazes upon the Pilot in silent judgement. As a result, the play's ending drives toward the kind of active spectatorship that Jacques Rancière describes in *The Emancipated Spectator*, in which viewing is itself a form of action, one which 'begins when we challenge the opposition between viewing and acting; when we understand that the self-evident facts that structure the relations between saying, seeing and doing themselves belong to the structure of domination and subjection' (2009: 17).

In its foregrounding of the audience's own spectatorship, both in the literal theatre in which they are sitting and in the theatre of war that they experience daily, through the screens of their portable devices, the play literalises Rancière's claim that spectatorship 'begins when we understand that viewing is also an action that confirms or transforms this distribution of processes. The spectator also acts, like the pupil or the scholar' (17). It draws attention to the technology of the theatre itself—that is, its basic technical elements (such as narrative, performance, lighting and spatial design)—and transforms them into a set of tools with the capacity to encourage in the audience a pushing back against both atmospheric circumscription and invisibilisation. Through its reflexive melding of what, on the one hand, is essentially a form of traditional oral storytelling, with what, on the other, is a more subtle manipulation of space through its deliberately abstract set design, the play offers a glimpse of a future in which the human and the technological might combine in ways that prioritises global coexistence and justice over the violently imposed policing of 'terror'.

References

Ahmed, Sara. 2004. *The Cultural Politics of Emotion.* Edinburgh: Edinburgh University Press.

Arendt, Hannah. 2006 [1963]. *Eichmann in Jerulsalem: A Report on the Banality of Evil.* London: Penguin.

Brant, George. 2013. *Grounded.* London: Oberon.

Bridle, James. 2018. *New Dark Age: Technology and the End of the Future.* London: Verso.

Butler, Judith. 2009. *Frames of War: When is Life Grievable?* London and New York: Verso.

Chamayou, Grégoire. 2015 [2013]. *Drone Theory.* Translated by Janet Lloyd. London: Penguin.

Dao, James. 2013. Drone Pilots Are Found to Get Stress Disorders Much as Those in Combat Do. *New York Times*, 23 February. https://www.nytimes.com/2013/02/23/us/drone-pilots-found-to-get-stress-disorders-much-as-those-in-combat-do.html.

ECCHR. 2017. Litigating Drone Strikes: Challenging the Global Network of Remote Killing. https://www.ecchr.eu/fileadmin/Publikationen/Litigating_Drone_Strikes_PDF.pdf.

Evans, Christine. 2015. Drones, Projections, and Ghosts: Restaging Virtual War in Grounded and You Are Dead. You Are Here. *Theatre Journal* 67 (4): 663–686.
Gibbs, Alan. 2014. *Contemporary American Trauma Narratives*. Edinburgh: Edinburgh University Press.
Gregory, Derek. 1994. *Geographical Imaginations*. Oxford: Blackwell.
Gregory, Derek. 2014. Drone Geographies. *Radical Philosophy*. January/February. https://www.youtube.com/watch?v=wfWsUqdVc4c.
Grewal, Inderpal. 2017. Drone Imaginaries: The Technopolitics of Visuality on Postcolony and Empire. In *Life in the Age of Drone Warfare*, ed. Lisa Parks and Caren Kaplan. Durham and London: Duke University Press.
Gros, Frédéric. 2019 [2013]. *The Security Principle: From Security to Regulation*. Translated by David Broder. London: Verso.
Harrop, Stephe. 2015. *Grounded*, Heracles and the Gorgon's Gaze. *Arion: A Journal of Humanities and the Classics* 23 (1): 169–185.
Jackson, Richard. 2005. *Writing the War on Terrorism: Language, Politics and Counter-Terrorism*. Manchester: Manchester UP.
Kaag, John, and Sarah Kreps. 2014. *Drone Warfare*. Cambridge: Polity Press.
Kapadia, Ronak K. 2017. *Insurgent Aesthetics: Security and the Queer Life of the Forever War*. Durham and London: Duke University Press.
Lacan, Jacques. 2006 [1949]. The Mirror Stage as Formative of the *I* Function in Psychoanalytic Experience. In *Écrits*, 75–81. Translated by Bruce Fink, with Héloïse Fink and Russell Grigg. New York and London: Norton.
Massey, Doreen. 2005. *For Space*. London, Thousand Oaks, and New Delhi: SAGE.
Massumi, Brian. 2015. *Ontopower: War, Powers, and the State of Perception*. Durham: Duke University Press.
Mbembe, Achille. 2019 [2016]. *Necropolitics*. Translated by Steven Corcoran. Durham: Duke University Press.
Meier, Inga. 2018. "Different Desert, Same War": The Simulacrum, the Real, and Drone Warfare in George Brant's Grounded. *Theatre Annual* 71:61–76.
Morrison, Elise. 2014. Ambushed by Empathy: George Brant's *Grounded*. *TDR: The Drama Review* 58 (4): 163–169.
Neocleous, Mark. 2014. *War Power, Police Power*. Edinburgh: Edinburgh University Press.
O'Gorman, Daniel. 2015. *Fictions of the War on Terror: Difference and the Transnational 9/11 Novel*. Basingstoke: Palgrave Macmillan.
Philippopoulos-Mihalopoulos, Andreas. 2015. *Spatial Justice: Body, Lawscape, Atmosphere*. Abingdon and New York: Routledge.
Pugilese, Joseph. 2017. How Drones Are Gamifying War in America's Casino Capital. *LSE US Centre Blog*. https://blogs.lse.ac.uk/usappblog/2017/09/15/how-drones-are-gamifying-war-in-americas-casino-capital/.
Ranciere, Jacques. 2011 [2008]. *The Emancipated Spectator*. London: Verso.

Samuel French Company. 2016. George Brant on Grounded, Interview, 4 January 2016. https://www.youtube.com/watch?v=wfWsUqdVc4c.

Shaw, Ian G. R. 2016. *Predator Empire: Drone Warfare and Full Spectrum Dominance.* Minneapolis and London: Minnesota University Press.

Sloterdijk, Peter. 2009 [2002]. *Terror from the Air.* Translated by Amy Patton and Steve Corcoran. Los Angeles: Semiotext(e).

Stanford International Human Rights and Conflict Resolution Clinic (IHRCRC), and Global Justice Clinic (GJC) at NYU School of Law. 2012. Living Under Drones: Death, Injury, and Trauma to Civilians from US Drone Practices in Pakistan. https://www-cdn.law.stanford.edu/wp-content/uploads/2015/07/Stanford-NYU-Living-Under-Drones.pdf.

Viskup, Jacqueline. 2017. Re-staging Surveillance Tragedy as Critical Resistance. In *Performance in a Militarized Culture*, ed. Sara Brady and Lindsey Mantoan. Abingdon: Routledge.

Weizman, Eyal. 2017. *Forensic Architecture: Violence at the Threshold of Visibility.* New York: Zone Books.

PART III

Disrupting Binaries: Self, Gender, Drone

CHAPTER 9

A Ghost in the Machine

Anne Scott Wilson

Background

If we imagine a top-down view on the world, and the power relations it begets, whether navigating with Google Maps as we drive across the digitised 'smart city', or the drone view of the city block that has just vaporised in Gaza City, we are wired to a new way of seeing the world dictated by a variety of technologies. Hito Steyerl suggests that from these aerial perspectives, we all are in freefall, in a scenario where the 'stable horizon', and a stable world with it, has been lost, because of a fundamental change in the way we orient ourselves in space. 'New types of visuality' are appearing through the increasing reliance on mapping, surveillance and artificial intelligence (AI) technologies that give us topographical overviews of where we sit in space and time—think Google Maps, satellite and drone perspectives. The illusion of linear perspective, and with it the horizon line, has been busted. What I point to in this text is a realignment of the tech to the body, where quite literally, I establish a horizontal dynamic of

A. S. Wilson (✉)
School of Communication and Creative Arts, Deakin University,
Burwood, VIC, Australia
e-mail: anne.wilson@deakin.edu.au

M. W. Azeem (ed.), *Human Rights in the Age of Drones*, Palgrave
Studies in Literature, Culture and Human Rights,
https://doi.org/10.1007/978-3-032-08191-9_9

vision and movement, as well as a shift in power relations between a performer and a drone. To follow Steyerl, we might analyse the performer and the drone as being in freefall, but together. In this tension, I argue, we find a potential moral view and emotional bond in the light of the technologies we seem to have ceded our vision to.

Numerous artists are offering critiques of the aerial view afforded by technologies in which the problem of our subjectivity gets stacked and jumbled with the tech we use to guide ourselves in the world. From Thomas Hirschorn's montage of war-torn bodies in his work *Touching Reality*, (2012) where we are inured to the horrors of dismembered, dead bodies to Pipliotti Rist's dream like affective positioning of the viewer in her largescale video projections, the eye has become ambient, detached from the retina and the moral view of what it witnesses. Drone cameras offer an 'out of body' perspective previously only possible by elaborate rigs. While military drone footage looks somewhat reduced in color and resolution, the drone camera can 'see' and rotate itself. It 'sees' more than the natural eye. 360-degree video cameras, capable of 8k resolution, can be trained to respond to human and non-human motion in the moment, offering viewers radically new and somewhat foreign visual patterns and rhythms. Additionally, AI now allows for more spontaneity in production as technology gets better, affording a more intuitive process for the artist.

With the help of new tools, artists can facilitate and mediate aspirational material. Artists like Wayne McGregor and Matthew Barney track and record movement patterns for different art contexts. McGregor, a contemporary choreographer, has been pioneering new ways to compose movement based on AI patterns derived from his DNA, which are then projected onto sculptures. His 2017 production '+/− human', made in collaboration with Random International, a programming company, utilised airborne pre-programmed 'balloons' in real-time swarming patterns triggering spontaneous choreographic patterns from the live dancers. In my project 'Seeing not Looking', I too responded to AI in real time, adapting to pre-programmed drone's movements and interactivity, which in turn reveal unexpected insights about power and ethics. Aside from the technical conditions that offer new processes, the aesthetics it produces are startling and seductive.

Large-scale LED light projections in galleries, for example, create a three-dimensional experience, pushing the boundaries of technology in profound ways. This mirrors the way the Eiffel Tower aesthetically exemplified technological progress and engineering capacities of the industrial revolution. Today artists like Refik Anadol use AI programming with real time data collection, to create awe-inspiring art, displaying movement patterns and light, which spill out from two-dimensional spaces into the audience in spectacular rhythmic motion and colour. In this way, art often showcases technological prowess. A quick survey of AI companies on the internet will inform you that in the near future military dominance will be defined by the performance of its algorithms. This may be one reason why the US Department of Defense has chosen Nvidia, the AI company that helps Anadol create 'the most boring dreams ever' as one of the recipients for funding from their new Advanced Robotics Manufacturing (ARM) institute (Lossin 2023).

While exploring the human desire that led to drone technologies is beyond this paper's scope, it is evident that these drones do not currently see or look in a human way. This echoes Gregoire Chamayou's argument in *A Theory of the Drone* that armed drones engage in identification that is generic rather than individual, often targeting innocent non-combatants. As technology becomes more attuned to human behaviour, the ethical and moral implications of its power over humans become increasingly problematic.

This project, using AI, drones, and video cameras, explores the binaries of us/them. The resulting video demonstrates how drone cameras, when removed from human control, interact with humans and what it means to be human when identity is mediated through automation.

Case Study

Excited by the prospect of an accessible (financial and functional) medium, I thought I could use the drone camera as if it were another actor, perhaps replicating human visuals of memory and imagination. I surmised that airborne footage, previously captured through complex rigs and out of helicopters and planes, could be improved upon by advanced capabilities of AI and the Osmo pocket camera attached to the drone. With its moveable eye and flying capabilities, it could be programed to respond to movement identified through sensors attached to human bodies. However, my expectations were dashed and instead of providing 'out of body' visuals an unexpected improvised narrative emerged that saw an uncanny relationship between the technology and the dancers, that as suggested, was more horizontal, than vertical. Based on this observation, I argue that power was not ceded to any one view, but distributed across a network of relations that included drone technicians, the artist (me), the performers and the drone. In this set of relations, I contend that an emotional and psychological bond became evident over seven days in the work, 'Seeing not Looking' (Fig. 9.1).

Initially, I attempted to use the drone camera to record imagery akin to mental visualisation used by dancers to remember sequences of choreography. By programming the drone in 3D space, I could integrate strange camera angles—a complex mnemonic function, to mentally connect physical technique with emotionally charged dance movements (Himberg et al. 2017). I thought technological innovations would reveal something that was impossible with older technologies. What I discovered was that the drone itself became intrusive. Eventually, however, our dancers, technicians and myself became enamored with the drone as if it were alive. Over the course of several days, emotions oscillated between anger, fear, affection and suspicion, serving to shape each performance (Fig. 9.2).

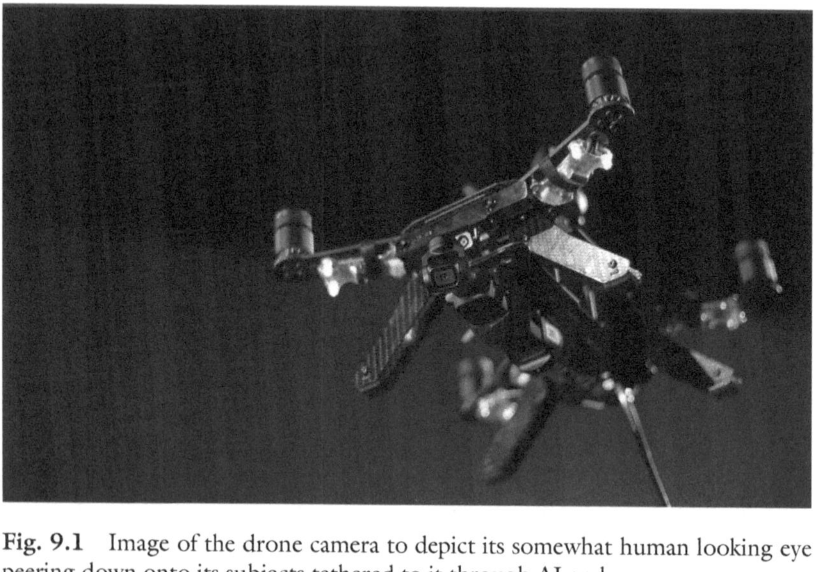

Fig. 9.1 Image of the drone camera to depict its somewhat human looking eye peering down onto its subjects tethered to it through AI and sensors

Fig. 9.2 Invitation to the premiere of 'Seeing Not Looking', 2021

Introduction

My art practice exists or emerges from the part of the imagination that is best described as the space between consciousness and dreaming. The actual time spent in the studio is underpinned by years of art practice, and by my career as a professional dancer, in which role my memories, emotions and imagination work simultaneously to guide my art practice.[1] My

[1] Artists such as Hito Steryl and Trevor Paglan provide a rich source of inspiration in their works and accompanying explanations, lectures and media that surround their practices. I

project began in an effort to harness, via video, a sense of embodied cognition,[2] imaging a virtual body by recording an imagined sequence (as a dancer) right before stepping on stage.

From my experience, emotionally charged dancing is a metaphoric conduit to transcend the body. I have found that emotions generate movement in the process of witnessing or performing dance. This aspect of inspired dance form distinguishes it from AI descriptors, such as movement, velocity, direction and so on. AI, in an art context, is a tool, like paint. At the same time, drone technology (AI) is perceived to threaten us with domination and control. Its panoptic view is more often regarded as controlling and surveilling rather than witnessing. Michael Richardson (2018) explores the drone in relation to the act of witnessing. Like a witness to a crime scene, a drone camera is assumed to be a recorder of truth, yet in a threatening way. It is confusing, because while we cannot trust a drone camera to be a medium of voracity; it sees from viewpoints that are unattainable to us, a god's eye view rendering humans as targets. By connecting dance, emotion, movement and the virtual body, could the drone camera, its AI language and function, be more clearly understood? (Fig. 9.3).

The Virtual and the Real

The drone camera can see us, but we cannot physically identify with how it works. Not only can it image or see better than us, but also its superior ability comes about through its programming—an alphabet of code we cannot naturally understand as a language. The language of AI is hidden within a virtual environment only accessible to programmers. As part of this project, I acknowledge and draw upon a virtual self that exists within me, within a kind of notional corporeal network of communication. Although imaginary, this virtual self is as real and important as my physical body when learning dance sequences. Repeated exposure to a mirror image teaches the dancer how to control, co-ordinate and perfect balance. A mental avatar emerges over years to assist, inspire, push and challenge the physical self.

work on a much smaller scale, yet think through similar problems using embodied knowledge that is the lived experience.

[2] Described by Evan Thompson (2015) as "always in process".

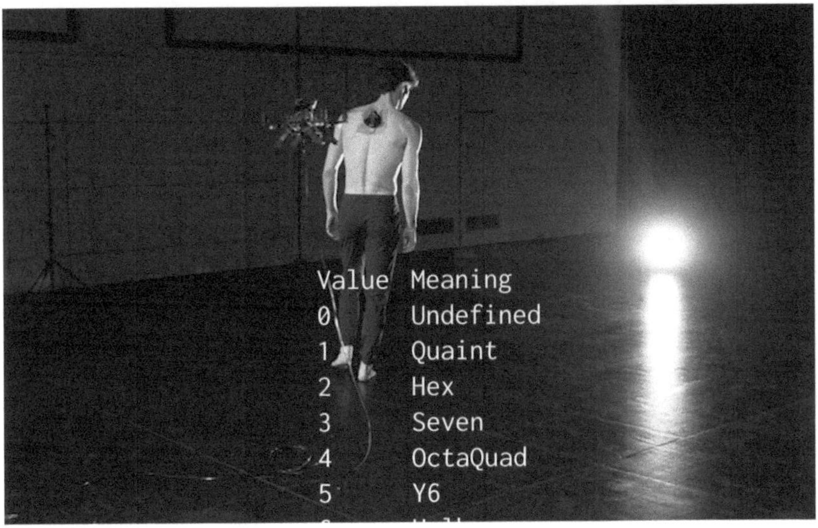

Fig. 9.3 video still from 'Seeing Not Looking', showing a juxtapose of coding language, the dancer, the sensor and the drone

My virtual self could perform perfect ballet technique. It assisted in acquiring mind/body coordination to form networks of communication (like cyberspace); its indefatigable capabilities diminishing the real self by contrast, messing with my sense of who I am, like a drone camera. The drone can see behind and in front at the same time—in dance this is called 'peripheral vision'—a critical ability required by a dancer in the corps de ballet. Space and motion is physically sensed, beyond one's own body, as group motion shifts and changes—the dancer must learn to adjust in the moment as if they have 'eyes in the back of their head'. Just as the drone camera is capable of flying, the virtual self defies gravity, performs technical feats, just out of reach of human capability. For example, to perform *grande jete* (big leap), I needed to have a mental image of my body taking off from the ground, hovering momentarily in the air, taking a breath while there, as if shocked, then landing like a feather, correctly taking the impact of gravity through the toes, metatarsal and the heel, holding my body weight away from the ground; my virtual self-performing in order to experience the movement in all its technical complexities. It provided a network, a conduit to other worlds, not unlike the way video games do.

My idealised body is formed through a desire to be something beyond myself. Not only is it physically superior to me—an idealised form—it draws together emotionally coherent dance sequences, making long compositions of dance feel effortless, as if second nature.

The virtual body evolved through actual performances and later helped to craft a choreographic practice. Today as an older person it is still with me, so much so that my physical body remembers what it now cannot do. I do ballet classes and it takes time to recover, my muscles and tendons pushed to their extreme once again. However, the fact that I still remember, through a mental imaging, and that my physical body engages muscle memory, attests to a sense of embodiment present in art practice.

In 2009, I tried to create a moving image that looked like the virtual self, by capturing an emotionally charged moment, a mental visualisation as if right before a stage performance. It was so difficult to achieve with the cameras of the time that I put the idea aside. After recently learning about the increased abilities of current technologies, I decided I wanted to try again.

The digital virtual world has a lot in common with my human virtual body, yet the differences emphasise some problems inherent in "the digital condition", a term coined by Felix Stalder (2018) which he exemplifies with an anecdote of unwittingly driving down a staircase following google maps.

To begin to unpack the emotional and psychological dimensions of the project, I will describe it.

The Project

The project started with a grant from the Australia Council for the Arts to integrate new technologies into my existing art practice. I have previously used video, sound, installation and performance in gallery and public contexts. I received a commission to make a work using AI—sensors that tracked individual audience members and triggered audiovisuals relative to their movements.[3]

This work challenged thoughts about audience participation. As the work came from a commission, I was obliged to try to fulfill the brief to draw out a physical real-time response in the viewing experience. Museum

[3] The artwork commission 'Every Day I Wait' accompanied 'Mao's Last Dancer' exhibition at the Museum of Brisbane, 2019.

of Brisbane feedback revealed that audiences danced in the museum and flash mobs came repeatedly to experience the work. I had aimed to evoke what it really feels like to do ballet, to transcend gravity momentarily and to experience emotionally charged dance. I worked with a programmer and technical staff at the museum and began to learn about the limitations and possibilities offered by new technologies. In addition, I had my ideas about audience participation, that art itself is enough to engage audiences, the works do not need any tricks or other intelligences to create an emotionally, intellectually and perceptually charged experience. Having seen how audiences responded to the commission, my preconceived ideas about what audience participation is and can be was challenged and the Australia Council grant allowed for further development to integrate this new knowledge into my practice. Supported by the newly formed ARS Electronica Australia, I was put into contact with digital technology specialists and I began to explore possibilities.

Perhaps the most difficult aspect of bringing AI into a visual art practice is that I can and prefer to operate as a solo entity. If I decided to use technology like a tool at the service of an idea, I needed to be able to communicate that idea to a programmer. The language of algorithms and ideas are so far apart, the chasm of comprehension lies in two distinctly different ways of thinking. One is a set of instructions brought about through a code I don't understand—the software together with the mechanics of the hardware, that is, the interface between the work and the audience in a gallery context. The other is where I simply imagine how I will explore a problem, draw the ideas, visualise various possibilities, test them out and maybe exhibit the works. The programmers and hardware specialists need to communicate what they can do within the parameters of the technology. I need to communicate my imagination, my thoughts; ideas that are often impossible to achieve physically.

While working with programmers I learnt about AI functions, binary thinking, feedback loops, and gaming technologies, and began to use these tools more frequently, contingent on funding and being able to communicate abstract ideas with programmers. 'Seeing Not Looking' (referred to as SNL for the remainder of the chapter) began after a conversation with programmers about how I had tried to capture a video of my virtual body. I explained that the technologies needed to do this well were not adequate then, and we surmised that with drone cameras it may now be possible.

We organised the project not being sure of what would emerge and approached it as an experiment. There was an element of the unknown for both the programmers and myself as we embarked on a five-day shoot in a studio with a seven-metre-high ceiling.

I searched for dancers who I thought could visually represent my virtual body—dancers accustomed to live performance, trained in ballet, robotic street dance, commercial dance and improvisation techniques. I describe this later in the chapter, as it is important how these qualities came into play over the period of the shoot and in the final work. I found two dancers who were capable and available to do the project, although only one dancer was available for the full five days. I worked with one dancer and a drone camera for the first few days.

I would give the dancers dramatic direction after each take and thought of the dancers as avatars—that is, an extension of my own body, at least my embodied memory that is in part unconscious and plays a part in how I directed the dancers. The drone camera was programmed with a sensor attached to its 'head', to track another sensor taped to the back of a dancer and travel at the same time. Starting with a choreographed sequence, I tried to stick to a method of filming each individual movement to capture how I visualised it. For example, if there was a step in which the head turned 90 degrees, I might see that through my virtual self, mentally imaged as starting from the base of the neck, in synchronicity with a sound in the music that is like a machine, a sound of metal on metal, a rhythm like a jack hammer. This image would be shot from a view of the base of the neck on the dancer's back, as well as from directly above, from the side and perhaps, given the nature of the movement—its mechanical sense. Sometimes it was shot from where the movement generated; for example, the solar plexus. The speed of that one shot might start quickly, then slow down, and then finish like a full stop, abruptly.

In reality, this detail was very difficult to achieve. The drone seemed to have a mind of its own, so instead of pursuing this detail, I eventually let go of my specific idea and allowed the human and artificial technologies take precedence.

If the technologies are thought of as a toolkit, it can help to explain how the imagery and performances present a way to explore what is actually happening between humans and AI.

The medium of AI *is* a toolbox much like paint. Just as paint, canvas and brushes have unique qualities, so do the programming, the space and dance styles, music and sounds. Each provides an opportunity to create form, but does not drive the project, yet informs it. The studio work using this toolkit created a library of media that I used, as if making a painting. But in the studio over the five days I began to learn about the medium, much like learning the difference between oil and acrylic paint, and I was able to use it while learning more about its limitations and possibilities.

Learning about the technology on the job offered a way for me to explore unconscious thoughts, feelings and subjectivities that influence our experience of the digital condition more broadly; however, it was only later that I could reflect on this.

The Toolkit

- Dancers
- Programmers
- Automated drone camera

  - Locked-off video camera (i.e. a camera on a tripod fixed in position)
  - A professional film studio with a lighting grid
  - Music used for the dancers to initiate movements

Dancers

In post 9/11 culture, the technologies we engage with are enmeshed into our experiences (Crawford and Paglen 2021) and I see the role of my project as revealing both how AI is training us and how we are affecting it. As stakes are the very things that cannot be measured as AI becomes more embedded into our lives. My thinking around this in the project was that beyond the emotional expression that dancers have unconsciously trained into their bodies, lies what has been, in my experience, a foundational quality of dance, that is to transcend the body.

Neural pathways form in humans through practice and repetition, a phenomenon found in machine learning[4] too (Mahesh 2020). The drone

[4]There are several different types of machine learning algorithms, including supervised learning, unsupervised learning, and reinforcement learning. In supervised learning, the algorithm is trained on a set of labelled data, where the correct outputs are known. Unsupervised learning, on the other hand, involves training the algorithm on unlabelled data, where the correct outputs are unknown. Reinforcement learning involves training the algorithm to learn through trial and error, using feedback from its environment. Its 'rein-

was programmed to do particular things, yet behaved unpredictably, partly because the dancers' movements helped to keep it airborne and partly because the drone and the dancers, through practicing repeatedly, learnt to know each other. This knowing occurred because of a deeply embedded body knowledge in the dancers, and I wondered whether the drone had some sort of consciousness like the robot in the baby chick experiment by Peoc'h (1995), which appeared to behave differently when it was with a living entity.[5]

In SNL, the symbiotic relationship between dancers and drone was a mash-up of two referents. The drone's referent was non-physical, while the dancer's was physical, and how we as a group apprehended the drone's movement encapsulated a dichotomy.

If the drone is airborne, its referent being non-physical, then the dancer learning to move in sympathy with the drone, learns the drone's programming. But as Stalder (2018) demonstrated, its 'alphabet', 'sentences' or 'syntax' cannot be known by the dancers. He cites a situation where, using his GPS, the route he followed led him to a flight of stairs—something only locals would have known—the map taking its information from a non-human source. The dancers and myself as dramaturg/dancer/artist cannot think of the project in terms of the language of the drone.

We start to embody a way of moving influenced by how the drone responds to human movement. At the beginning, it was simply a matter of the dancer learning to move in a particular way to keep the drone airborne. They needed to negotiate with each other through movement, how they would do this—if one dancer was more than 1 meter away from the drone they knew they were not in the recording, or rather they were partly in frame. As one dancer moved to allow the other dancer to come into frame, there were moments when the eye of the drone looked for something to reference. If it found nothing it would begin to descend, hover for a moment, then land. The purpose of the project evolved. It was now not to understand the language of the drone, but rather to see, through performance, how encountering the drone's behaviour, what human feelings are activated. That the emotions and drama are essential to

forcement learning' that mirrors dance training in how dancers repeat movements to perfect technique and master coordination and balance of the body in motion.

[5] It was found the robots, trained to respond to movement and space, stayed longer when the baby chicks were in the space than when they weren't. Baby chicks identify the first moving being as 'mother'.

the project is where the art has something new to offer in the discourse around cultural practices in the post 9/11 era. Studies into the politics of AI (machine training sets for example) implicate bias and presumption in how referents are labelled, while SNL facilitates human embodied cognition juxtaposed with a disembodied dead eye of the drone. The intensification of emotion and ways of moving focuses human with non-human movement, thus raising questions about human rights and dignity (Teo 2023).

Programmers

It is difficult to communicate ideas with programmers—not all programmers are equal. I found since making the first AI work that programming code is different from thinking through ideas. AI thinks through form and artists tend to think through ideas, imaginations, free association; the latter are philosophically driven. Reducing my original idea to make it understandable in binary code language was awkward and I found the problems of this manifested in the studio. The problems in communication then became the actual artwork.

Automated Drone Camera

The drone reduces humans to insects and humans reduce the drone to an insect. As we began to be dominated by the drone's presence, we thought of it as an insect or a living being, and the project took on a life of its own. It seemed as if we were forming a true relationship with the drone; as though we were affecting its behaviour through repeated practice and performance.

It is interesting to note that scientific experiments as far back as 1995 have shown that robots, programmed in algorithms similar to the drone, when put into a context of living beings, behave in unexpected ways. When baby chicks are born, they bond with the first moving thing they see, and in the experiment, it was found that a robot trained to move in a particular way also responded to the chicks, as if bonding with them over time and repeated exposure (Peoc'h 1995). I understand this phenomenon through quantum theory—simply that everything affects everything else at a quantum level, particularly within an observed/observer framework. Interestingly, recent experiments in neuroscience have revealed that theta waves, associated with memory and imagination, develop differently in a dancer's brain by repeated exposure to movement and music (Poikonen et al. 2018). When compared to a musician's brainwave activity, it was found that a dancer develops more strongly at a theta level. This indicates that emotions are closely linked to dance, memory, and imagination.

I needed the programmers with me in the studio to translate what the robot drone was doing, its limitations and capabilities. Using a type of inverse game technology, the drone was given a set of instructions that allowed it to be free from human control momentarily, thus creating a unique relationship between humans and the camera. Although the camera was tethered, to fulfil Occupational Health & Safety requirements, it was autonomous when recording the dancers. Three-dimensional space is a virtual precondition used for designing games.

When a game is being designed on a computer, the camera in virtual space usually stands in for the person playing the game, and the beings or animated characters are like the dancers with sensors. In this project, the programmers used real space instead of virtual space, thus inverting the process and allowing the drone to be free from human control at times. In reality, it felt something like watching an unsupervised toddler learning to play a game and learning rules through physical play. Thus, a virtual space familiar to a gamer became a real space and the drone camera, rather than standing in for the point of view (POV) of a gamer, was established in new physical relationship with the beings/characters it was following.

The dancers with the sensors could interact with the drone, released from its POV position, and freed to travel out of the virtual world it was designed within, into the real physical world of humans. Unlike drone warfare, where programmers remotely direct the drone and its sensors, in this case, the drone was given some agency (Fig. 9.4).

During the first shoot, which implemented a set of instructions for the drone to synchronise with the dancer's choreographed movements, the programmers and I began to see that certain dance movements destabilised the drone—ironically, the steps were robotic movements. The same movements humans use to emulate the machine caused the drone to shudder and lose its vision. A sensor on the drone's head was trained to see the sensor on a dancer's back, so as he moved, the drone's eye and body followed him. I submitted to technology, accepting its parameters that delineated what could and could not be done and began to rethink the project's aims.

I decided to let go of any idea of using a set choreography, and frame the project around a new set of rules that would allow the relationship

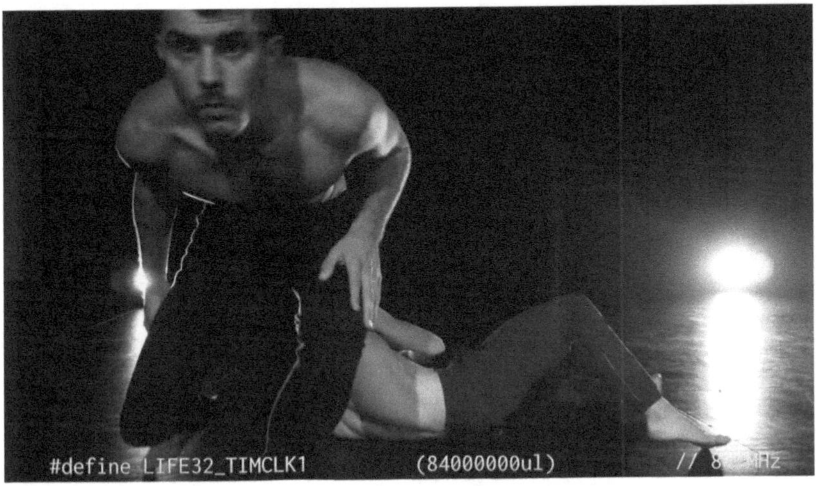

Fig. 9.4 Video still from the artwork 'Seeing Not Looking' showing code and bodily relationships between the two dancers navigating the eye of the drone spatially and with each other

between the programming and humans to be explored. Initially I started with just one dancer and the drone. The drone was programmed to travel in a diagonal direction, within a set space over about 30 seconds, while at the same time staying focused on the sensor on the dancer's back when he was 1 meter away. The dancer moved and travelled within the space defined by the drone's programming, so that a symbiotic relationship emerged in which the dancer was controlling the drone as the drone was controlling the dancer. Then after the dancer and the drone had practiced repeatedly, I introduced a second dancer. This meant that two dancers with sensors competed for the drone's attention and a physical game between the dancers and how they negotiated the drone's eye became a method of enquiry, pitching humans and AI in a live, spontaneous and unpredictable scenario (Fig. 9.5).

In order to see how we discovered more about the drone, I will describe the methods or rules used to construct the project after giving up on the initial idea.

Fig. 9.5 Video still from 'Seeing Not Looking' showing how it has been installed on a large screen. In this image the two figures are engaged in navigating the drone's eye in a dance-like relationship—changing places to keep the drone's eye on or off them

Rules of Engagement

1. Programming: drone camera looks at its target when a dancer is at 1 meter distance.
2. Dancers: two dancers have sensors on their backs, but the drone can only respond to one at a time, dependent on the dancer's distance from it.
3. Improvisation: dancers use improvisation techniques, responding to each other and to the drone, and do not consciously dance; rather they draw upon intuitive/instinctive responses to avoid creating habits born out of repeated performances and to draw out a more serendipitous quality. I assume the dancer's knowledge (even when not dancing) affects, colours and forms choreographic patterns, emphasising human/drone relationships.

4. Performance duration: the performance takes as long as it takes with no restriction on time.
5. Performance space: evolves over days as each entity negotiates how much space is available and its boundaries.
6. Dramaturgy: I exchange ideas about embodied human perspectives influencing actual movement/dance interactions.
7. The drone is considered through human terms: a body/being/machine that is like a partner for improvisation.
8. Drone rules: the drone is autonomous when shooting without direct human control.
9. Dance styles:

    (a) **Classical ballet** to engage techniques that help create movements akin to flight, as the drone is airborne. Classical ballet technique teaches dancers to momentarily defy gravity. From a metaphorical point of view, I think about defying gravity as a desire to be more than human. The desire to transcend our bodies is materialised in the drone itself, being a human creation; however, in classical ballet the desire to transcend materialises in stories of spirit figures and romantic notions of an afterlife, spelt out in ballet narratives—dramas of unrequited love, death and betrayal. To this end, the dancers I chose were at their physical peak and visually represented the possibility of achieving transcendence. In reality, classical ballet was never used overtly; it served as a precondition, as its form is what I understand in the virtual. Although ballet was not performed, the training affects human movement and sensibilities. Instead of a literal style of dance, our performances were improvised.
    (b) **Improvisation** responding to dramaturgical direction (Fig. 9.6).

A Symbiotic Relationship

At a subjective level, directing the dancers after each performance involved thinking of the drone as both a machine and a living being. We began to feel the drone's presence and understood it through unconscious identification with our bodies. By thinking of it as an insect, we anthropomorphised it. As the project developed over time, emotionally charged moments directed each take.

Fig. 9.6 Dancer keeping the drone airborne

The performances became more dramatic each time. We set the drone off, with its tracking function in the camera operating alongside the sensors. Then once it was flying, the dancer/s became more aware each time of how they were both being controlled and were controlling the drone. At this point the drone morphed into a living being in my mind and I conveyed this idea more emphatically with each take to the dancers.

After several takes and over the final two days, I asked the dancers to stop dancing, to see more clearly what was happening within each body. By removing 'dancing' altogether, whether learnt through improvisation technique or more formal contemporary or classical training, our focus laid solely upon the programmed fully automated movements and the dancers. If I took out any aspect of the performance that distracted from their interactions, I surmised that something interesting would happen. And it did. Each dancer seemed to be both captured and capturing (also keeping the drone airborne). In knowing that they were keeping the drone in flight, a dramatic relationship between them emerged. If one dancer was in the frame of the drone, they would keep the other dancer out of the drone's eye and its programming. While the drone's eye, its camera and sensor looked at one dancer, that dancer's movements were being controlled. If the dancer moved too sharply, changed direction too quickly or moved outside the delineated space—the dimensions factored into the original programming—and there was no other sensor for the drone to connect with, the drone lost its way. It would start to look for a body and

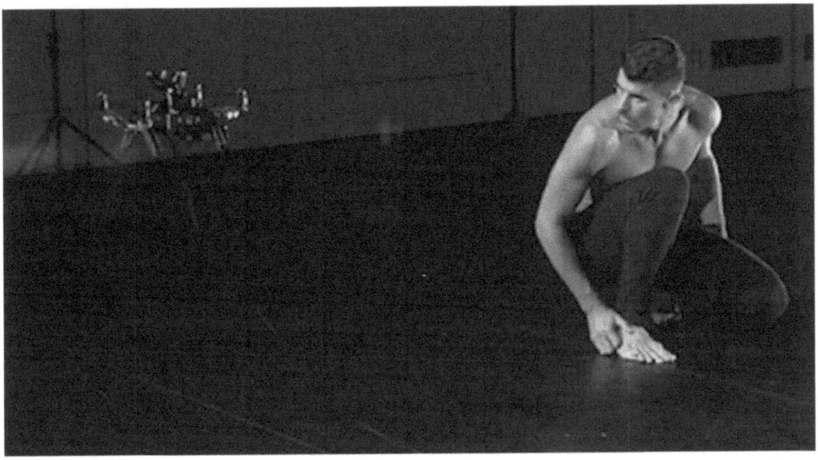

Fig. 9.7 Here the dancer is learning about how the drone sees them and learning how to move to keep it alight

at times focused on a shape made by the lights on the ground behind thinking it was a human shape. It would then fly towards the ground and eventually land, if it was not caught by one of the dancers before (Fig. 9.7).

The framing in the footage was fragmented and strange; while editing one scene into another I needed to sustain a flow of movement, which meant putting together different times, i.e. different takes and different cameras. This destabilised a sense of the human body, removing it from its groundedness and formed a choreography of shadow bodies, drone bodies and the dancers' fragmented bodies.

The two dancers with sensors therefore negotiated with each other over who was keeping the drone flying and how. Over a few improvised performances a Shakespearean drama[6] played itself out between the dancers as one dancer sacrificed himself to either allow the other dancer to remove themself from the scenario, thus completing one take, or by one dancer choosing to hold the drone's attention and allow the other to escape the drone's eye. Over several takes, a choreography of looping, falling,

[6] Shakespeare's plays are recognised as ground-breaking in how they depict the human condition through dramatic structure, plots and intense human relationships and in the same way the power of the drone enabled by human play forces new relationships between humans as demonstrated in the artwork.

holding and weaving began to create drama. Our attention was held amid moments of accumulated energy, emotional highs and lows, ebbs and flows, dynamic playfulness and serious, deeply felt dramatics.

Like an unsupervised toddler, the drone camera seemed to be learning the job within its spatial and behavioural limitations in respect of how the dancers moved. A purpose of AI is to give a computerised system agency. AI is excellent at chess and technically better than humans, but humans can change the rules spontaneously. Rather than connecting with the drone camera through us/them binary thinking, the project enabled a symbiotic relationship, offering a way to explore how we affect technology and how it affects us—at a physical and emotional level.

The catalogue essay that accompanies the artwork (video 'Seeing not Looking'), written by Jondi Keane, breaks down how embodied cognition is interdependent upon symbiotic relationships—the virtual (both my own as a director and the drone's). As dramatic as the performances became, it is by reflecting on those moments when it appears that dancer's movements are being controlled, partly by the programming of the drone and partly through how each dancer negotiated their movement relative to the drone.

A Drone's Sense of Self

The way the virtual world is disconnected from the physical world is described by Stalder as part of the digital condition and one of three elements that are influencing how technology is impacting culture and politics.[7]

I had thought of artificial and human intelligence in opposition: humans as emotional and AI as purely technical. Now I understood differently.

[7] Amid a confusing plurality, Felix Stalder argues that there are three key constituents of this condition: the use of existing cultural materials for one's own production, the way in which new meaning is established as a collective endeavour, and the underlying role of algorithms and automated decision-making processes that reduce and give shape to massive volumes of data. These three characteristics define what Stalder calls "the digital condition". Of the first, "the use of existing…" the lack of a physical referent relates to my project in that human bodies have the drone as a thing to refer to – its physicality as a whole makes up a referent. The drone, by contrast, is programmed in a virtual space – it exists in that virtual world as distinct from the physical one dancers respond to and refers only to itself, its programming and algorithms.

> All of us are already civilian soldiers, without knowing it ... The great stroke of luck for the military class's terrorism is that no one recognizes it. People don't recognize the militarized part of their identity, of their consciousness. (Virilio 1983: 18)

I understand now that engagement with AI in SNL enables humans to think and move differently and in synergy with the drone, thus internalising its effect on us as we adapt to its limitations. Could we extend this idea to Virilio's and be internalising terrorist ploys unwittingly, as if AI is training us? Just as a dancer learns through observation of a mirror image, drone imagery fashions a sense of self. While AI can produce a virtual body that interacts with human bodies, it cannot reproduce the desire to transcend, which also can be aligned with the fear of death. If we fully transcend the gravitational pull, either we are in space or we are dead, and so I think of this desire as a way of contemplating death. It is exhilarating as a dancer to fly momentarily, but it is not something that can be sustained. By contrast, the body of the drone can exist beyond gravity for long periods.

In anthropomorphising the drone, we identify with what we know. This thinking raises rhetorical questions about the drone. Where is the drone born? Who are its parents? From a human perspective, the lack of referents in virtual reality is the cornerstone of the problems and tensions inherent in post 9/11 culture more broadly, and specifically in SNL (Stalder 2018). The videos recorded during each 'performance' have been cut together with footage from three cameras to reflect a destabilised body.

We are changing through our exposure to and use of drones in cinema, everyday consumer use or as a surveillance tool. Our constant exposure to its imagery and how it operates in relation to our experience of the world, and our groundedness by contrast, alter our sense of embodiment. As predicted by Virilio (1983) and others, the technological revolution developed for military purposes perilously threatens our understanding of what it is to be human, yet it offers new ways of moving, a new choreographic language and new ways of relating to each other.

My project opened up this conversation and my thoughts about technology and distrust of how it images humans shifted from binary thinking into a more complex relationship. The project itself reveals tensions and power inequalities inherent in human/artificial technologies.

The Drone of Art History

As an artist, I am aware of how deconstructing dance makes way for new ways of moving, to choreograph and to process the physical world. When I performed I remembered sequences in both a technical and emotional way. My notations of sequences only made sense to me; I had my virtual self to rely upon, and my way of putting movements into a written form helped me to remember them. The notes were a kind of shorthand and I used diagrams and words to trigger memory. AI programming of movement patterns is much more precise; however, my project eventually challenged the function of AI by including unpredictable human emotions.

Artists such as Merce Cunningham have given audiences agency in real time to direct a performance.[8] Like Sol Lewitt, whose instructions allowed for his artworks to be made by others, the drone's programming reads and reproduces movement patterns. Movement scores can be reconfigured and materialised in various forms. My project has intentionally problematised this by using the sensors to track unpredictable human movement/dance. It was easy to destabilise the drone, but the tensions in keeping the performance going tested the limits of humans. I wanted to see what was left in human terms in my project, i.e. what cannot be measured as data.

In reducing dance to movement, we as the audience can experience these tensions. However, reducing dance to a movement makes it fodder for data harvesting.

Dance as a Language

I was a live performer for 30 years before transitioning into visual art. My embodied approach has been formed out of years of choreographing performances and performing. Today, I work with professional dancers because dance is a language, as distinct from movement. Years of practice, developing mind–body coordination skills, as distinct from sport, produces a very human quality that cannot easily be measured as data.

I started with a set of movements choreographed for the drone camera, thinking I could participate in the design of algorithms in collaboration

[8] Merce Cunningham embraced 'chance' in various ways. For example dancers could choose which sequence they would perform, when they would enter or exit. Common time is the binding principle in Cunningham methods. Another expression of using chance is when audience members (1964) were given cards, coins or other items and would be asked to flip them and this would direct the sequence within the live performance.

with a programming team, thus directing the drone eye to record subjective imagery constructed through my imagination.

I chose dancers who could perform a 'robot' dance, knowing this was absurd, yet I was curious about what would happen. I choreographed a small piece in collaboration with the dancers. I also selected dancers who had performed on stage professionally and were proficient in classical ballet, so as to draw upon different styles. I realised that a dancer's ability in live performance and emotionally engaged dance encapsulate what it is to be human, in contrast with the AI of the drone. Performing to a live audience develops emotionally charged movements that are distinct from a set of instructions given to a drone. Studies show that interactions between audience and performer affect the performance and this quality has a strong relationship with how a choreographed sequence is remembered (Bachrach et al. 2015; Himberg et al. 2017). Additionally, methods of remembering a dance performance are imbued with emotions; it was that aspect of professional dance practice that I was trying to capture in all its complexity.

Why Use Skilled Dancers and Not Pedestrian Movers with the Drone?

As the purpose of the project shifted and I was prepared to accept a certain amount of failure, the drone's presence became subsuming—we all, at some stage began focusing on the drone, anthropomorphising it. The purpose of the project changed and the point of using trained dancers came into question. Given that choreographic sequences were no longer needed, what difference would it make if they were not trained dancers? Does using trained dancers provide more understanding of how a drone camera sees us? It is important to discuss this in light of thinking through us/them binaries and the cultural context of drones in post 9/11 culture, because the algorithms produced out of machine learning mimic human functionally, especially in dance techniques such as ballet, which is a tightly scripted geometric and kinetic form.

For this project, I chose to work with those who have performed to an audience with other bodies. At the heart of this choice is the idea of language. Pitching two different yet highly developed languages onto the performance framework itself emphasises what is happening between humans and technology today. For example, the drone is automated through a set of instructions expressed in algorithmic code and dancers through technical embodied knowledge. AI is as a new language. This highly specialised form of language (see *The New Alphabet* HKW[9] 2019—a three-year program exploring algorithmic code) needs to be pitched against another equally specialised form of language—that which trained dancers possess, to make trouble for it and attempt to expose its characteristics.

Algorithms and the Language of Movement

An alphabet contains the singular elements which by themselves mean nothing, but when put together form relationships with each other. In artistic terms they may be thought of as concepts. In my project, the relationships between each element described in "The Rules of Engagement" section were where the problems between humans and technology revealed themselves.

The dancers' bodies intuit the drone's eye. They move, but they also dance in tangent with the drone because the drone's ability to stay airborne is partially controlled by how the dancers move. This relationship spells out a deeper problem about our human desire to transcend our body and defy gravity. Metaphors inherent in signification of gravity and ground are controlled by the drone, mediating metaphoric meaning at the same time. This speaks in a way to issues at stake in post 9/11 culture relating to "the digital condition" (Stalder 2018).

As mentioned earlier, recent studies in neuroscience reveal that dancers' brains develop differently from those of non-dancers at the theta level. Theta brainwaves are connected with emotion and memory (Poikonen et al. 2018; University of Helsinki 2018). Can AI only read and learn within physical parameters or is it possible that dancers bear witness to something beyond the physical, which in turn affects AI? Is there something beyond the technical/material/human/machine relationships that are evolving as humans become enmeshed in new technologies in every aspect of their life?

At the core of this project is dance—it is human, it is emotional, it speaks of desire by the very nature of its form, that is, like ballet technique

[9] Haus der Kulturen der Welt (HKW) is a pluri-disciplinary institution in Berlin whose work centers around the practices of visual arts, performative arts, sonic/music, architecture, literature and oraliture, as well as scientific and cultural discursive formats.

developed in part from a desire to defy gravity, so the trained dancer today embodies and develops, both physically and emotionally, through dance experiences and can be trained to achieve desires beyond the physical, i.e. to be airborne, to fly even momentarily. This comes from something that is entrenched in the human condition, in the search for purpose and knowledge of our mortality, the search for something beyond ourselves where the spiritual body or dreaming body is weightless.

Conclusion

Research into data harvesting of human biologies and neuroscience provide hope for medicine. Baudrillard (2005) and Virilio (1983) wrote about a post-human condition predicted as a result of technology, and others today are taking a philosophical position on what has been labelled "the digital condition" (Stalder 2018). What Baudrillard and Virilio predicted is further clarified in the new label in the twenty-first century and points to what is revealed through this artwork.

Drone cameras are not only capable of surveillance (from a god-like perspective), but they can also interact with humans through video-game programming. Our team learnt about the drone through repeated use. The dancers began to move in new ways. I initially thought of drones as bad military machines reflecting evil intentions of certain humans for the destruction of humanity, and as criminal beings that steal identity through surveillance. After the project, I realised that AI is constantly influencing our sense of identity. I directed the dancers through my response to the drone and my history as a dancer. I felt the drone's movements from my own memory of dance as distinct from movement. I did not think of dance as movement, but rather as a tool to investigate human drama, vulnerabilities and emotions, brought about through the ways each of us were relating to the drone over time.

By distinguishing between movement and dance, between emotions and intellect, between irrational and rational thought processes, between sleep and awake thinking and embodied cognition, the SNL project highlights what cannot be harvested as data and processed by technology. The project brought into focus what it is about identity that we give value to and why. The unknown may also be irrational and invisible, as is AI, yet identifying AI as the other, begs the question: do we unconsciously adopt binary thinking, mimicking programming? Do we begin to take what was once considered mysterious, unknowable, sublime in the human condition and unwittingly turn the wonder of thinking or pondering what extends beyond the body into binaries—finite measurements explainable through programming? The drone work in this experiment sought to visualise an emotionally charged dance, a virtual body. It eventually materialised as a sequence of destabilised images of bodies moving, bodies ungrounded and blowing around like the wind, struggling to find both the ground and a sense of something beyond gravity. The title, Seeing not Looking alludes to the ability to see yet not look, as looking is a human trait.

The word *look* could be applied to face-recognition technology on the camera of the drone and to the sensors programmed to find those on human bodies or targets. Does a drone look? I chose the title after being inspired by a story written by Oliver Sacks (1993) of two people who recovered sight after surgery, but only one could actually see. Sacks puts this down to the fact that to see one must want to see, to look. We know drones are machines without human desire, yet our desire to anthropomorphise them into something we can get to know confuses us. We cannot engage with their programming, so we try to know it through embodied knowledges. AI is hidden—its alphabet is only known by its experts and yet it has such a strong influence on us.

When the work is installed, it pilots the audience in ebbs and flows, stutters and groundless territories, where shadows stand in for the real body of the dancers, and the drone is the third performer. Each seems to re-spatialise the viewer, who is also implicated as an actor in a performance, relative to the architecture of the gallery. It's a new mapping that occurs in the gallery. In this picture of the gallery work, the figures dominate the viewer and, depending on where and how the viewer sees and hears their human experiences, subjectivities and embodied knowledges are activated in particular ways (Fig. 9.8).

The danger comes when digital data is fed back into itself, ever more reducing the possibility of being aware of what cannot be measured—those human things that lie beyond the physical. That dancers' brains develop differently compared with those of non-dancers through theta wave activity and conditioning, is both confirming and worrying. If we can identify through AI theta wave activity known to be connected to memory and imagination, both ephemeral qualities, what kind of rational extrapolation will be made by researchers in the future and how will that knowledge be used?

This project has explored these tensions—both the beautiful and the anxious, frightening aspects of drones—through a dramatic lens using

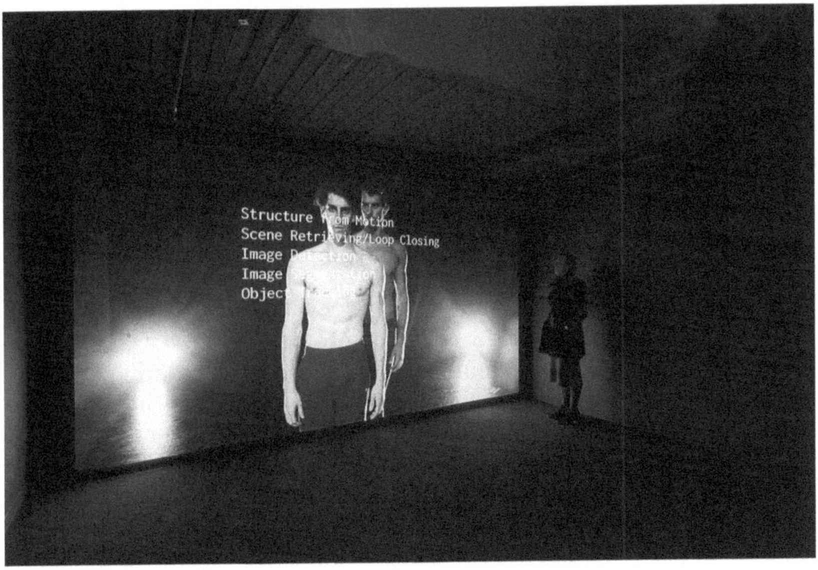

Fig. 9.8 Shows the scale of the virtual bodies in relation to the audience's body

embodied dancers who are aware of how emotions inspire dance, and using that to partner or improvise with the drone. It has provoked more questions. The science experiment with the baby chicks raises further questions: beyond the physical and mechanical, are we, as we observe and interact with the drone, causing an affect that cannot be rationally understood or analysed?

Neuroscientific tests showing theta waves develop differently in those who train and perform in dance, over a sustained period, point to something beyond what we know and expect. By this I mean science reveals something about embodied cognition and has measured theta waves in dancers under certain conditions to prove its findings (Poikonen et al. 2018).

James Bridle (2019) proposes human/technological development and its relationship to human rights, and is heavily influenced by the human tendency to see intelligence in a restricted way. He proposes that human rights and ethical development need to realign so humans take into account other intelligences we cannot understand and he gives an example of slime mould being used by engineers to design public transport routes—a task it is claimed cannot be done as fast by AI. Scientists do not understand how the single cell being does what it does—it seems irrational. Regardless, the ability to fully comprehend it hasn't stopped the awareness of its existence being included in developing humane designs for the benefit of humans. Artistic practice is also not necessarily rational in its design. I sense we affect the drone camera depending on how we choose to interact with it and through interaction can choose to use it for good or bad. I can further think through how identity is being framed in visuals, the implications of the interactivity with drones and humans in artistic terms, and begin to clarify what is beyond measurement and how and why in human terms this needs to be protected from data harvesting. While we embrace new technologies in art practice, it offers both an opportunity to reimagine the world we live in and a tsunami of knowledge that can neither be absorbed intuitively or without risk to humanity. "Four key interpretations of human dignity are identified, namely: non-instrumentalisation of the human person; the protection of certain vulnerable classes of persons; the recognition and exercise of inherent self-worth (including the exercise of individual autonomy); and a wider notion of the protection of humanity" (Teo 2023). In dance, human dignity is expressed through movement that can be influenced by AI bringing into play 'non instrumentalization of the human person'—and the incessant drive towards technological progress needs to be in collaboration with human rights, taking into account other intelligences (Bridle 2019). Whether AI within drone cameras is used in surveillance or to create a more intelligent being than a human, its dead eye creates power imbalances, and, as my project has revealed, enables violation of human rights with almost complete impunity.

References

Bachrach, A., Y. Fontbonne, C. Joufflineau, et al. 2015. Audience Entrainment During Live Contemporary Dance Performance: Physiological and Cognitive Measures. *Frontiers in Human Neuroscience*, 5 May. www.frontiersin.org/articles/10.3389/fnhum.2015.00179/full.

Baudrillard, J. 2005. *The Intelligence of Evil or the Lucidity Pact*. London: Berg.

Bridle, James. 2019. *New Dark Age: Technology and the End of the Future*. Unabridged ed. Tantor Media.

Crawford, Kate, and Trevor Paglen. 2021. Excavating AI: The Politics of Images in Machine Learning Training Sets. *AI & Society: Journal of Knowledge, Culture and Communication* 1–12, 8 June 2021. https://doi.org/10.1007/s00146-021-01162-8.

Haus der Kulturen der Welt (HKW). 2019. The New Alphabet 2019–2021. https://www.hkw.de/en/programm/projekte/2019/das_neue_alphabet/das_neue_alphabet_start.php.

Himberg, T., K. Förger, M. Niinisalo, et al. 2017. Social eMotions: Exploring Emotional Expression and Contagion in Contemporary Dance. In *ESCOM 2017 Proceedings: Expressive Interaction with Music*, ed. E. Van Dyck. Belgium: Ghent University.

https://www.hkw.de/en/. 2 July 2023.

https://www.kennedy-center.org/education/resources-for-educators/classroom-resources/media-and-interactives/media/dance/merce-cunningham%2D%2Dbiped/. 2 July 2023.

Lossin, R. H. 2023. Refik Anadol's "Unsupervised", Review Museum of Modern Art, MOMA, November 19, 2022–April 15, 2023E Flux Criticism, 29 May. https://www.e-flux.com/criticism/527236/refik-anadol-s-unsupervised.

Mahesh, B. 2020. Machine Learning Algorithms—A Review. *International Journal of Science and Research (IJSR).* https://www.researchgate.net/publication/344717762_Machine_Learning_Algorithms_-A_Review.

Peoc'h, R. 1995. Psychokinetic Action of Young Chicks on the Path of an Illuminated Source. *Journal of Scientific Exploration* 9 (2): 223–229.

Poikonen, H., P. Toiviainen, and M. Tervaniemi. 2018. Dance on Cortex: Enhanced Theta Synchrony in Experts When Watching a Dance Piece. *The European Journal of Neuroscience* 47 (5): 433–445.

Richardson, M. 2018. Drone Capitalism. *Transformations* 31:79–98.

Sacks, O. 1993. A Neurologist's Notebook: To See and Not to See. *The New Yorker*, 10 May.

Stalder, F. 2018. *The Digital Condition*. Translated by V. A. Pakis. Cambridge: Polity Press.

Teo, S. A. 2023. Human Dignity and AI: Mapping the Contours and Utility of Human Dignity in Addressing Challenges Presented by AI. *Law, Innovation & Technology* 15 (1): 241–279.

Thompson, E. 2015. *Waking, Dreaming, Being: Self and Consciousness in Neuroscience, Meditation, and Philosophy.* New York: Columbia University Press.

University of Helsinki. 2018. Dancers' Brains React Quickly to Changes in Music and Display Brain Frequencies Linked to Emotion and Memory Processes. *NeurosicenceNews*, 4 May 2018. http://neurosciencenews.com/dancer-brain-music-memory-emotion-8965/.

Virilio, Paul. 1983. *Pure War* (p. 18). New York: Semiotext(e).

CHAPTER 10

Transgressing Boundaries: Exploring the Warfare Drone in Contemporary Art Through the Gothic Lens

Susanne Schwertfeger

Drones in Contemporary Art: Navigating Aesthetics and Context After 9/11

The rise of drones as a subject in art and their growing use in both civilian and military capacities can be directly linked to the aftermath of 9/11. After the terrorist attacks, the United States accelerated the development and deployment of drones, particularly for military purposes. Drones became a cornerstone of counterterrorism strategies, enabling targeted strikes in regions like Afghanistan, Pakistan, and Yemen. Their prominence in military operations influenced public and artistic awareness of drones as tools of power and surveillance.

Drones were used extensively by the United States in the Iraq War, marking one of the early large-scale integrations of unmanned aerial vehicles (UAVs) into modern warfare. This war introduced a nocturnal

S. Schwertfeger (✉)
Christian-Albrechts-Universität, Kiel, Germany
e-mail: schwertfeger@kunstgeschichte.uni-kiel.de

M. W. Azeem (ed.), *Human Rights in the Age of Drones*, Palgrave Studies in Literature, Culture and Human Rights,
https://doi.org/10.1007/978-3-032-08191-9_10

aesthetic to media coverage, with green-tinted night vision imagery dominating the visual narrative of modern warfare, symbolizing technological supremacy and surveillance dominance, for their equipment allowed only US soldiers "to see order in the nocturnal chaos" (Robben 2011). Therefore, night vision footage highlighted the asymmetry of conflict, portraying US forces as almost omnipotent observers and actors in a technologically driven battlefield. The eerie glow of night vision created a surreal and almost cinematic representation of war, representing both reality and spectacle in public perception. This aesthetic marked a shift in war reporting, emphasizing remote control and invisibility, aligning with the broader cultural impact of post-9/11 security and surveillance technologies.

Drones also expanded into civilian applications, such as agriculture, and logistics, and post-9/11 culture is marked by heightened surveillance and the militarization of daily life. So much so that the commercial trend agency deathtostock recently on their Instagram account titled one of their posts "Panopticore", of course referring to Jeremy Bentham's Panopticon. This theoretical architectural design was intended for institutional surveillance, such as prisons. Its key feature is a central observation tower surrounded by cells, allowing a single observer to monitor all inmates without them knowing whether they are being watched (Foucault 2010). Deathtostock stated that "Surveillance is being aestheticized across social media, with brands and artists embracing voyeurism for views. In the process, society has to be contend [sic] with being constantly perceived and potentially broadcast to millions in any unsuspecting moment" (deathtostock 2024).

This dual-purpose technology intertwines civilian and military applications, a theme often explored in art. Warfare drones raise significant human rights concerns, particularly regarding the loss of accountability in targeted killings and the high risk of civilian casualties. Their use often operates in a legal and ethical gray zone, challenging international law and amplifying fears of unchecked power dynamics and the erosion of personal privacy (Human Rights Watch 2021). Drones became both literal and metaphorical extensions of these phenomena. In the introduction to the catalog *To See Without Being Seen* from 2016, the author states, "We are in the dawn of the drone age, a turning point in history when the technology of surveillance and remote engagement is changing the way we live and understand the world" (Malone 2016). A few years later, Michael J. Boyle adopted this as an established fact with the title *The Drone Age* for his exploration on "how drone technology will change war and peace" (Boyle 2020). In the realms the broadened range of applications, influenced by technological advancements and expanding applications in various sectors, an increase in production and sales volumes supports this notion. Military drone development has also seen remarkable advancements. The use of UAVs in warfare can be traced back to the early twentieth century. Round about 50 years later, drones became popular as a means of surveillance. With the Persian Gulf War in 1991, the drone became one of the most essential operational tools after the United States had used it extensively for reconnaissance (Kakaes 2015). The Russia–Ukraine conflict has further highlighted the strategic use of drones.

The rising accessibility and enhanced capabilities of drones have raised ethical and legal concerns, including privacy violations, autonomous targeting, and potential misuse in civilian and military contexts (Cavallaro et al. 2012). These concerns are increasingly reflected in contemporary art. Artists are engaging with those implications of the drone, and numerous notable exhibitions curated around the topics and the technical object, like *Fire and Forget: On Violence* (2015, Berlin, Germany), or the already mentioned *To See Without Being Seen* (2016, St. Louis, USA) as well as *The World of Drone Art*, a virtual Exhibition accompanying the Being Human Festival in Sheffield, England, in 2020. This artistic engagement reflects a broader dialogue about how drones embody power structures, question ethical boundaries, and explore the intersections of technology and humanity.

The Gothic: Themes and Concepts

But how are the Gothic, an enduring literary genre that emerged in the eighteenth century, and the questions of the twentieth century and its art connected? The Gothic is often characterized by its dark atmospheres and an inventory of familiar motifs, such as decaying castles, hidden passageways, and mysterious happenings. These tropes created a formulaic structure that defined the perception of early Gothic literature for authors, critic, and readers. An anonymous critic in 1798 humorously encapsulated this approach, presenting Gothic fiction as a 'recipe':

> Take—An old castle, half of it ruinous.
> A long gallery, with a great many doors, some secret ones.
> Three murdered bodies, quite fresh.

> As many skeletons, in chest and presses.
> An old woman hanging by the neck, with her throat cut.
> Assassins and desperados, *quant. suff.*
> Noises, whispers, and groans, threescore at least. (Anonym 2000 [1798])

Today, the Gothic is understood on a more abstract level, transcending its surface inventory to explore themes of radical boundary transgression (Botting 1996). From the collapse of physical and metaphysical borders to the destabilization of identity, Gothic literature serves as a vehicle to confront fears of the unknown, unravel societal anxieties, and question the limits of the human experience. Even early texts such as Horace Walpole's *The Castle of Otranto* (1764), *The Fall of the House of Usher* (1839) by Edgar Allan Poe, and Mary Shelley's *Frankenstein* (1818) exhibit these aspects. The following analysis uses these texts as examples of boundary transgressions in Gothic literature, establishing a foundation to later connect them to contemporary art that explores drones as a theme.

However, this text argues, that two additional concepts are central to the Gothic, and are also central to the understanding of the drone: Sigmund Freud's notion of the Uncanny, which explains psychological responses to unsettling, repressed phenomena, and the Sublime, as an experience of overwhelming sensory grandeur. While the Sublime evokes awe through grandeur and overwhelming power, the uncanny elicits terror through disruption and unease. Yet, the two concepts frequently overlap in Gothic literature. Freud's concept of the Uncanny was introduced in his 1919 essay *Das Unheimliche.* It explores the unsettling experience when something familiar becomes eerily unfamiliar (Freud 1919). He associates the uncanny with repressed fears or desires resurfacing in distorted forms. Central to this idea is a paradox: the Uncanny arises from what is simultaneously known yet hidden, creating a sense of discomfort. The Uncanny is a cornerstone of Gothic literature, which thrives on exploring liminal spaces where the ordinary morphs into the extraordinary.

The Gothic also intersects with the Sublime, an aesthetic category that grapples with extremities of human emotion. The Sublime describes an overwhelming emotional response to something vast, powerful, or awe-inspiring, often linked to nature or experiences of grandeur. Philosophers Edmund Burke and Immanuel Kant explored the tension between fear and admiration, evoking both terror and beauty (Burke 1792). The concept relies on a safe distance from the object of fear, allowing the observer to experience awe without direct physical threat. Whether trough reading of a Gothic novel or the contemplation of the size of the universe and the realization of one's own insignificance: terror is mediated through imagination or perception rather than immediate danger. Crucially, the Sublime is never linked to bodily harm but instead thrives on the tension concerning admiration and fear, contained within a framework of safety (Morley 2010).

A striking example of this is a photograph that combines vibrant atmosphere with subtle but unsettling elements, inviting deeper reflection on the underlying themes (Fig. 10.1): Trevor Paglen's *Untitled* (2010) welcomes us with a warm, inviting mood. The image is visually divided into two distinct segments based on color: the lower portion is dominated by yellow and ochre tones, while the upper is imbued with pale blue hues. White structures serve as intermediaries between these zones. This segmentation recalls the American color field painting of the 1950s and 60s,

Fig. 10.1 Trevor Paglen: *Untitled* (2010); Chromogenic print, National Gallery of Art, Washington

and the picture could easily be seen as nonfigurative. Upon closer examination, however, the subject reveals itself as a depiction of the sky. What first appeared as abstract streaks become clouds and contrails illuminated by sunlight. This newfound recognition invites comparisons to Caspar David Friedrich's art or, given the atmospheric phenomena, to J. M. W. Turner's *Rain, Steam, and Speed* (1844). While the viewer's gaze traverses the surface of the artwork, a persistent sense of disorientation emerges. The absence of spatial markers provides no geographical anchors, leaving the viewer untethered in their perception. This phenomenon intensifies as one moves closer to the piece, where the edges of the print dissolve from view.

However, a small dark point disrupts the harmony produced by the interplay of light and color and the impression of overwhelming vastness. The subtitle of the piece *Reaper Drone*, anchors the otherwise sublime image in a Gothic mode, inserting an aspect of transgression and unease.

The Reaper drone—alongside its counterpart, the Predator—represents one of the most commonly deployed military drones. Initially, they provided real-time video feeds to military commanders, which were essential for monitoring insurgent activity, tracking high-value targets, and identifying potential threats. Weighing 2223 kilograms when empty, the Reaper can remain airborne for up to 25 hours, reaching speeds of approximately 482 kilometers per hour. Unlike surveillance drones, its primary function is close air support. Typically armed with two laser-guided 500-pound bombs and four laser-guided air-to-ground missiles, its maximum takeoff weight increases to 4763 kilograms. The first squadron of Reaper drones was stationed at Creech Air Force Base in Nevada in November 2006, and the first weapon was fired in combat in 2007. Its main area of operations is Afghanistan—a distance of over 12,000 kilometers from Nevada, where pilots execute strikes via remote control (U.S. Air Force 2021). The act of killing is executed at a distance of 12,000 kilometers, rendered as 'clean' as a video game—by a simple press of a button. There is no physical exertion, no pulling of a trigger, no direct sight of the victim except through the mediated images captured by the drone itself. Paglen's work vividly illustrates how the dehumanization of victims and the disembodiment of killing mechanisms have transformed modern warfare. The separation of the human operator from the act of killing and the violent transgression of the victim's body through the effortless digital crossing of thousands of kilometers in near real-time evokes a haunting presence—a contemporary visitation by a distant, foreign spirit. The sublime distance remains intact for the viewers, allowing them to experience the beauty and vastness of the imagery, yet the underlying horror is embedded within the composition, subtly evoking the unseen violence and ethical ambiguities represented through the drone.

In his works, Trevor Paglen examines surveillance as well as visibility and invisibility, particularly in military contexts. In addition to his artistic practice, he holds a degree in technology and earned a Ph.D. in Geography. These interdisciplinary influences manifest in his photographic projects, which often use telescopic lenses. This reversal of subject and object in surveillance and visibility offers a profound critique of power dynamics.

In the photograph's depiction, elements come together that, according to our perception, do not belong together. Also, the destructive power and far-reaching consequences of the drone are irreconcilable with the tiny dot in the image. Initially, the beauty of the photograph might still align with the Sublime, evoking a secure sense of awe. However, this sense of security unravels in the twenty-first century when we realize that we are not merely assuming the perspective of potential victims. The sublime distance—once celebrated, for example, in the landscape depictions of the Hudson River School—is no longer ours to bridge. Instead, it belongs to a command center thousands of kilometers away.

In both literature and art, multiple forms of transgression often overlap and intertwine, reflecting the complexity of human experience. Gothic literature, for instance, frequently combines spatial, temporal, and bodily transgressions within a single narrative, just as contemporary art dealing with drones explores intersecting themes. However, for the purpose of this analysis, the focus will be placed on specific texts where particular aspects of transgression are especially pronounced. By isolating and examining these elements, it becomes possible to establish a clearer framework for understanding how they manifest in drone art and to offer a more targeted interpretation of this evolving artistic discourse.

Spatial and Geographic Transgressions

Gothic literature often uses space and geography to challenge boundaries. These spaces, marked by decay, isolation, and otherworldly elements, form the narrative's foundation, shaping its tension and atmosphere. Their architectural features—such as crumbling castles, labyrinthine corridors, and desolate landscapes—serve as metaphors for psychological and societal ruptures. However, the ownership and control of these spaces, alongside their symbolic significance, also drive the plot, revealing themes of power, fear, and the unknown.

Horace Walpole's *The Castle of Otranto* (1764), widely regarded as the first Gothic novel, exemplifies this use of space. Set in a medieval castle filled with secret paths, spectral apparitions, and ancestral curses, the story follows Prince Manfred's desperate attempts to secure his lineage after the mysterious death of his son. Manfred's pursuit of Isabella, his son's fiancée, through the castle's labyrinthine cellars reflects his assertion of dominance, not just over the physical space but also over Isabella's autonomy. The castle becomes a central character, its hidden passageways and decaying structure symbolizing liminality, where past sins intrude upon the present. Manfred's mastery of the castle's layout mirrors his control over those within it, reinforcing themes of surveillance and patriarchal power.

Modern surveillance technologies, particularly drones, resonate strongly with the Gothic's exploration of spatial authority and disruption. Drones grant operators an elevated perspective, enabling real-time monitoring of vast territories while remaining unseen. This aerial vantage point creates a god-like authority, analog the Gothic's use of space to assert dominance and control. Much like the labyrinthine environments of Gothic literature, where characters navigate twisting corridors and hidden chambers, drones reconfigure traditional notions of geography by reducing them into a single, surveilled field of view. This manipulation of space transforms landscapes into strategic zones governed by observation and control. Like Gothic tales where secrets lie behind locked doors or within hidden rooms, drones penetrate inaccessible spaces, creating an omnipresence that amplifies vulnerability and unease for those under observation. The drone also embodies the ultimate overcoming of spatial boundaries, connecting locations that were once separated by insurmountable distances. Through its technological capabilities, otherwise disconnected regions are unified within a single visual field. From thousands of kilometers away, operators gain an intimate view of remote landscapes. This boundary-crossing occurs not only in a functional sense but also at a symbolic level, as drones create a new geography where space is reimagined as interconnected and controllable. This profound spatial transgression aligns with the Gothic's use of liminal spaces, where the fixed and the separate dissolve into a disorienting continuum, challenging traditional notions of distance and autonomy. Through the use of drones, foreign governments bypass national borders and legal frameworks, asserting control over airspace and territory, effectively appropriating these areas in acts that challenge sovereignty and redefine geopolitical boundaries, intertwining these actions with colonial themes of domination, exploitation, and the erosion of self-determination.

Time-Bound Transgressions

In Gothic literature, time is manipulated, disrupted, or transgressed in various ways. The texts examine themes like the distortion of time, temporal instability, or the obscuring of past, present, and future. The classic phenomenon of ghosts is a prime example of temporal transgressions. Ghosts represent an eerie disruption of time, as they are figures from the past who intrude upon the present, challenging the natural frontier of life and death. Their appearance often suggests that time is not linear but cyclical, with past wrongs or unresolved events resurfacing to haunt the living. In this way, the ghostly presence becomes a manifestation of time's unsettling power. This cyclical return of the past, embodied by ghostly figures, can be identified as Freud's Uncanny.

This is also addressed in Edgar Allan Poe's *The Fall of the House of Usher*. This Gothic short story centers around the narrator's visit to the decaying mansion of his childhood friend, Roderick Usher. Upon arrival, the narrator is struck by the eerie, almost sentient atmosphere surrounding the house, which is reflected in its physical deterioration. Usher, suffering from both mental and physical ailments, reveals that his twin sister, Madeline, is also gravely ill and confined to the mansion. The guest himself can be interpreted as an outsider, seemingly from another time, whose presence only deepens the sense of temporal dislocation within the story. Roderick Usher constantly shifts between the layers of his family's troubled past, his haunting present, and his anxiety about the future of his lineage, and memory, current reality, and impending doom are merging. Through these transitions, the narrative itself distorts the perception of time, immersing the reader in a world where the boundaries between past, present, and future are continually questioned. Over the course of the story, the house's oppressive, mysterious presence seems to influence the fates of its inhabitants. Eventually, Madeline dies—or so Roderick declares—and is entombed within the house, but later reappears, alive and vengeful. The story ends with the dramatic collapse of the mansion, symbolizing the literal and metaphorical fall of the Usher family.

This dynamic resonates with the temporal distortions introduced by modern drone technologies, which alter traditional perceptions of time by merging past, present, and future into a single, manipulable continuum. Unlike human observation, drones can compress or extend time through their advanced imaging capabilities, such as high-speed cameras or time-lapse technologies (Stubblefield 2020). This temporal manipulation allows drones to capture events invisible to the naked eye, such as the unfolding of a single moment in extraordinary detail or the gradual changes in landscapes over years. By doing so, drones disrupt the linear flow of time. At the same time, drones are able to create a permanent now. Through real-time surveillance, drones provide live feedback to operators, presenting a continuous stream of the present that can be archived for later review. This creates a paradoxical relationship with time: while the drone captures the fleeting moment, it also transforms it into a retrievable artifact (Gusterson 2016). The experience of time becomes elastic, where the immediacy of observation merges with the historical permanence of recorded data.

Drone operators act on live feeds, but their actions are informed by hours of surveillance footage and data analysis, allowing them to anticipate and control potential futures. The Gothic also shows a fixation on the inevitability of fate, where characters, like Usher, are simultaneously trapped in and shaped by time's relentless flow. Moreover, the sense of timeless anxiety pervasive in drone warfare reflects the Gothic's psychological disorientation. Drones create a state of perpetual anticipation for those under surveillance, much like the oppressive temporal atmosphere in Gothic tales. Communities under constant drone surveillance often describe a sense of timeless anxiety, where the persistent presence of drones creates a state of suspended temporality (Chamayou 2015). Days and nights merge into a continuous state of anticipation, as the threat of action looms without a fixed timeline. For both the observed and the observer, time becomes elastic and fraught, amplifying a sense of dread. The asynchronous nature of drone warfare, where actions and consequences are temporally disjointed, further challenges conventional ideas of cause and effect in time.

Bodily Transgressions

Bodily transgressions in Gothic literature often involve the violation of physical integrity or identity, exemplified through grotesque transformations or the merging of human and non-human elements. These disruptions evoke the Uncanny, as defined by Freud, by threatening familiar notions of the human body and exposing repressed fears of mortality and monstrosity. Gothic literature uses these bodily violations not only to provoke terror but also to question the boundaries of identity and the limitations of physical existence.

Mary Shelley's *Frankenstein* (1818) tells the story ofVictor Frankenstein, an ambitious scientist whose quest for knowledge leads him to create life artificially. Driven by a desire to conquer death, Victor assembles a creature from body parts of different humans and brings it to life using scientific experimentation. However, he is horrified by the monster's grotesque appearance and abandons it. The creature, left alone and rejected, struggles to survive and seeks companionship and understanding. Initially benevolent, it learns language and observes human interactions, but repeated experiences of prejudice and isolation embitter it. When the creature seeks acceptance from Victor and is spurned, it vows vengeance against its creator. The narrative unfolds as a series of tragic events: the creature kills Victor's loved ones to punish him for its own suffering. Victor, consumed by guilt and a desire for revenge, pursues the creature across Europe and into the Arctic. Ultimately, Victor dies from exhaustion, and the creature, overcome with remorse, vows to end its own life.

Mary Shelley's *Frankenstein* exemplifies bodily transgression through the creation and animation of the creature. Victor Frankenstein's act of reassembling corpses into a new lifeform lifts the veil that separates life and death, human and inhuman, resulting in a grotesque violation of natural laws. The creature represents the ultimate bodily transgression. His towering figure and patchwork appearance evoke the sublime, inspiring awe through his physical power and unnatural origin. Yet, his uncanny presence unsettles; he is both familiar and disturbingly other, a mirror of human fragility and the consequence of overreaching ambition. The creature also acts as Victor's doppelgänger, embodying his unacknowledged desires and the monstrous consequences of his ambition, creating a stark physical transgression. The doppelgänger in Gothic literature often represents a fractured identity, the self and the other are no longer safely separated, threatening the integrity of the body and the psyche. This doubling blurs the line between creator and creation, echoing the Gothic's exploration of bodily violation and the uncanny confrontation with one's darker self.

Drones represent a profound form of bodily transgression, disrupting the boundaries of physical presence and identity for both operators and those they surveil or target (Stubblefield 2020). Surveillance drones dehumanize their subjects, reducing individuals to mere visual data captured and analyzed from afar, stripping them of autonomy and transforming their bodies into objects of observation. This can also be found in the Gothic's uncanny disruption of identity, as those observed are simultaneously present and absent, visible yet unreachable. Armed drones intensify this transgression by shrinking the physical distance between operator and target, enabling acts of violence to occur remotely. Gusterson states:

> This distanced voyeurism is counterbalanced by a sense of immersive intimacy when drones patrol the same terrain over and over and operators come to feel they know the people below. (2016)

The relationship between operator and drone, which remains physically separated yet deeply interconnected and mutually responsive, finds a fitting analogy in Gothic theory through the concept of the doppelgänger. The doppelgänger can manifest as a human figure (e.g., Mr. Hyde to Dr. Jekyll) or even as a shadow, as seen in Hans Christian Andersen's *The Shadow* (1847). The doppelgänger typically serves as a haunting reflection of the other identity, often revealing not only familiar aspects but also previously hidden or unsettling facets of one's personality (see Freud's concept of the Uncanny). Similarly, the drone casts its shadow onto the earth, echoing the symbolic shadow of the doppelgänger—a dark, inseparable presence that magnifies the drone's role as an extension of the human operator. It can be read as the operator's decisions, carrying out actions remotely, and introduces a sense of disembodiment, as the operator observes and acts without direct physical presence. This doubling questions the human agency in the wake of machine autonomy, reflecting the Gothic's preoccupation with fractured identities and unsettling extensions of the self. Also, in traditional doppelgänger narratives, the coexistence of both entities often becomes unsustainable, as one must ultimately perish to restore balance. The presence of the doppelgänger destabilizes the original identity, creating a conflict that can only be resolved through the destruction of one (Rank 1993 [1925]). The Gothic's exploration of fragmented identities often culminates in an unavoidable confrontation with one's hidden, repressed self.

This dynamic foreshadows the psychological toll on drone operators, whose detachment from their actions creates an internal conflict that manifests as guilt and trauma, as though one part of their identity must be sacrificed to reconcile the moral consequences of their role. The act of killing becomes disembodied—a push of a button detached from the visceral reality of its consequences, turning the human operator into a distant force of destruction. For those targeted, drones violate bodily integrity on a terrifying level, transforming the body into a vulnerable site of both surveillance and annihilation, often without warning or the possibility of defense. This dynamic copies the Gothic's exploration of the fragile boundary between life and death, where the body becomes a symbol of vulnerability and terror. Even for drone operators, bodily transgression occurs; the psychological toll of remote warfare, combined with the detachment from physical combat, creates an unsettling rupture between action and accountability—one that extends beyond the regular detachment imposed by the chain of command, as the drone becomes both a tool and a disembodied proxy, amplifying the operator's sense of alienation and ethical ambiguity.. Thus, drones inherit different entities: human and machine, observer and observed, present and absent, making them a modern embodiment of bodily transgression.

Transgressions in Totality: The Unified Impact of Moral and Ethical Dimensions

All the aspects discussed—spatial, temporal, and bodily transgressions—inevitably culminate in a moral transgression, where the restrictions of responsibility, accountability, and ethical judgment are profoundly and irreversibly breached. Responsibility and morality are central themes in *Frankenstein*, as Victor Frankenstein's creation of the creature raises profound ethical questions about accountability for one's actions and the consequences of surpassing natural boundaries. Victor's failure to take responsibility for his creation leads to destruction and tragedy, as a broader exploration of unchecked ambition and moral negligence. Similarly, in Walpole's *The Castle of Otranto*, Manfred's obsession with securing his lineage disregards ethical boundaries, resulting in manipulation and violence, while in *The Fall of the House of Usher*, Roderick Usher's inability to confront his family's legacy reveals the collapse of personal and moral responsibility. His moral failing lies also in his neglect and psychological dominance over his sister, Madeline, as he isolates her within the decaying family mansion, ultimately prioritizing his own fears and obsessions over her well-being and autonomy.

These narratives resonate strongly with the use of drones in contemporary warfare and surveillance, where moral accountability is similarly obscured—whether on the side of the operator or the subject of surveillance. Drones, particularly those used for targeted strikes, detach operators from the immediate consequences of their actions. The physical distance between operator and target enables a disembodiment of responsibility, much like Victor's abandonment of his creature. Decisions made from a remote command center can result in immense human suffering, as well as the lack of direct physical involvement creates an ethical ambiguity reminiscent of the Gothic's exploration of moral lapses. The drone operator experiences a strange dissonance, working a 'shift' that alternates moments of intense focus and mundane routine. Seated thousands of miles from the conflict zone, the operator transitions seamlessly from controlling life-or-death situations to returning home, as though performing any ordinary job. This normalization of war and surveillance within the framework of a standard workday creates a psychological distance, opening a dilemma of ethical responsibility and detached efficiency. The unsettling juxtaposition of such high-stakes actions with everyday tasks highlights the moral and emotional complexities of this experiences.

For those under drone surveillance or attack, this moral transgression is experienced as an erasure of autonomy and humanity, reducing individuals to data points or targets. As in Gothic literature, where actions driven by ambition or negligence ripple outward to affect others, drones symbolize the expansion of moral and ethical consequences beyond immediate visibility. The narratives of Frankenstein, Manfred, and Usher similarly also depict the transmission of curses or unresolved guilt across generations, meaning trauma in communities subjected to constant surveillance or drone attacks can linger, shaping the experiences and psyches of future generations.

The Uncanny Eye: The Gothic in Drone-Focused Art

In the following section, two works of art on the theme of warfare and drones will be analyzed and contextualized through the lens of Gothic motifs. By closely examining these examples the analysis will highlight how Gothic tropes inform the representation of drones, be it in the form of the object itself or the people impacted by it.

Omer Fast's 2011 film *5000 Feet Is the Best* centers on two interviews conducted by the Israel-born artist with a former U.S. drone operator suffering from PTSD. The pilot agreed to discuss his work, and at one point—off camera—he briefly admitted that the UAV frequently targeted both soldiers and civilians, leading to his psychological struggles. Fast brings these fragmented interviews to life in his film through the technique of montage. He seamlessly weaves together blurred real interview excerpts, a staged interview featuring an actor in a hotel room (Fig. 10.2), and sequences of seemingly unrelated side stories told by the actor, all interspersed with drone footage.

At one point, during a break in the interview, the actor stands in the dimly lit hotel hallway and smokes. When he attempts to return to the room—according to both his perception and that of the viewer—he realizes he has been knocking on the wrong door. This moment captures a disorienting loss of spatial certainty. Just as Gothic narratives often manipulate geography to evoke unease Fast uses the actor's misstep to destabilize the viewer's sense of orientation. The mundane hotel hallway becomes a liminal space, where the distinction between familiarity and alienation dissolves, reflecting the film's broader theme of fragmented perception and control.

On the audio level, the film also alternates the actual pilot's voice, the actor from the staged scene, and the interviewer. During the smoking break sequences of the actor the actual pilot takes over the narration: He describes the visible details captured through the drone's camera, and conveys an unexpected perception of beauty in these minutiae and their

Fig. 10.2 Omer fast: *5000 Feet Is the Best* (2011), Filmstill

aesthetics—only to seamlessly transition from this very human conception into describing the screen's view as the computer takes over, evaluates the situation and the target acquisition begins:

> I mean if someone sits down let's say on a cold surface for a while and then gets up you'll still see the heat from that person for a long time. It kind of looks like a white blossom just shining up into heaven. It's quite beautiful. I mean – heck – if you see someone light up a cigarette, that's a huge Beacon. You see a very white glow coming from that area and you're just on a preset path flying a circular orbit watching him as they smoke from two or three miles away. You can be following them and they wouldn't hear nor see you. And I'll set the laser on a spot, you'll see a box pop up. What it does is it locks in those pixels as we circulate, and the computer will figure out the trajectory, the distance, and the speed and come up with an estimated time that it would take for the missile to impact. (Fast 2011)

At this interplay of sound and image, a haunting parallel between the actor's actions and the pilot's narration is created: Shortly after the pilot described the moment when human observation is handed over to the computer, the actor seems to have lost his own sense of control and orientation within the space (also while smoking).

When asked to speak about his mission in Afghanistan, the actor leaves the room once more. The scene repeats the earlier break, but this time the man watches himself exiting the room a second time. His doppelgänger slowly strolls down the hallway, eventually stopping at an open door, from which the faint sound of radio chatter emanates. Again, the pilot takes over and recounts his routine of work and winding down time. He contrasts prolonged observations with cases of emergencies "where stress comes into play". The statement demonstrates the temporal elasticity enabled by drones, where real-time monitoring allows operators to anticipate and respond to events instantly. He admits that sometimes he makes "mistakes" and recalls how after five years he had to reflect on the death that were the direct results of his actions. His legitimations for those actions and the reasons to go on were that otherwise "some new kid would be doing, it but worse" (Fast 2011). The term "kid" sounds irritating regarding his job, but the pilot reveals that he himself at this point was 26 years old, meaning he started this career at 21.

In the next scene, the doppelgänger actor enters the spare room—which turns out to be the correct on. Omer Fast also manipulates the viewer's perception of time and space, paralleling the Gothic's disruption of linearity. The doppelgänger actor's repeated exit and re-entry into the room creates a loop-like structure, echoing the non-linear experience of memory and trauma. The same conversation opening unfolds once again, with the actor appearing reluctant about being filmed before bringing up the payment for the interview, and then being asked about the difference between him and someone "who sits in an airplane" (Fast 2011). At this point in the conversations, a high-pitched, piercing tone overlays the audio, perceptible only to the viewers and the actor, who is visibly hurt by it. In the last little story, the doppelgänger pilot tells, our view follows a western middle class family as they drive out of town that suddenly gets hostile. Warm colored traveling footage of the drive change back and forth into black and white bird's eye surveillance material that showcase some data as they have to stop at a country road because of a group of men working in the middle of it. When listening closely, the narrated story implicates a setting in the middles east, using the phrase "In schāʾa llāh", and rejecting the idea that the guys are shepherds because there are no "camels" in sight. The film here critiques Western complacency regarding drone warfare. The recording recounts an incident involving an Afghan family but uses a cast of white American actors, forcing the audience to confront cultural biases and the disparity when witnessing distant suffering and Western detachment. The narrative and visual elements in this scene evoke a phenomenon of bodily exchange; it highlights not only the interchangeability between the humans represented and narrated but also let the viewer experience both perspectives. This duality mirrors the Gothic's trope of doppelgängers and fractured identities, as the observer becomes both the watched and the watcher.

After a tense few seconds, the family's car slowly passes the men, and only now does the camera reveal that what initially appeared to be tools in their hands are, in fact, machine guns. Just shortly after a missile strikes the scene and kills the men. When the camera pans over the family's car it gets clear that they also died (Delmont 2013). However, after a few moments, they leave their car and simply walk away in a zombie-like state. The pilot's narration of striking men on the ground illustrates the dehumanizing nature of the drone, where individuals are reduced to data points or targets.

The doppelgänger actor states: "Time passes. Time is on my side. Seeing the world from above doesn't just flatten things, it sharpens them. It makes relationships clearer" (Fast 2011) Again, the interview is interrupted, this time by the doppelgänger actor's phone. But instead of taking it when outside, he just rejects it without hesitation. Meanwhile the pilot narrates the real-life events that we just witnessed in the fictional sequence from his side, as drone footage fills the screen with impressions of the nightly Las Vegas with increasing glitches.

The phrase "Time is on my side" underscores how the drone's ability to compress and control time sharpens power dynamics. But in this constant loop, it is only enabling the operator to act with god-like precision on a surface level. Instead, it keeps him in a constant state of waiting, decision-making, and violence and can hardly be seen as a reliable force. Moral ambiguity is central to both the pilot's reflections and the film's narrative. The pilot's justification for his actions—believing he performed the job better than a "new kid" might—highlights a rationalization that shifts accountability rather than addressing it. This can be linked to the fact that "[...] the interpretation of such images is an art, as well as a science - because it inherently involves imaginative leaps—the putatively scientific and objective interpretation at the service of governments and commercial institutions tell only *a* story, not *the* story, of what is going on in these images" (Kurgan 2013). Therefore, the operator not only bears the responsibility for making life-altering decisions but also holds—or is forced to represent—the authority over the narrative surrounding those actions. Omer Fast explores this dynamic through the counter play of visual and textual elements, where the tension between what is seen and what is narrated highlights the complexities of accountability and perspective. This also can be linked to Gothic literature's moral conflicts, where characters like Victor Frankenstein or Roderick Usher evade responsibility for their destructive actions. The pilot's recollections of mistakes and the deaths he caused expose the ethical dilemmas of remote warfare, where decisions are made in sterile environments detached from their devastating consequences. The statement, "Seeing the world from above [...] sharpens relationships," offers a chilling rationalization of the drone's god-like perspective, suggesting clarity while obscuring the moral weight of such actions.

Fast's work intricately weaves these transgressions into a cohesive and complex critique of drone warfare. *5000 Feet Is the Best* explores how drones transcend physical and psychological limits, creating a chilling commentary on the erosion of moral and human boundaries. The film leaves viewers questioning not only the technology itself and the structures of power and control it reinforces but also the perception of reality by creating an additional layer of disorientation.

Fragments to Wholeness: The Dual Role of Drones in Art and Investigation

While drones are often associated with destruction and the deconstruction of spatial, temporal, and bodily boundaries, their imagery also holds the potential for reconstruction and understanding. In artistic and investigative contexts, drone footage is increasingly used to piece together fragmented narratives, reveal hidden truths, and recontextualize events. The following section examines how drone-generated imagery is repurposed in art and research to rebuild narratives and provide new perspectives on conflict and space.

The composite image *Drone Strike in Miranshah* (2014) from the research agency Forensic Architecture, based at Goldsmiths, University of London, presents a strikingly different approach compared to the initial analysis of Trevor Paglen's work, shifting from abstract aestheticization to a detailed, investigative reconstruction of events (Fig. 10.3). The

Fig. 10.3 Forensic Architecture stitched together multiple still video frames to recreate the scene of the destroyed room. (Forensic Architecture using footage from the Rachel Maddow Show on MSNBC (22 June 2012), 2016)

previously romanticized, warm, and soft atmosphere is now replaced by a fragmented image that lays bare its composite nature through visible frames. This shift emphasizes the constructed and mediated quality of the visual narrative, moving away from a seamless representation to one that reveals the process of its own creation. Forensic Architecture is specializing in spatial and architectural analyses to investigate cases of state violence and human rights violations (Forensic Architecture 2014). Their interdisciplinary team employs advanced architectural and media techniques to reconstruct and analyze events, providing critical evidence for legal and political forums.

One of their notable investigations is on the 2012 Drone Strike in Miranshah, North Waziristan (Pakistan). A video documenting the strike's aftermath was secretly transported out of the region and broadcast by MSNBC. While the CIA has neither confirmed nor denied the attack, Forensic Architecture through their work on the 43 second clip could confirm that four people were killed, deduce the location of the building, and the munition used. It seems that the missile detonated mid-air within a room, indicating the use of a delay-fuse missile, likely a 'Romeo' Hellfire II AGM-114R. The distribution of shrapnel marks on the walls allowed the team to infer the positions of individuals present during the explosion, effectively capturing their silhouettes in the spatial damage. The traces of the victims, evoke an unsettling ghostly presence, akin to a spectral imprint of the individuals who once occupied the space. Although they are absent they remain present. The outlines of human figures, typically a marker of life, now appear as haunting voids that emphasize their absence. The room becomes a liminal space.

The drone-generated images are now countered by alternative visuals that challenge their narrative authority and offer a different perspective. Here, the images of the interior, derived from stills of the MSNBC footage, were instrumental in this analysis. By reconstructing the room's three-dimensional model and mapping the shrapnel trajectories, Forensic Architecture provided a detailed spatial understanding of the event. This method exemplifies their approach of using architectural and media analysis to uncover and present evidence of human rights violations. The group's artistic strategies hold users of warfare drones accountable by meticulously reconstructing events to make the invisible visible, transforming abstract violence into tangible evidence that demands ethical and legal scrutiny.

Conclusion

The intersection of drones, surveillance, and civil rights presents a powerful and necessary area of exploration for contemporary artists. They are drawn to the intensified surveillance and control enabled by drones, seeing them as emblematic of modern power structures. By reinterpreting drone imagery and its implications, artists reveal how surveillance alters the dynamics of freedom and agency. Drone warfare, with its asymmetrical and detached nature, provides another focus for artistic inquiry. Through their creations, they highlight the ethical tensions of technological advancements and the human cost of their implementation, as does the Gothic's exploration of unchecked power and its unintended consequences. The Gothic's ability to expose liminal spaces and unseen horrors aligns closely with this cultural and artistic critique, offering a means to interrogate how drones both materialize and mask violations of human rights, such as the right to live free from surveillance and violence.

By framing drones as Gothic figures—tools of disembodied violence and surveillance—this analysis reveals the unseen forms of immiseration they perpetuate, from psychological torment to the erasure of privacy to the dehumanizing act of killing at a distance. The physical and psychological distance afforded by drone operations, though subject to conflicting claims about its impact on operators' susceptibility to PTSD (Phelps 2021), is often perceived as reducing the emotional and ethical toll. This ambiguity further obscures accountability and reinforces the divide between the self and the other. This distance enlarges the boundary between the self and the other, diminishing the perceived significance of harm inflicted on the observed, rendering their suffering less visible and less urgent. The dehumanization inherent in drone operations, where individuals are reduced to abstract data points, is another critical concern for artists. Mistakes in targeting, leading to civilian casualties, expose the fragility of the systems that claim precision. By addressing this in their work, artists restore humanity to those affected, emphasizing the consequences of disconnection and objectification. This focus resonates with the Gothic's preoccupation with fractured identities and the human cost of transgressing boundaries.

For artists, the psychological impact on drone operators themselves is equally important. The detachment experienced by operators, who make life-and-death decisions from thousands of miles away, reflects a profound moral estrangement. Artists bring attention to this alienation, portraying the ethical and emotional burden borne by those behind the screens. These works often serve as a space for reflection, encouraging viewers to grapple with the complexities of accountability in an age of remote warfare.

Finally, the manipulation of drone imagery offers fertile ground for artistic critique. Drones create powerful visual narratives that shape public perception, often serving political agendas. Artists challenge these narratives, reframing the imagery to reveal hidden truths and alternative perspectives. This engagement with perspective and interpretation also is a critical Gothic strategy to highlight concealed realities and the power of storytelling.

Artists like Trevor Paglen, Omer Fast, and the collective Forensic Architecture approach drone imagery to *de-* and *re-*construct narratives and expose biases as well as human rights violations. Their work shifts from the Gothic's focus on decay and destruction to one of restoration, yet it retains the genre's motif of uncovering hidden truths. By making visible the invisible—whether through composite images or spatial reconstructions—they counter the drone's narrative of control with one of accountability. The Gothic, with its emphasis on the Uncanny, Sublime, and fragmentary, provides a powerful metaphorical language to grapple with the cultural and political challenges posed by drones in the twenty-first century.

References

Andersen, Hans Christian. 1847. *Skyggen [The Shadow].* In Nye Eventyr. Copenhagen: C.A. Reitzel.

Anonym. 2000 [1798]. Terrorist Novel Writing. In *Gothic Documents. A Sourcebook 1700–1820*, ed. Emma J. Clery and Robert Miles, Robert, 182–184. Manchester/New York: Manchester University Press.

Botting, Fred. 1996. *Gothic.* London/New York: Routledge.

Boyle, Michael J. 2020. *The Drone Age. How Drone Technology Will Change War and Peace.* Oxford: Oxford University Press.

Burke, Edmund. 1792 [1757]. *Philosophical Enquiry Into the Origin of Our Ideas of the Sublime and Beautiful.* Basil: J. J. Tourneisen.

Cavallaro, James, Stephan Sonnenberg, and Sarah Knuckey. 2012. *Living Under Drones: Death, Injury and Trauma to Civilians from US Drone Practices in Pakistan*, New York: NYU School of Law.

Chamayou, Grégoire. 2015. *A Theory of the Drone.* New York: The New Press.

deathtostock. 2024. Are We Being Watched RN. https://www.instagram.com/p/DDiWiw2yGTx/?hl=de. Accessed 14 December 2024.

Delmont, Matt. 2013. Drone Encounters: Noor Behram, Omer Fast, and Visual Critiques of Drone Warfare. *American Quarterly* Vol. 65, No. 1: 193–202.

Fast, Omer, director. 2011. 5000 Feet is the Best. 32 min. https://www.youtube.com/watch?v=K-8dW1dg7KY&t=478s. Accessed 10 August 2024.

Forensic Architecture. 2014. https://forensic-architecture.org. Accessed 10 December 2024.

Foucault, Michel. 2010. *Überwachen und Strafen. Die Geburt des Gefängnisses.* Frankfurt am Main: Suhrkamp.

Freud, Sigmund. 1919. Das Unheimliche. *Imago. Zeitschrift für Anwendung der Psychoanalyse auf die Geisteswissenschaften* 5/6: 297–324.

Gusterson, Hugh. 2016. *Drone: Remote Control Warfare.* Cambridge, MA: MIT Press.

Human Rights Watch. 2021. US: End Impunity for Civilian Casualties. Lack of Accountability Goes Beyond Kabul Drone Strike. https://www.hrw.org/news/2021/12/14/us-end-impunity-civilian-casualties. Accessed 10 December 2024.

Kakaes, Konstantin. 2015. From Orville Wright to September 11: What the History of Drone Technology says about its Future. In: D*rone Wars: Transforming Conflict, Law, and Policy*, ed. Peter L. Bergen and Daniel Rothenberg, 359–387. New York: Cambridge University Press.

Kurgan, Laura. 2013. *Close Up at a Distance: Mapping Technology & Politics.* New York: Zone Books.

Malone, Meredith. 2016. Introduction. In *To See Without Being Seen: Contemporary Art and Drone Warfare*, ed. Svea Bräunert and Meredith Malone, 6–9. Chicago, IL: University of Chicago Press.

Morley, Simon. 2010. *The Sublime* (Documents of Contemporary Art). London: Whitechapel Gallery.

Phelps, Wayne. 2021. *On Killing Remotely. The Psychology of Killing with Drones.* New York: Little, Brown and Company.

Poe, Edgar Allan. 1839. The Fall of the House of Usher. *Burton's Gentleman's Magazine* 3:145–152.

Rank, Otto. 1993 [1925]. *Der Doppelgänger. Eine psychoanalytische Studie.* Wien: Turia und Kant.

Robben, Antonius C. G. M. 2011. The Dead of Night. Chaos and Spectacide of Nocturnal Combat in the Iraq War. In *War, Technology, Anthropology*, ed. Koen Stroeken, 34–44. Oxford: Berghahn Books.

Shelley, Mary. 1818. *Frankenstein or, the Modern Prometheus.* London: Lackington, Hughes, Harding, Mavor, & Jones.

Stubblefield, Thomas. 2020. *Drone Art. The Everywhere War as Medium.* Oakland, CA: University of California Press.

U.S. Air Force. 2021. Fact Sheets: MQ-9 Reaper. https://www.af.mil/About-Us/Fact-Sheets/Display/Article/104470/mq-9-reaper. Accessed 10 December 2024.

Walpole, Horace. 1764. *The Castle of Otranto*. Strawberry Hill: Strawberry Hill Press.

CHAPTER 11

The Ticking Bomb Drone Strike: Drone Warfare and Emergency Ethics in *Eye in the Sky*

Alex Adams

Introduction

One of the major reasons that narratives and representations are socially and politically meaningful to their audiences and consumers is that they provide ways of staging political and ethical debates. Although aesthetic and cultural production cannot be reduced to this didactic function, by dramatizing debates and arguments as coherently organized and readily comprehensible stories, texts such as novels, comics, TV shows, video games, and films help us think through, articulate, and debate what is at stake in our ideas, values, and political positions. Military fiction is a particularly charged genre in this respect: a great range of representations, from popular action franchises such as the *Rambo* series (1982, 1985, 1988, 2008, 2019) through TV shows such as *Homeland* (2011–2020) to high culture artefacts such as *Syriana* (2005), engage in moral and ethical debates about the legitimacy and conduct of war, global policing, state

A. Adams (✉)
Independent Scholar, Jarrow, UK

M. W. Azeem (ed.), *Human Rights in the Age of Drones*, Palgrave Studies in Literature, Culture and Human Rights,
https://doi.org/10.1007/978-3-032-08191-9_11

violence, and the protection and promotion of human rights. Representations that explore the moral and ethical conundrums of war can be influential ways of framing and contributing to public discussions about one of the most serious uses of state power, so cultural texts that attempt to provide explanations of the complex issues associated with it are of substantial importance.

However, they often provide us with compelling yet misleading explorations of the issues at stake. Like any critique, representation, or understanding of state violence, the examination of drone warfare must consider broader political questions to generate meaningful insights; in the case of unmanned vehicular warfare, attention should be given to matters of geopolitical power, coloniality, sovereignty, racial and economic inequality, and surveillance, for instance. This essay examines Gavin Hood's 2015 film *Eye in the Sky*, in which civilian and military authorities disagree over the ethics of authorizing a drone strike in a militia-controlled area of Nairobi. I argue here that while contemporary theoretical discourse may now be generating valuable insights into the political, material and philosophical implications of drone warfare, thriller narratives such as this film that rely on an evaluation of emergency ethics—that is, narratives that consider whether any given urgent situation may or may not legitimize a violent act—thus far remain unable to fully account for it and therefore represent ahistorical, depoliticized, and impoverished interventions in the debates of which they are a part. Specifically, this chapter argues that *Eye in Sky*'s ethical debate is structurally analogous to the ticking bomb scenario, a very popular but gravely misleading narrative about torture, and that as a consequence, it frames the moral quandaries of drone warfare in a way that integrates it into the existing rhetorics of military necessity that underpin liberal humanitarian interventionism—that is, it examines it in a way that allows many of the most troubling and controversial aspects of drone warfare to be left unexplored and for its violence to appear morally and politically defensible.

Torture, Drone Warfare, and the Structure of Violence

In an astute re-evaluation of Elaine Scarry's *The Body in Pain* (1985), Kevin McSorley (2019) notes that the structure of modern drone warfare is analogous to the structure of political torture. Scarry's classic book is a political phenomenology of interpersonal violence, and in it, she writes that torture is a process through which the 'insignia of power' is repeatedly written on the physical body of the victim, amplifying the illegitimate power of the torturing regime and coercing the sufferer into confirming the authority of their torturer (Scarry 1985: 27–59). McSorley draws on Scarry's analysis of the ways that physical violence creates 'a sense of the incontestable reality of the torturing regime's power' and identifies an 'underlying mechanism of the transubstantiation of pain and injury into political power' that he claims can be read across both torture and drone warfare (McSorley 2019: 3, 19). Both forms of state violence are, for McSorley, marked as strategies of violent biopolitical governmentality by their concern with total control over and knowledge of the people and populations against whom they are violently mobilized. That is, both forms of violence are political tools for the imposition of power over people—at the level of the individual body and at the level of the wider population—through the exercise of force, intimidation, and wounding.

There is much to explore here. One of Scarry's major arguments in *The Body in Pain* is that by exercising total control—in the form of the infliction of injury and suffering—over the body of the tortured person, the torturer permanently redefines reality for their subject, annihilating their ability to feel safe in the world and endeavouring to produce the political effect of obedience or defeat. Likewise, McSorley writes, drone warfare redefines reality in traumatic terms for the populations against whom it is mobilized.

> For those populations living under drones, predatory war is experienced primarily as a form of pervasive sensory terrorism, its effects widespread, unpredictable and seemingly arbitrary [...]. Feelings of constant fear, incomprehension and becoming prey led to an undermining of the normal routines of everyday living, the sense of a stable interaction order, and community trust. [...] Predatory war has been experienced in terms of widespread feelings of ubiquitous surveillance, of enclosure and being held hostage, and the increasing penetration, desecration and inversion of a sense of hospitality and safety everywhere and at all times. (2019: 12–15)

The permanent potential for arbitrary destruction built into the military drone produces the effect of terror in the lives of those it targets: by terror, I mean here permanent knowledge of the annihilatory whims of the regime to which one is subject. The most important aspect of this, however, is the political meaning of the erasure of bodily safety. Much as torture inscribes power on the fabric of the individual body, drone warfare inscribes the power of the US drone regime across the fabric of the zones—Pakistan, Afghanistan, Gaza, and elsewhere—that it subjects to weaponized drone surveillance.

The reason that I draw here on McSorley's observations is, of course, that there are wider parallels to be drawn between torture and drone violence. The similarities do not end with the phenomenology of vulnerability—the world-unmaking sense of one's perpetual availability to the Hellfire missile—to which he refers. Torture and drone warfare need to be understood as parts of an integrated military-political apparatus, a broad and deep system of imperial power that relies on the exercise of extraordinary violence to enforce its hegemony. Drone warfare, that is, is the latest stage of a multifaceted historical process in which imperial space and colonized populations become subject to violent securitization in order to enable capitalist expansion and resource exploitation. In turning sections of the world into open prisons that can be remotely policed, drones are as integral a component of a global carceral system as torture prisons. In addition, drones are the latest iteration of a long historical process in which certain areas of the world are surveilled and bombed by Western powers; therefore, they also need to be understood as what Derek Gregory calls 'a profoundly colonial modality of air power' (2011: 189). The power that drones wield, that is, has deep roots. Drone networks of surveillance and control are, although potentially omnipresent, in practice differentially distributed and disproportionately focused in certain areas. Indeed, since much drone violence is perpetrated by states in the Global North and West against states and populations in the Global South and East, modern drone technologies, whilst revolutionary and innovative in engineering terms, reinscribe and deepen historically persistent constellations.

Drone warfare is concerned not with the military logic of *invasion* and the strategic logic of a *temporary exercise of force* in the pursuit of *specific and limited objectives* but with the colonial logic of *occupation* and the policing logic of *permanent control* in the pursuit of *generalized and adaptable objectives.* Torture has been described as the colonial political technology that most clearly expresses the nature of the political relationship entailed by colonial occupation; Robert Young (2009) writes that torture, as well as a definite political phenomenon with clear material effects and physical consequences, is also 'an expression of the occupant-occupied relationship'. Drone warfare could well be on the way to displacing it as the ideal mechanism and perfect metaphor for the exercise of imperial power-knowledge. An important caveat should be observed here, however: in describing the revolutionary nature of drone technology and the totalizing ambitions of those who wield it, we critics should not embrace too readily the rhetoric of total control and military omniscience in which such descriptions are too often couched. Embracing this rhetoric uncritically risks inadvertently praising the technology or, worse, suggesting that the coloniality it represents and reproduces cannot be resisted.[1]

While it would be irresponsible to claim that drones are as all-powerful as some of their giddier advocates claim, the range and scope of the power that drones potentially enable is in fact troubling, and more thoroughgoing than may be expected. For instance, Mike Bourne draws on Bruno Latour to argue that

> the relationship between technology and warfare and subjectivity can be argued to be closely entangled, whereby new technologies enter the networks of war through processes of non-linear adaptation, innovation and faltering assimilation, and affect how the humans (soldiers, policy makers, weapons scientists) behave and conceive of themselves. [...] For Latour, it is the process of composition in which technology and society are co-emergent that assembles power relations in particular configurations and renders them fixed, invisible and logical. (2012: 158–159)

That is, at stake is not simply the fact that technology is folded into warfare to pursue existing aims but rather the fact that the insertion of ever-developing technology into warfare itself affects not only the everyday conduct of war but also the parameters of possibility. Drone warfare, in integrating surveillance, policing, and assassination, is a radical composition, an incredibly sophisticated and dangerous assemblage of technologies that enables new forms of thought, experience, and conduct on the part of those operating and designing them and that opens up the possibilities of planning and executing new forms of total warfare. Torture, too, is a transformative political technology that renegotiates and fixes power relations. By making populations aware that they can be made available to torture if they commit certain acts or express certain views, torturing powers in authoritarian or colonial societies use force (and the wider threat of torture) to redefine the parameters of political possibility.

[1] For this point, I am indebted to an exchange with Derek Gregory at Beryl Pong's *Aesthetics of Drone Warfare* conference at the University of Sheffield in 2019.

On a more granular level, another parallel between torture and drone violence can be found in the rhetoric of bureaucratic dehumanization that both forms of violence have accumulated. As Jeffrey S. Bachman and Jack Holland write, the Obama administration 'employed innovative techniques of dehumanization' in the course of the rhetorical justifications of their drone warfare, 'adopting a sanguine, bureaucratic language to veil the act of killing' (2019: 3). This has its corollary in the bland language used to describe the forms of violence used against prisoners in the post-9/11 torture programme. That is, both torture and drone warfare have attracted a specialized bureaucratic vocabulary: where targeted assassinations are referred to as 'surgical strikes' and innocent people murdered (by mistake or design) are referred to as 'collateral damage', torture is described as 'enhanced interrogation'—with specific torture techniques having their own banal denotations, such as 'dietary manipulation' for starvation or 'close confinement' for shackling in a locked box, for instance. The function of such language is not, of course, to change the character of the violence it describes for the person or people enduring it; the function is to enable its incorporation into a body of bureaucratic and legalistic procedures and to present imperial violence as legitimate, proportionate, and compatible with international law.

It is also important to acknowledge that in some respects, the drone programme has, as a historical process, grown directly out of the torture programme. Jeremy Scahill (2013), in particular, shows how the torture programme and drone programme arose as interlinked forms of covert warfare after 9/11 and that as the torture programme came under pressure to shut down, the drone programme was building up a head of steam. For their part, drone advocates are rarely coy about this. 'It has become more politically palatable,' wrote journalist Daniel Byman, 'for the United States to kill rather than detain suspected terrorists' (2013: 34). Conflict incarceration during the post-9/11 wars in Afghanistan and Iraq has proven to be consistently politically problematic and the object of much public controversy because of the extent to which it involved the US in violations of international law and exposed lawmakers and the military to sustained criticism from human rights groups. The drone programme seemed to represent a neat solution to this because killing on the battlefield (as drone strikes were often misdescribed) was more easily described as a legitimate, proportionate, and fair act of conventional warfare than were concentrationary incarceration, indefinite detention, and systematic torture.

Likewise, and perhaps most important for this chapter, cultural narratives about torture and drone strikes sometimes display interesting similarities. In some ways, classic science fiction franchises such as the *Terminator* or *Robocop* movies remain the most prescient and insightful explorations of robot warfare and policing, due in part to their emphasis on the intimacy of the connection between technological innovation and merciless authoritarianism. They do not, however, capture the planetary ambitions of modern robotic warfare, and neither do such fictions, as Jordan Crandall (2016: 324) notes, capture its specifically vehicular (rather than anthropomorphic) character; the 'rendering of drone warfare on film via the established Hollywood idiom necessarily involves a blindness to, precisely, drone warfare's non-human aspect', writes Yasco Horsman (2020: 306). Nor are such texts the limit of cultural representations of drone warfare. In an article exploring how 'drone warfare is mediated through literature, film, and video games, and what the particular mode of mediation reveals about the effects of drones on those who work with or live around them', Tobi Smethurst and Stef Craps have identified the very broad scope and range of contemporary fiction, film, TV and video game cultural productions that engage with drones (2018: 3). I do not, of course, contend that most or even many of them are torture narratives. A range of forms of narrative, however, engage with or stage moral debates about violence, and productive parallels can be drawn here because of the intriguing similarities between the ways in which torture and drone strikes are debated. They are both signature political technologies of state terror; it is perhaps only logical that they are debated and narrated in the same impoverished and abstract terms in hegemonic popular culture.

The Ticking Bomb Scenario

The ticking bomb scenario is a thought experiment that aims to demonstrate that torture can be permitted in certain emergency situations. It is also one of the most culturally prevalent narratives about torture and can be found throughout a wide range of cultural productions, including novels, film, TV, graphic novels, and video games (Adams 2019). It dramatizes a falsely unambiguous decision point—a bomb is ticking, and a prisoner is tortured until they reveal the information that can prevent the bomb from going off—to frame a persuasive narrative that attempts to justify torture. It aims to demonstrate that if an atrocity of some kind can be prevented in this manner, then torture can, in some limited circumstances, be defended; it aims to demonstrate that the absolute ban on torture in mainstream ethics is, theoretically, unsustainable. This simplistic framing requires us to answer in the affirmative the misleading question that it poses about torture. Of course, if it were a decision between the right of one criminal not to be tortured and the right to life of many innocent individuals, we are supposed to think, then yes, torture is the lesser of two evils and can be condoned. David Luban writes that the thought experiment is 'a remarkably effective propaganda device' because 'it is simple, easy to grasp, emotionally powerful, and – above all – it seems to have only one right answer, the pro-torture answer' (2008: 4). Its framing makes it almost impossible for us to choose not to torture, and as such, it is a very powerful intervention in discussions about torture. The question can be dismissed and critiqued, but it cannot be answered on its own terms in the negative.

In many ways, the ticking bomb scenario echoes another thought experiment, the trolley problem, in which the driver of a train with defective brakes must choose whether to take a track that will result in the train hitting and killing five people or to take another available route that will result in the death of only one person; most people, writes Judith Thompson (1985), would agree that even though we may feel discomfort about causing the death of the solitary innocent, it is difficult not to agree that minimizing harm is the right choice. The ticking bomb scenario is structurally analogous and allows those who deploy it to frame torture as a compassionate form of harm reduction rather than a grotesque human rights abuse. Thought experiments are often ways of exploring ideas to critically examine our habits of thought or our unconscious biases; the ticking bomb scenario flattens the multifaceted and potentially reflective potential of the trolley problem into a misleading justificatory discourse.

Crucially for the present discussion, the most troubling effect of this thought experiment is to naturalize the idea that limited emergency situations require us to forgo our legal and moral commitments to the absolute prohibition of torture. As Luban writes elsewhere, 'ticking-bomb stories depict torture as an emergency exception, but use intuitions based on the exceptional case to justify institutionalized practices and procedures of torture' (2005: 1427). There is a subtle yet definite slippage in the principle that is established by the hypothetical: by agreeing that an exception can be made, we undermine the absolute prohibition on torture.

Similar rhetorical positions can be found in discussions about drone warfare. The discussion about drone warfare most closely resembles the ticking bomb scenario when it concerns collateral damage—that is, when it concerns the unintended yet nonetheless deliberate deaths of noncombatants, such as those that occur when drone strikes are used against populated areas. Both positions share a kernel of utilitarian argumentation: the idea that we may sometimes have to commit an atrocity—commit torture or kill innocent bystanders—to save a large number of innocent lives. Lisa Hajjar (2016: 65) writes, for instance, that Israeli state lawfare has integrated the notion of a ticking bomb into its justification for targeted killing: if individuals are considered to pose an imminent and grave risk, their assassination is considered legally warranted. (Naturally, these assessments of risk are rarely clear-cut and frequently result in the deaths of civilian, noncombatant victims.) In his 2013 *Foreign Affairs* article, 'Why Drones Work', Daniel Byman writes that 'sometimes imminent and intolerable threats do arise and drone strikes are the best way to eliminate them' because they 'offer a comparatively low-risk way of targeting these areas while minimizing collateral damage' (35, 32).

In his 2005 article 'A Defence of Torture', Sam Harris draws a particularly bold comparison between unintentional killing in smart bomb strikes and ticking bomb torture. He argues that since we are willing to accept the unfortunate necessity of collateral damage, we should be willing to accept the unfortunate necessity of emergency torture.

> There is no escaping the fact that whenever we drop bombs, we drop them with the knowledge that some number of children will be blinded, disemboweled, paralyzed, orphaned, and killed by them. [...] If we are willing to drop bombs, or even risk that rifle rounds might go astray, we should be willing to torture a certain class of criminal suspects and military prisoners.

Modern war, he writes, is inconceivable without unintentional harm to the innocent; therefore, because one must sometimes do a thing that is wrong in itself to achieve larger, more just aims, then some limited degree of atrocity is morally permissible. In *Drone Theory* (2015: 102), Grégoire Chamayou criticizes this ethics of violence as 'tautological, and reduced to a flatly Jesuitical justification of ends that justify means'. Chamayou observes that the understanding of military heroism, bravery, and valour that underpins drone operations is that 'bravery consists in doing the dirty work' (a formulation found throughout ticking bomb torture arguments) and that this notion of some people getting their hands dirty to guarantee the security of others is a reflection of a generally impoverished moral debate.

'With the right feelings,' write Jeffrey S. Bachman and Jack Holland in their discussion of Obama's drone policy, 'it is easy to justify killing' (2019: 8). Positioning collateral damage as *regrettable but inevitable if the right thing is to be done in the pursuit of justice* is a major tactic found throughout rhetorical justifications of drone violence, just as torture is positioned as regrettable but necessary in certain articulations of the torture debate. The important point here, however, is that discussions of limited interrogational torture and unintentional blast zone deaths are misleading ways of framing ethical discussions about contemporary warfare. A critique, however detailed, of the moral rationale for any given decision is effectively meaningless. What, after all, does one limited act of warranted interrogational torture have to do with the seedy murk of a globally institutionalized torture programme? How does an understanding of the moral calculations behind any one missile strike give us any insight into a globally networked robotic security apparatus? The way to challenge the ticking bomb scenario is not to say that the imaginary terrorist should not be tortured but rather to reveal the ideological service that the thought experiment performs in relation to a sustained *regime* of torture; to understand what is at stake in the system of global militarized surveillance, one must aim for a comprehensive understanding of the *regime* rather than the moral minutiae of any one act of killing. In what follows, I argue that *Eye in the Sky*, by dramatizing drone warfare as a ticking bomb scenario, reflects the generally politically impoverished condition of debates that utilize such hypotheticals.

The Ticking Bomb Drone Strike

Eye in the Sky stages, simply, one decision. Three al-Shabab terrorists occupy a house in Kenya. They are under constant drone surveillance, and an international coalition of American, British, and Kenyan military forces plans to collaborate on a capture operation. However, there is an unexpected development: the targets move to another location, in a district that is inaccessible to the capture team (it is controlled by al-Shabab and as such cannot be entered without a firefight) and begin to prepare two young recruits for imminent suicide attacks. The operation immediately changes drastically, and everybody involved has to reassess whether it is appropriate for the objective of the operation to change from capture to kill. That is, should the drone operator fire upon the house to kill the terrorists and stop their attack, even though their house is in the middle of a densely populated zone?

Although the military officers in charge are immediately certain that a Hellfire missile is warranted, the civilian characters and the drone operator himself are unsure, and their uncertainty constitutes the dramatic focus of the movie. The operation is being observed by COBRA, a British emergency security committee, so that some members of civilian government can witness the operation; reluctant to assume political responsibility for the missile strike, they pass responsibility for the decision to the British Foreign Secretary, who passes it to the US Secretary of Defence, who ultimately (without hesitation, in the middle of a ping pong game) approves it. However, there is an additional complication. The drone operator, noticing that a young girl is within the projected blast radius, demands that the military reassess the likelihood of killing her along with the terrorists. A military intelligence officer is pressured to manipulate the calculation of the estimated blast zone (or CDE—Collateral Damage Estimate) to artificially lower the official estimate of the probability of killing her in the course of the strike and thereby enable the launch of the missile. Ultimately, of course, the strike goes ahead, and the girl is killed along with the terrorists.

The film emphasizes this central question: is it morally right to kill the girl in the course of killing the terrorists? What should be our moral priority? Is an innocent death an acceptable price to pay for the achievement of a justified aim? They calculate that if the attacks are not prevented, at least eighty civilians are likely to die. In a novel riff on the trolley problem, the film asks whether the *chance* of preventing eighty possible deaths is worth the *certainty* of murdering at least one innocent. Ultimately, the film concludes, yes: though it is sad, it is probably right; it is sad that this is the only right thing to do in this situation, that our ethics have forced us to accept something terrible. Nothing can disrupt the teleology of military necessity: it is never in question, truly, that the missile will be launched. The point of the film is, simply, the discomfort caused for all involved by the obvious fact that the girl will be killed along with the al-Shabab cell.

On a purely utilitarian basis, it is represented in the movie as straightforwardly operationally justified to kill enemies in pursuit of a military objective. The British military representatives and the US Secretary of Defence find it frustratingly obvious that the drone operator should pull the trigger and prevent the terrorists from detonating their suicide weapons. However, many of the other characters find the situation upsettingly ambiguous and consider it morally wrong to kill a young girl regardless of the circumstances. The movie ends tragically, with the death of the young girl foregrounded; before the credits roll, we see an elegiac slow motion shot of the girl dancing in the sun. Everybody seems able to agree, however, that they did the right thing, and that the reason that the girl's death is sad is that *it had to happen*, that *they could not have acted otherwise.* If we choose to read it as a condemnation of drone violence, then the film's moral and political horizons only allow us to read it as a condemnation of drone assassinations in which an indisputably innocent victim is killed alongside terrorists. That is, the film engages the moral problem of collateral damage at the expense of the many broader moral and political questions raised by the regime of drone warfare itself. The goal-oriented nature of the narrative, which telescopes towards an inevitable closure, necessarily misrepresents the messy complexity of drone warfare.

The framing of this movie fundamentally misrepresents the nature of the moral and philosophical problems that drone warfare poses. The scenario is, of course, exaggeratedly clear-cut: due to the miraculous power of high-definition surveillance, they are able to be certain that these five terrorists are definitely preparing for two suicide operations (and not merely to suspect it, or to have credible evidence that it may be the case); they know for certain that they have a short window of time in which to act, or as an exasperated general emphasizes, that they 'have a situation here which could result in massive loss of life in the next ten minutes'; they know for certain that there is one little girl who will have to die to prevent the al-Shabab attack. The ticking bomb scenario presents a falsely unambiguous situation in which torture seems acceptable because the reality of what torture entails is not visible. Concentrationary imprisonment, degradation and corruption of state institutions, and other issues central to the reality of systematic state torture as it actually occurs in the world must remain invisible for the thought experiment to work. Likewise, the framing of drone warfare in *Eye in the Sky* focuses on whether it is right to kill innocents in the course of otherwise morally unproblematic operations. This reflects a certain debate around drone warfare in which the issues of extrajudicial assassination, global surveillance, and planetary enclosure simply do not surface or are assumed to be unproblematic. Incredibly (not to say unrealistically) detailed high-definition real-time global surveillance, for instance, is integral to the narrative perspective of the movie, as everyone shares multiple screen views of the district in which the terrorists are based. Such invasive, panoptic access into the households of Nairobi must be presumed acceptable in order for the movie to make sense. The COBRA committee, epicentre of the moral objection to the missile strike, only develops qualms once the objective changes from capture to kill. Watching the events in intrusive surveillant detail is an uncontroversial prerequisite for the development of the narrative.

Do Not Kill Me: Compassion and the Imperialism of Human Rights

The ticking bomb scenario is, at its core, an argument about the necessity of violent protection. As such, it is an image in miniature of the liberal argument for humanitarian intervention. This may seem to be a provocative claim, as liberal interventionism is consistently positioned as a matter of the promotion of peace and the installation of democratic institutions into political spaces blighted by authoritarianism or anarchy, and not as a fringe argument defending specific atrocities. It is an article of faith for liberal interventionists, for instance, that 'intervention can be right when human rights are being denied, either by repressive state authorities or as a side-effect of internal conflict' (Lipsey 2016: 416), and another of the central pillars of the justification of humanitarianism is that liberal states have the moral duty 'to *rescue* victims of tyranny or anarchy, if we can do so at reasonable cost' (Tesón 2003: 93. Emphasis in original.). Where the ticking bomb scenario claims that violence against prisoners is justified in order to defuse hypothetical bombs and rescue huge amounts of innocent civilians, the rhetoric of liberal interventionism likewise justifies wholesale invasions in order to rescue civilians and to promote, by force, human rights. In both cases, violence is rendered innocent through appeals to its supposedly protective effects. If Radhika Desai's tone is polemical when she writes that the contemporary West 'festoons its imperialism with the rhetoric of human rights and democracy' (2022: 170), her substantive point stands.

This iconography of conquest is found throughout the discussions surrounding twenty-first century wars in Iraq, Syria, Libya, Ukraine, Iran, and elsewhere. Therefore, it is perhaps no surprise that it was not long before drones were integrated into the humanitarian rhetoric of contemporary imperialism. In 2014, Kristin Bergtora Sandvik and Kjersti Lohne warned that 'drone strikes may, over time, be appropriated as a specific technological expression of humanitarian reason' (164); their concern was proven warranted a year later, as in 2015, the same year that *Eye in the Sky* was released, Caroline Kennedy & James I. Rogers argued in *The International Journal of Human Rights* that drones are, because of the reduction of potential harm to peacekeeping personnel, a virtuous and ethical peacekeeping technology. Although *Eye in the Sky* is perhaps not this bold in overtly claiming that drones are virtuous, it certainly makes the case that their violence can be warranted and that their surveillant gaze can enable protective humanitarian activity.

Perhaps the most significant aspect of *Eye in Sky*'s engagement with the humanitarianism of liberal interventionism is the girl in red dress. This young African girl, the innocent victim who complicates what would otherwise be a straightforward matter of the remote elimination of an imminent terror threat, is learning mathematics, reads a picture book about London, and enjoys playing with a hula hoop, and is as such one of the people who liberal interventionism positions itself as defending (one of the victims, in Tesón's terms, who 'we' are morally obligated to rescue): a young girl who wants, despite the prevailing political authoritarianism and misogynist patriarchy of 'her culture', to be educated, to travel, and to express her bodily autonomy. These aesthetic and political coordinates establish her death as particularly tragic, as the drone strike is shown as destroying that which it is designed to protect. Although she is a vibrant example of a prominent paternalistic cliché in human rights discourse—the innocent, tragic native—she also contributes to the film's engagement with the moral legitimacy of the drone strike by underscoring the material costs of imperial violence.

Her red headscarf is visually significant too, as it echoes the young girl in Steven Spielberg's Holocaust drama *Schindler's List*, described by film scholars as representing the 'universal victim—childlike and female, thus innocent, passive, and powerless' (Rapaport 2002: 59), a fragile innocent whose death is 'terribly more wrenching than any other single image might have been' (Eley and Grossmann 1997: 56). Witnessing the death of the girl in the red coat—a little girl whose clothing is rendered in striking red against the monochrome of everything else in the film—is a key moment in Schindler's moral development, and it forces Spielberg's protagonist to become more resolute in his desire to rescue Jews from Nazi extermination camps. *Eye in Sky*'s red-garmented innocent is important in similar terms: she is a vivid reminder of our responsibility to protect the vulnerable. More specifically, however, she underscores the tragedy and waste of the sacrifice that the drone operators have had to make, as they have had to annihilate the very virtue and vulnerability that they were seeking to protect. She is the essence of human innocence that is enshrined and valued by the very concept of human rights. In killing her, they grievously offend against the principle of humanity itself.

Matthew Robson (2020) writes that the film's emphasis on this young innocent girl is an attempt to engage a Levinasian ethics of responsibility. Levinas's philosophy, committed to nonviolence and interpersonal compassion, foregrounds our mutual responsibility for one another's suffering: by recognizing our ethical obligations towards one another, we are enjoined by what Levinas (1969) calls simply 'the face' of the Other to reject violence and the exercise of power over our fellow humans. Levinas's work—rendered intuitively attractive by its reference to love and compassion and yet stylistically opaque enough to admit a range of interpretations—has been hitched to many political projects, but Robson's article, which claims that *Eye in the Sky* is a counterhegemonic cultural artefact and which positions Levinas as a possible candidate for the future of counterterrorism ethics, must be the most preposterous yet. 'With the drone strike imminent and the risk that she too will be blown up in the attack, the radically interdependent nature of Being comes to the fore along with the undeniable obligation to the Other felt as a responsibility without limits', Robson writes, continuing: 'her face calls out "do not kill me"' (2020: 109). It is true enough that the young girl is lavishly humanized in a way that makes violence against her appear obscene. However, this invocation of Levinas—who was always explicitly critical of visuality, sentimentality, and representation and who expressly denied that any form of plastic art could capture the essence of his ethics (Crignon 2004)—as a philosophical legitimation of this fetishization of an 'innocent African girl' both misunderstands Levinas and misses the far simpler point that the girl exists as a pretext for the characters to display remorse over their actions, actions that are never seriously in doubt.

Most significantly, the effect of the film's relentless attention on the girl in red is to attenuate the extent to which the targeted assassination of five terrorists is seen as problematic. In comparison to the innocent girl, who is emphatically humanized and whose murder represents so pronounced an obstacle to the moral righteousness of the attack, the terrorists register in the film's narrative only as objects of surveillance whose deaths are so clearly warranted that they barely register as murders at all. In fact, the terrorists' deaths are the reason that the attack is righteous in the first place: the drone strike is a sanctionable act *because* the terrorists will die, and this righteous status is put into question by the fact that the girl will die too. The film does not have a problem with killing, but only with situations in which it cannot be done *cleanly*.

In the movie's closing moments, the girl's father relies upon al-Shabab soldiers to rush his daughter to the hospital in which she finally dies. It seems that the murder of the girl may force her father to embrace al-Shabab, and perhaps himself therefore come to constitute a future terrorist threat. This echoes a fairly common critique of what is often considered the strategic shortsightedness of done assassinations; drone warfare 'kills today's enemies but creates tomorrow's in the process' (Byman 2013: 39). We might call this a blowback critique because it focuses on the danger of the possible resistance that drones might cause, rather than the substantive reasons that drone violence engenders resistance. It may admit that this one man has a personal reason to resent drones—the tragic loss of his daughter—but it fails to provide any structural reasons more broadly for resistance to drone warfare and the contemporary colonial politics of which it is the essence.

From the Sky: Concluding Remarks

Roger Stahl writes that drone culture 'promotes an exquisite understanding of how this technology functions but a stillbirth debate about whether its deployment aligns with the rule of law' (2013: 672). That is, by understanding how drone optics have been integrated into contemporary popular culture, we are able to empathize with drone operators and gain insight into the domestication of warfare. However, many of the texts that undertake this task, because of their focus on the private effects of warfare, also make it difficult for audiences to consider broader political and moral questions that drones raise. *Eye in the Sky* is a perfect example here, as it gives its audience an insight into the political decision making behind unmanned assassinations but fails to fully engage many of the most pressing questions raised by such assassinations. Its debate about the legality of the attack is restricted to one clear-cut situation and does not engage the broader geopolitical questions raised by planetary securitization. 'Postcolonial politics', writes Inderpal Grewal, 'concerns more than that which can be seen, since it is the scale of the widespread and dispersed violence of empire, capital, and postcolony that cannot be captured by the visual' (2016: 362). Narratives of limited emergency cannot show us the dispersed, rhizomatic nature of the global military-economic-political apparatus of which drones are the new enforcers.

Eye in the Sky may show us the networked nature of military violence as its narrative shuttles between many interiors dispersed across the globe (Nevada, Whitehall, Nairobi), and it may well foreground the way that drones put national sovereignty into question; one of the British characters foregrounds the novelty of the military situation, embarrassing everybody present, by asking whether there has 'ever been a British-led drone attack on a city in a friendly country that is not at war?' Likewise, elements of the legalistic debate about the proportionality of a drone strike in an imminent crisis are articulated with considerable sophistication. However, what the film cannot show us is the psychopathology of postcolonial capitalism to which Grewal refers, which has established the globally integrated securitizing violence the abstract ethics of which the film takes as its direct focus at the expense of its material and political realities. To return to McSorley's analysis of Scarry, what is simultaneously most fundamental to an understanding of drone warfare and most glaringly missing from *Eye in the Sky* is the insight that drone warfare is a form of authoritarian colonial state terror. Its horizons are narrowed to the consequences of one decision, with the structural violence of the drone programme hinted at but ultimately unexplored.

Zubairu Wai (2014: 494) writes that contemporary liberal interventionism is a form of power that 'adjudicates its own legality which in turn provides the basis for reproducing and maintaining its power and authority.' The persuasive structure of *Eye in the Sky*—which, although it may appear to morally problematize drone warfare, in fact convinces us that the drone strike is tragically necessary—is an example of how cultural production participates in this broader process of adjudication. The primary moral and political question with regard to torture and drone warfare should not be a managerial inquiry into when they can be used most effectively or how they can be used in a way that is compatible with a principle of harm reduction, but rather should perform analysis of the relations of power that they enable. The moral and political risk of debating state violence in terms of the trolley problem or the ticking bomb scenario is that it positions massive, destructive state power as inevitable and beyond question, which leaves us with a critical inquiry—which people should we kill with our unquestionable power?—so impoverished as to be meaningless. *Eye in the Sky* is an interesting artefact in this specific regard: it shows us the radical narrowing of critical horizons that is necessary for certain major framings of the debate over drone ethics to be politically and philosophically comprehensible.

References

Adams, A. 2019. *How to Justify Torture: Inside the Ticking Bomb Scenario*. London: Repeater Books.

Bachman, J. S., and J. Holland. 2019. Lethal Sterility: Innovative Dehumanisation in Legal Justifications of Obama's Drone Policy. *The International Journal of Human Rights* 23 (6): 1028–1047. https://doi.org/10.1080/13642987.2019.1592159.

Bourne, M. 2012. Guns Don't Kill People, Cyborgs Do: A Latourian Provocation for Transformatory Arms Control and Disarmament. *Global Change, Peace & Security* 24 (1): 141–163. https://doi.org/10.1080/14781158.2012.641279.

Byman, Daniel. 2013. Why Drones Work: The Case for Washington's Weapon of Choice. *Foreign Affairs*, July.

Chamayou, Grégoire. 2015. *Drone Theory*. Translated by Janet Lloyd. London: Penguin.

Crandall, Jordan. 2016. Materialities of the Robotic. In *Life in the Age of Drone Warfare*, ed. Lisa Parks and Caren Kaplan, 324–342. Durham: Duke University Press.

Crignon, Philippe. 2004. Figuration: Emmanuel Levinas and the Image. *Yale French Studies* 104:100–125.

Desai, R. 2022. The Imperialism of Democracy and Human Rights vs the Democracy and Human Rights of Imperialism. *International Critical Thought* 12 (2): 169–178. https://doi.org/10.1080/21598282.2022.2065719.

Eley, Geoff, and Atina Grossmann. 1997. Watching *Schindler's List*: Not the Last Word. *New German Critique* 71:41–62.

Eye in the Sky. 2015. Directed by Gavin Hood.

Gregory, Derek. 2011. From a View to a Kill: Drones and Late Modern War. *Theory, Culture & Society* 28 (7–8): 188–215.

Grewal, Inderpal. 2016. Drone Imaginaries: The Technopolitics of Visuality in Postcolony and Empire. In *Life in the Age of Drone Warfare*, ed. Lisa Parks and Caren Kaplan, 343–365. Durham: Duke University Press.

Hajjar, Lisa. 2016. Lawfare and Armed Conflicts: A Comparative Analysis of Israeli and US Targeted Killing Policies and Legal Challenges Against Them. In *Life in the Age of Drone Warfare*, ed. Lisa Parks and Caren Kaplan, 59–88. Durham: Duke University Press.

Harris, Sam. 2005. In Defense of Torture. *The Huffington Post*, October 17.

Horsman, Y. 2020. Drone Bomb Me: Cinema & Warfare in *The Good Kill* and *Eye in the Sky*. *The Senses and Society* 15 (3): 299–310. https://doi.org/10.1080/17458927.2020.1820192.

Kennedy, C., and J. I. Rogers. 2015. Virtuous Drones? *The International Journal of Human Rights* 19 (2): 211–227. https://doi.org/10.1080/13642987.2014.991217.

Levinas, Emmanuel. 1969. *Totality and Infinity: An Essay on Exteriority*. Translated by Alphonso Lingis. Pittsburgh: Duquesne University Press.

Lipsey, David. 2016. Liberal Interventionism. *The Political Quarterly* 87 (3): 415–423.

Luban, David. 2005. Liberalism, Torture, and the Ticking Bomb. *Virginia Law Review* 91:1425–1461.

Luban, David. 2008. *Unthinking the Ticking Bomb*. Georgetown Law Working Papers. http://ssrn.com/abstract=1154202. Accessed 3 June 2023.

McSorley, K. 2019. Predatory War, Drones and Torture: Remapping the Body in Pain. *Body & Society*. https://doi.org/10.1177/1357034X18822085.

Rapaport, Lynn. 2002. Hollywood's Holocaust: *Schindler's List* and the Construction of Memory. *Film & History: An Interdisciplinary Journal of Film and Television Studies* 32 (1): 55–65.

Robson, Matthew. 2020. Re-visioning the "Eye in the Sky": Targeted Drone Strikes and an Ethics of the Encounter. *Critical Studies on Terrorism* 13 (1): 100–117. https://doi.org/10.1080/17539153.2019.1658414.

Scahill, Jeremy. 2013. *Dirty Wars: The World is a Battlefield*. London: Serpent's Tail.

Scarry, Elaine. 1985. *The Body in Pain: The Making and Unmaking of the World*. New York: Oxford University Press.

Smethurst, T., and S. Craps. 2018. Towards an Understanding of Drone Fiction. *Journal of War & Culture Studies*. https://doi.org/10.1080/17526272.2018.1514759.

Stahl, R. 2013. What the Drone Saw: The Cultural Optics of the Unmanned War. *Australian Journal of International Affairs* 67 (5): 659–674. https://doi.org/10.1080/10357718.2013.817526.

Tesón, Fernando. 2003. The Liberal Case for Humanitarian Intervention. In *Humanitarian Intervention: Ethical, Legal and Political Dilemmas*, ed. J. Holzgrefe and R. Keohane, 93–129. Cambridge: Cambridge University Press.

Thompson, Judith Jarvis. 1985. The Trolley Problem. *The Yale Law Journal* 94 (6): 1395–1415.

Wai, Z. 2014. The Empire's New Clothes: Africa, Liberal Interventionism and Contemporary World Order. *Review of African Political Economy* 41 (142): 483–499. https://doi.org/10.1080/03056244.2014.928278.

Young, Robert. 2009. The Violent State. *Naked Punch*. http://www.nakedpunch.com/articles/38. Accessed 4 July 2022.

Index

M. W. Azeem (ed.), *Human Rights in the Age of Drones*, Palgrave Studies in Literature, Culture and Human Rights,
https://doi.org/10.1007/978-3-032-08191-9

FSC
www.fsc.org
MIX
Papier | Fördert
gute Waldnutzung
FSC® C083411

Kolibri 360 GmbH
Ferdinand-Jühlke-Straße 7
99095 Erfurt, Deutschland
produktsicherheit@kolibri360.de